ATTAINING
PERSONAL
GREATNESS

ATTAINING PERSONAL GREATNESS

❖

ONE BOOK FOR LIFE

Melanie Brown, Ph.D.

WILLIAM MORROW AND COMPANY, INC.
New York

Excerpt from *The Common Reader* by Virginia Woolf. Copyright 1925 by Harcourt Brace Jovanovich, Inc.; renewed 1953 by Leonard Woolf. Reprinted by permission of publisher.

Excerpts from *Granite and Rainbow* by Virginia Woolf. Reprinted by permission of Harcourt Brace Jovanovich, Inc.

Excerpts from *Women and Writing*, edited by Michele Barrett. Reprinted by permission of Harcourt Brace Jovanovich, Inc.

From *Markings* by Dag Hammarskjöld; translated by Leif Sjoberg and W. H. Auden. Translation copyright © 1964 by Alfred A. Knopf, Inc., and Faber and Faber, Ltd. Reprinted by permission of Alfred A. Knopf, Inc.

Excerpts from *TM and the Nature of Enlightenment* by Anthony Campbell. Published by Harper & Row, 1976. Used by permission of the author.

Library of Congress Cataloging-in-Publication Data

Brown, Melanie.
Attaining personal greatness
Bibliography: p.
1. Success. 2. Self-realization. 3. Identity
(Psychology) I. Title.
BF637.S8B725 1987   158'.1   87-1553
ISBN 0-688-06343-8

Printed in the United States of America

First Edition

1 2 3 4 5 6 7 8 9 10

BOOK DESIGN BY RICHARD ORIOLO

PREFACE

At some moment in our lives, we all have the thought "I want to be great."

Whether we consciously think of wanting to be great or whether it is just a fleeting feeling of which we are hardly aware, everyone has such desires. They are entirely natural and the spur for our unique growth. Wrote Helen Keller: "One can never consent to creep when one has the impulse to soar." Indeed, the desire to be great, though it may be unexpressed, lies deep within all of us, and it exists in every aspect of nature, as we shall see. This desire is universal and innate because wanting to be the best you can be--what you are proposed by nature to be--is nature's way of becoming better, of optimizing, of evolving, *through you.* So we are, in this sense, designed to be great.

Greatness is not something separate from ordinary life; it is the best of ordinary life. And this "best" applies to one's physiology and one's psychology in all experiences. Greatness may not necessarily require hard work or perseverance or even good luck. But it does demand growth.

Adult development requires both new and more complex patterns of awareness. We need continual growth to foster our tremendous capacity for learning and for creativity. For example, we all have the ability to draw well, at least much better than we do. As art instructor and author Betty Edwards reminds us, most of us still draw the way we did when we were seven years old, even though we could be drawing in adult ways within hours of learning how. Great people are generally those who continue to grow past childhood, who develop more of their abilities and strengths, use them, and live them.

Many psychologists now believe that the past, no matter how unfortunate, is not as important as our attitudes toward the present. The bottom line seems to be: The more potential we activate in the present, the less our past habits, experiences, and attitudes dominate us. And thus, the best thing we can learn about ourselves from a psychological viewpoint is how much potential for growth there is left in us once we reach adulthood. For example, the brain, once suspected of dying as we grow older, has now been found to contain so many cells and neurons that the average person uses up less than 1 percent in a lifetime!

We rarely hear of a single human being who has made full use of his or her abilities. Even Einstein estimated that at the height of his productivity, he was using no more than 20 percent of his thinking capability. Even so, neurophysiologists have recently found that Einstein's brain was far more developed than average. Not surprisingly, the more we use the brain, the more it is stimulated to continue its growth. Creativity, intelligence, compassion and wisdom, and all the other hallmarks of greatness are just beginning to grow by the time we reach adulthood. Yet this is where so many of us stop. We think it's all fixed at that point.

But the journey does continue, although you don't really ever arrive at a station marked "GREATNESS" and get off. It is more, to paraphrase Margaret Runbeck, "a manner of traveling."

Gail Sheehy's study of "passages" some years ago informed us that at different ages in our adult lives, we all pass through and experience certain psychological landmarks. However, the greatness journey does not appear to be correlated with particular phases of one's life; instead, it seems to transcend one's individual psychology. Certainly the journey toward greatness has its passages, but they are not necessarily connected to the passing of time; rather, they are born from *deepening levels of awareness* that can occur anytime during our lives. We could say that greatness comes about through continually progressive experiences of knowledge and integration inside us. It is available to everyone, but not everyone goes for it.

It requires tuning into the laws of nature that regulate and stimulate growth in all life. These laws, which make plants grow to their fullest, are necessarily the ones that enable people to grow, too. We could say that greatness requires the kind of growth that nature intends for us. If there is one single secret to becoming great, it is that great people have access to the laws of nature hidden beneath the surface of life.

The purpose of this book is to establish a comprehensive picture of greatness and its characteristics, and to approach it as something tangible and attainable, to explore greatness as it pertains to real life, and to offer a way in which one can develop one's own qualities of greatness and start to live them.

We can understand greatness from three main angles:

1. From descriptions of great people and the works they leave behind;
2. From modern scientific research, which identifies how the laws of nature operate and are expressed in human life; and
3. From personal experience--through knowing great people and discovering our own greatness as we experience it within our own lives.

Ultimately, what we're really interested in is to locate the essence of human greatness, because then it could apply to any one of us.

"One Book for Life" refers to the inherent gift with which we are all born--the ability to write our own life, to create the best life we can. Quite simply, great people are those who allow greatness to blossom. It's not so much the kind of activity they are involved in-- be it music, gardening, raising children, or finding the cure for a disease--it's the effect they have on all of us. It doesn't matter whether they are well known or not--great people create great effects even on the quietest levels of life.

There's no doubt that we need greatness in our society more than we need any other single human and/or natural resource. Fortunately, for perhaps the first time in history, we can think about the possibility of an entire society of great individuals. And anyone who is willing to take on the responsibility of his or her own greatness is giving the rest of us and all societies in the future the best gift possible.

One is not born a genius; one becomes a genius.

SIMONE DE BEAUVOIR

The success of undertaking of great people comes from the goodness of their lives, not from what they do.

VEDIC PROVERB

You must come to know that each admirable genius is but a successful diver in that sea whose floor of pearls is all your own.

RALPH WALDO EMERSON

ATTAINING
PERSONAL
GREATNESS

1

———— ❖ ————

WHAT IS GREATNESS?

❖

Recognizing Greatness

Perhaps it is that Nature has traced in invisible ink on the walls of the mind, a premonition which these great artists confirm; a sketch which only needs to be held to the fire of genius to become visible. When one so exposes it and sees it come to life one exclaims in rapture, "But this is what I have always felt and known and desired."

VIRGINIA WOOLF

Have you ever stopped to watch a group of teenage boys play basketball and noticed that, although they're all playing well together, your attention is drawn instantly to one of them--you feel a rush of recognition and think, "This player is great"? As you watch him, you

13

might notice that what he intends to do in each play seems to be effortlessly carried out without mistakes--with the absolute cooperation of every element of his mind and body working together, creating a kind of perfection in motion. Transfixed by his performance, you discover that *you* are feeling great.

Or maybe while watching a musical, you've mentally picked out the one dancer in the troupe whose performance has something great about it; she makes you aware of an essence--a palpable zenith of human expression--which you identify, or could identify, as greatness.

In whatever field, there are certain individuals who inhabit a clearly recognizable dimension of greatness. You hear Ella Fitzgerald sing, and it is obvious there is something more there than just vocal technique. There are lots of excellent singers, but there is a quality in her singing that is beyond excellence. Indeed, she has the ability to create what conductor André Previn calls "pure sound." Says Previn, "Orchestras tune to an A given by the oboe, because it is the purest sound. They could just as easily tune to an A given by Ella."

This recognition of greatness doesn't occur only in performances. You can also experience it just by being in the presence of certain people. It's in the qualities they display--their grace, their generosity to others, their ease of being in the world.

You see it in the behavior of a dynamic business person. You remember certain teachers who captured your complete attention in their classrooms, no matter what subject they were teaching. You see parents whose loving, flexible relationship with their children brings out that feeling in you--and you think, "They are great." And the thing that makes you notice each of these individuals and draws you to them is that they make *you* feel great.

For it seems that greatness compels us toward it. We can see it, feel it, and recognize its power in ourselves. And we notice it immediately. It's almost as if the boundaries of great people have a kind of incandescence. You may see lots of people whom you could measure with physical and psychological tape measures, and they would come out exactly the same as the greats, but they wouldn't have that radiance.

We can feel the influence of a great person the moment she walks into the room. Such individuals have what Thoreau called the ability to "affect the quality of the day." It's not so much what they do, it's the *effect* they have on the rest of us. It doesn't seem to matter what they have produced or achieved or whether they are well known; by creating an influence around them, great people directly help us experience our own greatness. Wrote Phillips Brooks: "Greatness, after all, in spite of its name, appears to be not so much a certain size as a certain quality in human lives. It may be present in lives whose range is very small."

Most of us are admittedly fascinated by great people and want to know what the something is that makes greatness stand out in the crowd. Because we recognize greatness when we see it, we may have an idea of what it is, but we often experience some difficulty putting this feeling into words because the concept of greatness seems remote and far removed from daily life. We tend to think that being great is something separate from ourselves--reserved for just a few special people.

In fact, many of us sincerely believe that great people are "born great." Success may be achieved without that initial gift, but greatness is somehow more a matter of destiny, somehow unattainable for most of us. We may have learned to dismiss greatness, to see it only as rarified difference, not inclusive but exclusive, more unreal than real. But is this true?

By way of an answer, the first thing we need to do is to look at some long-held misconceptions about greatness. They fall basically into three categories: (1) Greatness is something "extra"; (2) greatness is really rare; and (3) greatness is synonymous with success and fame.

The Three Myths About Greatness

MYTH #1:
GREATNESS IS SOMETHING EXTRA

I'm personally very deeply convinced that I have no faculties with which all human beings are not endowed. I do not think I am any exception whatever in this matter.

BUCKMINSTER FULLER

15

What we identify as greatness was called the "X factor" by the Russian novelist Leo Tolstoi: He described it as that "extra" something that seems to be visible in great people.

But perhaps the X factor is better described not as a "plus" but as a "minus," a "lack of something" rather than an "extra" something. We might call it a *lack of restriction*, a lack of those impediments that prohibit us from developing into what we could become if allowed to bloom as nature would have us--in the same way that it is natural for a rose to blossom and become great.

The truth is, we don't think there is anything unusual about a full-blooming rose. We don't believe that a beautiful rose has something extra; we merely assume that it is doing its proper job. We take it for granted that the vast majority of flowers are perfect; we don't believe that nature only comes up with just a few great ones. And actually, if we see a wilted flower in the bunch, that's the one that looks odd or wrong.

So, according to nature, greatness is what ought to be normal, and those who are less than great may be the odd ones, the wilted ones. Yet for some reason, we tend to see great human beings as "abnormal" and the rest--the not-so-great--as "normal." And no matter how extraordinary we are, most of us are convinced we want to be thought of as normal. In his research on self-made millionaires, psychologist Srully Blotnick found that even in our money-oriented culture, many people who have a lot of money feel they are abnormal and may go to great lengths to present themselves as being "just like you and me."[1]

Indeed, when we think of great people, we often relegate them to that inhuman status called "genius"--people we think of as living apart from "our" world and "our" everyday thoughts and activities. And we may even withdraw from genius or push it away from us as if it were less human instead of more. To make great geniuses seem more ordinary, to prove their normalcy, we like to hear about them in terms of their daily lives--how they eat breakfast, read the paper, etc., just like the rest of us. Somehow this is comforting.

But what might be an even more appropriate and long-lasting comfort is if we could all be geniuses. The poet W. H. Auden wrote, "Geniuses are the luckiest of mortals because what they must do is the same as what they most want to do . . . ."

Surely we all ought to want to be geniuses. After all, many geniuses accomplish a great deal with very little effort. And because their lives are often full and developed, they are generally ready to help others develop, to take responsibility. As Thomas Carlyle observed, "Genius is the transcendent capacity for taking trouble." And perhaps we are nervous about genius because it reminds us that we really have a lot more to give to the world than we're giving at the moment. If we're not geniuses, we don't have the responsibilities that genius might demand.

We could call this the "Einstein Excuse": E = MC². My Capabilities are only a tiny fraction, a square root perhaps, of Einstein's or, Einstein's = *My Capabilities* Squared. So we may think, "Einstein was great. Einstein was a brilliant physicist. I can't be great because, after all, I'm no Einstein!"

Essentially, the real distinction between being great and being less great seems to be the extent to which we are willing to be pushed along by our own best desires. The idea is not a new one; it has long been held throughout world history that our deepest desires are in some way also the desires of nature. And by allowing them to shape the direction of our lives the way great people do, we are living closer to what Mother Nature expects of humanity, to what we, in our finest hours, expect of ourselves.

When we say that someone is "extraordinary," maybe what we really mean is that they are nature's best representatives. In this way a great individual can be considered an open channel for "the flow of life," which Emerson described as the desire of nature to express itself through every person: "When it breathes through his intellect, it is genius; when it breathes through his will, it is virtue; when it flows through his affection, it is love."[2]

In his research on human development, psychologist Abraham Maslow made a major contribution to understanding what it means to be great when he evaluated great people as *more* rather than less human. Maslow believed that "what a man can be, he must be." To support his theory of self-actualization, he demonstrated that great people are those who have "actualized" their best characteristics; they have become most loving, most open, most integrated, most spontaneous, most stable, and most creative, and thus most like the kind of person everyone really wants to be.[3]

Maslow was not alone in his view of greatness. Carl Rogers's "fully functioning person," Carl Jung's "individuated person," and Erich Fromm's "productive character" were all similar psychological descriptions of great people who continued to unfold their highest qualities in keeping with the natural tendency of all life to progress to maximum capability. Thanks to these researchers and others, geniuses have started to look very much more normal.

So perhaps we can say that great people are great, not because they are "supernormal," but because they measure up to what normal ought to be. In effect, greatness may be *the* most natural state of life and anything less than great may be truly unnatural. In this sense, greatness is perhaps best understood as *the ability to be what you naturally already are, but fully, without restrictions.*

MYTH #2:
GREATNESS IS REALLY RARE

The first lesson that students of economics learn is the "lesson of scarcity" versus the "lesson of plenty." "Why," they are asked, "if we can't live without water, is water free, and diamonds, which are purely ornamental, so costly?" The answer, of course, is that there's plenty of water, but diamonds are rare. Yet, if there were equal amounts of both, water, since it is so precious to life, would be infinitely more valuable.

When we think about greatness in terms of diamond-like scarcity, we value it for its rarity; to maintain that value, some of us will have to live without it. This is a highly restrictive view of greatness, reminiscent of the ethic of material scarcity, which has been disproved in the past two decades. As Professor Julian Simon, author of *The Ultimate Resource,* has said: "The amount of copper that is available to us in economic terms is essentially infinite. You can't put any limit on it because there's no way to say we can't keep finding more and more, or discovering suitable substitutes, or using it more efficiently. Human ingenuity is the ultimate resource."[4] Economists Harold Barnett and Chandler Morse have also argued against the scarcity view by noting that "Nature imposes particular scarcities of specific materials but not a general scarcity."[5] Similarly, we could observe that nature imposes a particular scarcity of, say, *musical* greatness but not a general scarcity of greatness itself. ("We do have to be careful," wrote Elizabeth Minnich, "not to confuse specific skills with human worth. Good piano players are not always good people.")[6]

Thus, the idea that there can only be a few greats per era is as outdated and inappropriate as the idea that the economic resources of the world are insufficient and some people will therefore have to do without.

It is also obvious that an abundance of greatness in our society would benefit each of us. This principle of abundance has already been well-articulated in business. In his "Theory X versus Theory Y" productivity analysis, Douglas McGregor called Theory X, "the assumption of the mediocrity of the masses." Theory Y, by contrast, assumes that "the capacity to exercise a relatively high degree of imagination, ingenuity, and creativity in the solution of organizational problems is widely, not narrowly, distributed in the population." Therefore, Theory Y says that a long base line of greatness can be upheld within any organization. And, indeed, it has been found that when a company like IBM expects great talent to be widespread among its employees, widespread greatness occurs.

In *In Search of Excellence*, Thomas Peters and Robert Waterman described the generous way in which IBM supports success in its employees--with awards given to more than two thirds of the sales force. "The real key to success at IBM," they suggest, "is helping the middle 60 percent a few steps up the ladder." They conclude: "Given the supports, the would-be champion population turns out to be enormous, certainly not limited to a handful of creative marvels."[7] Using this Theory Y approach to all areas of society, it is possible that *everyone* could end up great. And this would be to the advantage of everyone else.

Of course, we may ask, if greatness were like water, common instead of rare, would it be less precious? Certainly, even though greatness would be appreciated, it would no longer be noticed. And the situation could arise whereby, as Gilbert and Sullivan observed, "If everybody's somebody, then no one's anybody." With similar logic, one could conclude, "If all roses are perfect, there are no perfect roses." Or if all people were great, there wouldn't be any more great people. Then how could we judge and distinguish among ourselves?

Would we still need to allocate the "10s"? We might also wonder how *People* magazine would gain or lose readership if we were all great. Would the situation, for example, require that we all be famous?

MYTH #3:
GREATNESS, FAME, AND SUCCESS ARE SYNONYMOUS

Be grateful as your deeds become less and less associated with your name, as your feet ever more lightly tread the earth.

DAG HAMMARSKJÖLD

Greatness is . . . not about fame, fortune, how many people you reach. It's about the quality of your life.

DEBRA WINGER

If we are confused about greatness, it may be because we associate it with being famous. We often say "great people" when we mean "famous people." We may even think people have to be famous to be great.

There is a story in England about a longtime university librarian who was being asked about the various people with whom he was acquainted. Had he met Karl Marx who had frequented his library? "Karl Marx? . . . Yes, of course. Used to come every day, he did, stay all day and leave quietly every evening. Then he stopped coming. I don't think anyone has heard of him since." So much for Karl Marx.

Even though fame is one outer confirmation of greatness, it is not necessary to be famous in order to be great, nor does fame necessarily confer greatness. It may be a measure of greatness, but not its equivalent.

Because fame is exciting to us, we are always ready to catch a rising star; we want our heroes and we are willing to confer heroism on anyone who can offer a glimmer of hope and inspiration. Not only do we love the famous, but we have built Halls of Fame to enshrine them for eternity. More than fifty thousand people have been "inducted" into over six hundred Halls of Fame. There are Halls of Fame for bowlers, cowboys, dog mushers, and even pickle packers.

Once we select our heroes, we adore them; we give them all our love and best wishes. And thanks to us, in no time at all, whether they want to or not, they're dining with heads of state, having streets named after them, and becoming models for our children to emulate.

Nowadays, fame and "media fame" are nearly identical. To paraphrase Dean Martin's old hit, "You're nobody 'till somebody loves you. You're nobody 'till two hundred million people care. . . ." And if we're asked, "Who are the current famous?" we find it easy to name five people who bring us the news on TV. Or five popular singers. But less easy to think of five scientists or five artists, five inventors or even one philosopher. Our heroes today are the heroes of the visible marketplace whom we all know and share. Some we call "stars," "superstars," or "legends in the making." Stars are indeed "real" people, and some try very hard to remind us of who they really are. When asked, most of them say they do not feel like stars at all; they point to others as the real stars. Now at the height of her career, comic Joan Rivers still says, "I'm very shy and very intimidated by the greats."

In most cases, whether "real" or not, our heroes and stars serve a vital purpose--to help unite and unify the family aspect of our society and the whole world, and to help us feel connected to the immediate culture. So fame is actually a connecting force but ephemeral.

To a large extent, fame is what is in fashion at a given moment in time. But fast fame, like fast food, doesn't last long and quickly becomes tasteless. In his now famous remark, artist Andy Warhol suggested that by the end of the century, we will each get fifteen minutes of fame. Perhaps to accomplish this unusual possibility, we dethrone our heroes just as easily as we create them. Says baseball hero Steve Garvey:

> We praise them, we glorify them, we put them up on a pedestal, and slowly they're chipped away. . . . We have to be very careful that we don't chip away at these heroes for the sake of bringing them back down to earth, because a lot of these people lead exemplary lives and they should be allowed to do what they feel is best, to be true leaders.[8]

Fame becomes fleeting when the personal characteristics that appear to attract and nourish it are not in fact related to the person's

21

true inner life. Fame then is no more than the superficial and transient attention we pay to externals. It's the outside looking at the outside, and something that can be given and taken away by others can't have much to do with the real person inside. "In the last analysis," wrote the poet Rainer Maria Rilke, "fame is only the epitome of all the misunderstandings which gather about a new name." Being *called* "great", therefore, and actually *being* great are often very different realities.

For most of us, the desire for fame is usually tied in with the desire to be worthy of it, to have done something to deserve it. Geneticist James Watson has written that, as a young man, he wanted to solve a problem that would be important enough to win him the Nobel Prize. His vision of his own potential was clear: He went ahead and discovered DNA. But his motivation was less to win the prize than to do something tremendous, something worthy of that level of recognition.

Since the real pleasure comes from the performance of the act itself, the "something tremendous," many great people do not need personal confirmation of their achievements. Thomas A. Dorsey, the founder of modern gospel music, advised, "Remember me, not for me, but for the work I've done." And Brandeis University research psychologist Teresa Amabile had found that when people are seeking fame, fortune, and success, their creativity actually declines, but when they focus on the *intrinsic* rewards of pleasure and satisfaction, their creativity increases dramatically. Says Amabile: "The key to creativity is to concentrate while you're working on a task on what is enjoyable about it, what is intrinsically satisfying. Don't think about consequences and evaluations until the job is done."[9]

Often the people who win honors and awards are the ones least interested in public approval. In a TV interview, physicist Richard Feynman talked about receiving the Nobel Prize:

I don't know what's worth what--I have nothing to do with the prize. The honor is unreal. The prize is the pleasure in finding the thing out. That's the real thing. I don't need anything else.

"Fame," observed Justice Oliver Wendell Holmes, "usually comes to those who are thinking about something else." And it almost seems as if fame arises in inverse proportion to the desire to be famous.

The most sought-after people are often the most private. One thinks of the reclusive Greta Garbo, who is famous for avoiding fame. If you want to see her, your best chance is to watch her movies, where she obviously prefers to be known.

Great people are usually well aware that fame is a reflection of yesterday, not of today and certainly not of tomorrow. Pianist Arthur Rubinstein couldn't listen to recordings he had made only months earlier. "I had changed," he said, "but the recordings did not." To avoid the pressure to be "fixed," many famous people try not to be stuck with an easily attainable but ultimately dissatisfying kind of fame. Writer Virginia Woolf declared: "I will not be 'famous' great. I will go on adventuring, changing, opening my mind and my eyes, refusing to be stamped and stereotyped."

Albert Einstein knew how important it was for society to have famous people, but he did not accept his own renown as personal glory. At age seventy, he wrote to a relative:

> It is a curious thing to see how one appears from the perspective of others. It was my fate that my accomplishments had been overvalued beyond all bounds for incomprehensible reasons. Humanity needs a few romantic idols as spots of light in the drab field of earthly existence. I have been turned into such a spot of light. The particular choice of person is inexplicable and unimportant.[10]

If fame in itself does not constitute greatness, what about success? Is success a requirement for greatness? Yes and no. Yes, greatness usually enjoys success; but no, not all success is a reflection of greatness.

Success vs. Greatness

Some are born great, some achieve greatness, and some have greatness thrust upon them.

WILLIAM SHAKESPEARE, *Twelfth Night*

We can't judge a person's potential for success. All we can say is that "she succeeded" or "she didn't succeed." Thus, success is an a priori proof in which only the results of a certain activity can be judged successful, i.e., the products of action, not the process itself. "The world is not interested in the storms you encountered," wrote William McFee, "but did you bring in the ship?"

Whereas greatness necessitates being in touch with the universal values of life, often transcending time and place, success requires tuning in on the specific needs of the particular culture. It requires immediate approval. Therefore, to be successful, greatness is localized as much as it is universalized.

Successful people of every age have been able to be in tune with the societal values of their time. They are able to identify the "right time and place" parameters for success. For example, some years ago Dr. Robin Cook, an eye surgeon, decided he wanted to write a money-making first novel. He read a large number of best-selling books in order to discover the basic formulas that structure contemporary best sellers. Then he wrote his own best seller, *Coma,* and accomplished his goal.

However, for a work to carry beyond the year, the decade or the century, more powerful formulas may have to be called upon. The music of Bach has lasted through four centuries because, no matter how much we may love New Wave music, to experience more delicate feelings at a wedding or a funeral, Bach still expresses them better. Greatness has to have the capacity to travel well from one era to another.

Yet greatness does not always produce immediate success. Herman Melville wrote *Moby Dick* at the height of his creative achievements, but it did not sell. Unable to support himself as a writer, he worked as a minor business clerk. Eventually, the culture caught up with him and applauded. The work of Henry David Thoreau who wrote the classic *Walden* went unnoticed in his day, and he died in obscurity.

Not only have many great people been abysmal failures within their own societies and lifetimes, but many have been considered heretics. Commenting on authors of great books of Western civilization, former Columbia College Dean Peter Pouncey noted "how many of these great thinkers went into exile or were burned at the stake for their eccentricities in forming these theories. . . ."[11] In some societies, it seems, being burned at the stake meant you had made it.

Because of this gap between lack of immediate success and eventual acknowledgment, we often say that great people are ahead of their times. But are they? When the renowned piano teacher Nadia Boulanger was asked whether she believed great innovative composers to be ahead of their times, she replied, "Why don't we just say the audiences are late?" Actually, great people are more likely to be those individuals who are very much in the center of their culture, at the nerve center of change, tapping the resources of their age, and able, through a universality of thought and vision, to express the transformative needs of the culture. In fact, some historians suggest that we remember great individuals specifically *because* they represented the transformation of their culture so perfectly. If they had been completely out of step with their times, no one would even have understood what they were talking about.

Because they often represent the beginning of change, great people may *seem* unique, and even isolated and out of touch. As a result, the depth of their contribution and their full worth may not be recognized for as long as five hundred years. This happened to Leonardo da Vinci, many of whose major ideas and inventions, such as the airplane, the helicopter, roller bearings, air conditioning, and the self-driven car, weren't even comprehended until twentieth-century technology became available.

If success and greatness don't always connect, it is due to the distance a culture may have to move along the path that its best representatives have already traveled. For example, while Socrates, Rembrandt, and Galileo were not exactly in tune with the immediate values of their respective cultures, they were certainly in tune with the deeper laws of nature--truths they knew they had to express despite adversity. In Blake's words, they "kept the Divine Vision in time of trouble."

There is yet another form of greatness, about which questions of fame, success, and recognition by contemporaries or later generations are entirely irrelevant. These are people whose greatness results simply from the nature of their being and need not be translated into external accomplishments.

Observed philosopher Elizabeth Haich:

They neither write literary works nor compose music for the public, nor do they strive after glory or worldly success; instead they radiate their creative energy purely as divine-spiritual intelligence, as universal, divine law.[12]

For these people, greatness is lived solely on the inside, through thoughts and feelings, not necessarily through deeds. Their stories do not make for dramatic biography--the significance of their lives is not in what happens to them, in what they do or produce--rather, they lead lives of inner silence. They represent the other side of greatness, greatness without success *or* fame. We don't think of them as "making it" in societal terms, yet they have a total commitment to the best of life and the betterment of society. "One can be helped by a great man," wrote Seneca, "even when he is silent."

Some of these quiet greats have been religious contemplatives whose lives provide an affirmative answer to the question philosophers love to ask: If a tree falls in the forest and no one hears it, has it made any sound? Within religious life, writes Thomas Merton in *The Silent Life*, "the monk remains a potent, though hidden, force in the world . . . even though he may never leave his monastery, never speak a word to the rest of man, the monk is inextricably involved in the . . . society in which he lives."

Others are not religious per se, but may have only limited contact with the wider world. Your sweet and generous next-door neighbor who is loved by the whole community may not be remembered "by history" after she is gone. But in terms of real personal greatness, her profound ability to enliven the value of love in others, she is as great as a Marie Curie, it's just that her territory of influence is less comprehensive. However, through her developed qualities, she will teach greatness to her family and friends and thus deeply influence her world, albeit a small one. Therefore, in the history of great people, the distinction is not so much between being great and not great, but between greatness manifesting itself in a small arena of life or in a very large one.

* * *

Now that we've explored some of the mythology surrounding greatness, have we come closer to locating the essence of greatness? We've seen that greatness is normal, natural, necessary, and beneficial for all, although it may have little to do with fame or even success. We can conclude that while success is dependent upon external circumstance and local criteria, greatness is an inner contract between the individual and the universe to create and discover deepening qualities of life and how best to express them.

We might say that unlike local success, which can rise and fall quickly, greatness is lasting and is achieved and lived on the basis of a permanent connection, intimately binding the great person with all human progress. The depth of knowledge and experience that is powerfully communicated over the centuries emerges based on the depth of greatness within the individual. Wrote Emerson, "According to the depth from which you draw your life, such is the depth of your accomplishment, manners and presence."

It seems that what lasts continues to be an appropriate expression of knowledge and values for each ensuing culture. Researcher Irvin Child showed that aesthetic judgment--the awareness of what is good-- always transcends cultural boundaries. If a work of art is enjoyed across a variety of eras and cultures, if it touches the deepest feelings of people everywhere, it is said to have crossed the boundaries of culture and will have a resulting broad influence.

And besides *crossing* cultures, greatness must also *extend* the boundaries of each culture. There has to be a certain degree of the eternal, an unshakable permanent value once you eliminate the popular context. Jane Austen's writing, observed Virginia Woolf, demonstrated this:

> . . . It has the permanent quality of literature. Think away the surface animation, the likeness to life, and there remains, to provide a deeper pleasure, an exquisite discrimination of human values.[13]

It is this quality of *permanence* that may best begin to describe greatness. Mythologist Joseph Campbell has identified our need to "attach ourselves to that which survives." Embedded in great achievements is a measure of immortality; they have survived even though the achiever has not. We naturally want to know what gives greatness its permanent characteristics.

Melanie Brown

"I Go on Forever": The Permanence of Greatness

But all the time each private life possesses, deep down as a
treasure, the fundamental permanence of consciousness which
depends on nothing.

PAUL VALÉRY, *Selected Writings*

Not in entire forgetfulness,
And not in utter nakedness,
But trailing clouds of glory do we come . . .

WILLIAM WORDSWORTH, *Ode: Intimations of Immortality*

The poet Wordsworth had a not uncommon insight into the nature
of life--that there is a possibility of continuity, of immortality, that
we are born not empty but full, not ignorant but knowledgeable.
Instead of a blank, one's mind at birth may be, as another great poet,
William Blake, observed, "like a garden ready planted." Or, as psychologist Jerome Bruner has proposed, maybe the infant mind is already "programmed, . . . a bud, ready to bloom," ready to be
awakened to its own full nature.

This continuity is akin to a permanency of life that each of us
sustains. Yet at the same time, we know that life is always changing
--down to our very cells. Most recent scientific data reveals that 98
percent of what we are physically--the atoms of which we consist--
changes completely every year. Still, something remains to keep us
going in an organized manner.

Perhaps the best way to envision this curious combination is the
way Buckminster Fuller did, as a coral reef "where new life is going
in and old life is going out." He further suggested that we view ourselves as a passenger liner--like the *Queen Elizabeth*--"a kind of form
. . . with life going on inside. The atoms get changed, the people
on board change, yet there is a sum-total form that goes on."[14]

If we are a *form* rather than a substance of some permanency, what
is inside each of us that makes us *feel* permanent? Constantly changing life is called "relative existence," and it is what makes some
philosophers, singer Peggy Lee, and others ask despairingly, "Is that

all there is?" It certainly doesn't seem to be all, because that's not what we *really* experience. We sense there is something about life that feels very permanent and very unifying.

How do we experience this permanent feeling? If you look at a picture of yourself when you were a baby, and then at one taken when you were a child, and then at one of yourself as a teenager, and if you remember something of how you felt at each of those times, you have a definite feeling of "me" or "I" that each of those pictures has stirred. Your interests have changed, your life-style is different, your friends have changed, your appearance, even your bones, skin, and cells have changed, yet "you" are still the same. *You* are always there. As Gertrude Stein put it: "We are always the same age inside." So what is it that always remains?

What Is Always There?

Amidst all the mysteries by which we are surrounded, nothing is more certain than that we are in the presence of an Infinite and Eternal Energy from which all things proceed.

HERBERT SPENCER

Almost all cultures throughout history have identified an underlying part of life that they describe as eternal and infinite. The Sioux Indians call it the *Wakan.* Philosophers, religious leaders, artists, scientists from all cultures have given powerful and clear descriptions of this absolute, unchanging basis for all change. In the *Symposium,* Plato envisioned it as:

An everlasting loveliness which neither comes nor goes, which neither flowers nor fades, for such beauty is the same on every hand, the same then as now, here as there, this way as that way. . . .[15]

In *Archetypes of the Collective Unconscious,* Carl Jung saw it as:

. . . a boundless expanse full of unprecedented uncertainty, with apparently no inside and no outside, no here and no there, no mine and no thine, no good and no bad.

Educator Harold Rugg has written that "pervading each human being there is an intrinsic and unchanging inner nature."[16] Great people come to know this absolute source of their greatness, through their intimate and personal experiences of it. Saint Augustine saw it as "the mountains and hills of my high imagination . . . manifold and spacious chambers, wonderfully furnished with innumerable stores." The ancient historian Heraclitus pictured it as "an enormous space whose boundaries, even by traveling along every path, could never be found out."[17]

It is the joy of discovering this unchanging basis of life that is singled out by the greats as the most captivating part of nature's draw. Indeed, many great people have reported that the main discovery of their creative lives was not the particular achievements or creations for which they were best known, but the discovery of something universal *underlying* their own creation that actually gave rise to their creativity, to their ability to discover anything at all.

Einstein described it as "being":

There are moments when one feels free from one's own identification with human limitations and inadequacies. At such moments, one imagines that one stands on some small spot of a small planet, gazing in amazement at the cold yet profoundly moving beauty of the eternal, the unfathomable: life and death flow into one, and there is neither evolution nor destiny, only being.[18]

Yet despite its all-pervasive nature, this field has remained somewhat elusive. According to writer Thomas Carlyle, it is hidden "underneath": "Of our thinking, we might say it is but the mere upper surface that we shape into articulate thoughts . . . underneath is the vital . . . force of creation." What many greats report is that by going to deeper levels of awareness, they experience greater unification, greater wholeness, and, it seems, greater *contact* with this infinite source of creation. And since this source underlies everything, we can arrive at it from anywhere. To discover and experience fully this permanent inner source of greatness may be the prime motivation for people to become great. Let's look at how this process takes place.

The First Four Steps to Personal Greatness

Now that we've seen that greatness exists and is recognizable everywhere, that all of us, rather than just a few of "them," are its purveyors, that it is linked to an intangible but all-encompassing sense of permanence, we can look more closely at four steps that can lead us to personal greatness. We start by admiring greatness in others, choosing it for ourselves, generating it for society, and validating it inside.

STEP ONE: SEEING GREATNESS IN OTHERS

Joe Louis was my inspiration. I idolized him. He wrote the book on boxing. . . . I just give lip service to being the greatest. He was the greatest.

MUHAMMAD ALI

And then there is the incentive of any great figure doing good work. It sets off a lot of others.

ALFRED NORTH WHITEHEAD

Our experience of great people is not just *knowing* that they are great, but experiencing their energy and achievements along with them--of communicating with them on a deep, delicate level of feeling, as they break boundaries. By seeing patterns broken, we are taught to break a few ourselves. Someone has beaten the odds, has kicked the door open, has reawakened human adventure.

Certainly we're all different on the surface, but in going deeper, we are more and more alike. So it would not be surprising if we were to find that what Thomas Edison did and what a wise grandmother does and what Beverly Sills does and what Napoleon did share more similarities than differences. "All men are alike," observed artist Joan Miró, "and they differ only in their habits, their customs. The . . . painter of the cave of Lascaux was like you, like me. I sincerely believe if you get to the bottom of one man you get to the bottom of every man."[19]

Therefore, successful people may help us to get to the top, but great people can help us most effectively to "get to the bottom" because they have discovered and communicated the most precious aspects of human development. If we are all connected to one another at the most basic level, then those who have accessed this level of life, and are enlivening it through their creativity and intelligence and through their ability to love, will make us feel more connected to this part of our selves. Thus, they become our teachers.

Interviews with or biographies of great people always seem to reveal one special person whom they credit with their success. Neurosurgeon Wilder Penfield described his teacher, Sir Charles Sherrington, as: ". . . the least prejudiced man I've ever known. . . . Sherrington's mind was so open that he expected each of us who was working under him to teach him something."[20]

What we can identify in these mentors is their ability to elicit personal greatness. Television reporter Bill Moyers has written:

> An amazing number of creative people have been touched and moved by another person at some point in their lives. It might have been a parent, grandmother or very often a teacher. That person has communicated to them a sense of "you matter" and made them aware of their own intrinsic worth as a human being.[21]

No doubt each of us has met some of these magical people who bring out the best in us. We may feel the same degree of awe toward them as that we might feel around a great but unknown genius. Their particular attraction may not be due to the power of their intellect, but may take various forms. We may wonder how a particular person can be so loving and cheerful in the face of undeserved anger, another so willing to take on enormous responsibility, or a third so courageous in the face of a personal disaster. These are the people who become our real guides. And even a single one can inspire us for a lifetime.

Yet you don't always have to have direct contact with a great person to be inspired. Fortunately, many great individuals have left us their works and thoughts, so their personal greatness carries across centuries and cultures. You can read their books or see their works of art or study their ideas in any field. And as long as you feel greatness stirring within yourself, you are benefiting from the contact, no matter the time and distance.

You can also start consciously looking for greatness in everyone. The next time you walk down the street, think to yourself, "I'm going to look at the next five people I see as if each were a Nobel Prize winner." After this, walk farther and think, "The next three people I see are self-made multimillionaires; this one walking toward me is the president of a Fortune Five Hundred company." Or try thinking, "The next person who walks by me is the most talented musician (or artist or writer) of our day." Or, "The next person I see has jumped into an icy lake to rescue a stranger."

Now look at each passing person as a caring father or a wise mother or a most loving friend or in any way you can to give beneficial value to their presence. What do you notice in this experiment? First, you might notice how your reaction to each person is heightened. You actually see each one more clearly. And because you are seeing them in a positive light, you are opening your awareness to their best qualities. You may feel you want to learn from them. And you'll be on the road to greatness, because great people tend to see greatness in others. Henry Cardinal Manning pointed out: "It is no sign of intellectual greatness to hold other men cheaply. A great intellect takes for granted that other men are more or less like itself."

You might also think of one person you consider to be great. Then ask yourself, "Do I think this person is great because she is famous? Or does this person really inspire me?" Make sure this person is real to you and excites your interest and captures your heart. Then think about what it is that makes you admire this individual. What qualities of greatness are you looking at?

Different people see greatness in others differently. The identifiable admirable qualities of a particular person are a tremendous source of knowledge about yourself. This is because we tend to admire other people for two main reasons: for what we are and for what we want to be; for those qualities that are most developed in ourselves, and for those qualities we most want and may feel we lack.

We admire what we personally have in abundance because we can experience the depth of that quality in someone else. We've all heard the expression "It takes one to know one." If you have a great sense of humor, for instance, you'll pick up quickly on the humor of a talented comic.

On the other hand, if you lack some quality that you deeply desire, it may loom even larger in others. "Gerry is so easy around new people; he seems to have no fear of being himself." Or, "Notice how Debra makes eye contact with everyone in the audience. Each person feels she's speaking only to him."

In any case, you may find that you want to adopt those admirable qualities for yourself. This is a common way in which great people develop their strengths. As the late Egyptian president Anwar Sadat revealed, "Whenever I see a good quality in someone else that is not in me, I always try to take it and put it in myself."[22]

And when you feel admirable yourself, it's even more rewarding to be around someone you admire. This is really a principle of all love relationships: You can only fully love and admire someone to the extent that you feel loving and admirable yourself, to the extent that you are self-sufficient and not needy. If you are overshadowed by someone, your love for that person cannot help but be diminished. And when you meet a great person, depending upon how you feel about yourself, you'll either feel small and perhaps shaky inside, or very full and great around him.

It's said that what you give your attention to is what you become. If this is true, then by associating with the best qualities of great people, you can start to live up to their standards and values. In this way you can also learn how great people think and work, and can apply some of those principles to yourself. Being around a great person gives you a wonderful chance to experience your own greatness. It's like playing tennis with someone who's more skilled than you. You play better.

In a Princeton University study, a list was compiled of the ten people who have done the most to advance human life. The following were chosen: Socrates, Plato, Aristotle, Galileo, Leonardo, Pasteur, Shakespeare, Newton, Darwin, and Einstein.

Historian Arnold Toynbee made his own list and chose Confucius,

Lao-tzu, Buddha, the prophets of Israel and Judaea, Zoroaster, Jesus, Mohammed, and Socrates.

You might have your own list of great people--those you feel have done most to advance *your* life. They need not be famous. Try to think of the qualities they display in their presence, personalities, behavior, ideas and/or achievements that draw you to them. You'll start to identify your own qualities of greatness, no matter how well hidden.

Once we've recognized and identified these personal qualities of greatness, we can then make choices that favor them over our less impressive qualities.

STEP TWO:
CHOOSING YOUR BETTER SELF

No one ever achieves his real self until he is his best self.

JULIAN HUXLEY

Many of us are faced with an incredible choice at present--unique in world history--what to do with our lives. Until now, very few men and almost no women had such a choice available to them. Today, technology has raised the quality of life and freed many of us from the constant chore of taking care of basic needs. Now we are challenging ourselves and each other to make the kind of life choices this freedom allows. In making those decisions, there are two things we can learn from great people. First, when they make a choice, they choose to be themselves; and second, they choose their "best" selves.

Choosing your self is of course no small task. It requires complete personal integrity. But it is a major requirement of greatness. Former U.S. Secretary General Dag Hammarskjöld observed:

> At every moment; you choose yourself. But do you choose *your* self? Body and soul contain a thousand possibilities out of which you can build many *I*'s. But in only one of them is there a congruence of the elector and the elected. Only one--which you will never find until you have excluded all those superficial and fleeting possibilities of being and doing with which you toy, out of curiosity or wonder or greed, and which hinder you from casting anchor in the experience of the mystery of life, and the consciousness of the talent entrusted to you which is your *I*.

He concluded: "What you have to attempt--to be yourself. What you have to pray for--to become a mirror in which, according to the degree of purity of heart you have attained, the greatness of life will be reflected."[23]

When Picasso was asked if he considered Van Gogh his favorite painter because he was the best, he replied, "No. Because he is Van Gogh. He is not always good but he is always Van Gogh."[24] And so it is with each of us; we can be great in terms of ourselves only. Whatever we do, it has to be the best of us, not the best of someone else. Writer Isaac Bashevis Singer says that when he writes a story, he has to have the feeling that only *he* could write that story.

Letting yourself be yourself--"To thine own self be true"--is perhaps the most significant contribution you can make to your own greatness. In this regard, Barbra Streisand made the following observation:

> When I was fifteen, I remember seeing things like--most people, even if they were nothing much--I mean, no charisma, no particular aura--if they pretended to be something they were not, they were nothing. But if they just were themselves, if they were just being, they were fascinating. Just by being human. Once they acted, it was false. They were their inadequacies. But once they were just nothing, they were something.[25]

Once we are truly ourselves, our choices become ways to fulfill all our desires. Maybe some of us don't want to be great per se. Yet we may desire to be knowledgeable, loving, creative, happy, and fulfilled, and as we aspire to these qualities, we are really aspiring to be great. Greatness may be the natural by-product of a fulfilled life.

It is certainly different to consider living one's life always keeping the best in mind. But it is noticeably the most satisfying. To have what we ultimately want, we may have to reject whatever comes along first in order to go for something better. It may mean waiting a month longer for a promotion so that someone else can gain the needed experience to replace you and succeed; it may mean making less money so that your heart's desire to teach music to children is satisfied. By rejecting something lesser for something greater, we are acknowledging the natural flow of our own lives, of personal evolution. We are choosing the best for ourselves and, by no mere coin-cidence, the best for everyone else. This is exactly what great people ultimately do.

Whatever your occupation, your greatness can rise within it. True, most of us live lives that will not lead to a Nobel Prize in shopping or an Olympic gold medal for getting the change in the tollbooth receptacle every time. But we do create the worlds we live in. We know we create our own happiness and contribute to the happiness of others. Whatever our strengths, we can learn to recognize and structure deeper levels of thinking, perception, beliefs, and attention in order to produce ideas, connections, relationships, businesses, books, and paintings enlivened with all the best of life.

Said Pope John XXIII: "Each person has something of value to offer; in the process of offering it, one raises one's station in the world." We all have the ability to create the best life we can. And because of this ability, we each have the birthright to become great.

Greatness is neither a psychological nor a sociological description of a type of person; it is not a personality profile of a given individual. It is, however, a picture of a "full-bloomer," someone who can say, as opera singer Leontyne Price has said, "Who I am is the best I can be."

To bring about this transformation, each of us obviously becomes responsible for his or her own greatness. It's not at all complicated. It's really a matter of finally growing up and becoming the person you always knew you could be when you were a child.

STEP THREE: MOVING TOWARD GREATNESS --THE SOCIETAL PUSH

Unlike children, who typically have no difficulty thinking up some-thing great to be or do, adults in our culture somehow learned that wanting to be great was either a gigantic ego problem or, at best, a childish fantasy.

And as a result, the goal of greatness was somehow replaced by the goal of being like everyone else, of being just a regular person. For some of us, being "ordinary" was like wearing an old shoe; it was familiar, it was comfortable, it was easy--but it wasn't what we really wanted to wear. Yet we were taught that ordinary people are much closer to us than extraordinary people because they were more "real," more like us, more human than the extraordinary ones. As a result, Norman Cousins wrote, "We have cheapened our goals by cutting them down to accessible size and separating them from a concept beyond infinity. It is as though we had been preparing for Beethoven by listening to hyenas."[26]

Then something started to change and as Buckminster Fuller, whose prophetic vision of the future remained accurate for fifty years, observed:

> . . . I find that everybody is getting to be an Einstein or a Christ, finding principles and understanding. I expect that we'll come to a point where humanity will spontaneously do the logical things together. It's a question of encouraging man to be aware of his great potential and not throw away his chance for success. . . . We are coming to success by virtue of all the people who have fallen in the fantastic continuity of sacrifice that has been made by humanity all down the line.[27]

It does seem that a highly opportune time has now come in our society for us all to become great. The recent emphasis on success gives a clue to the possibility of a major transformation toward greatness. Success has become the ideological thrust of recent times. Entrepreneurship, yuppiedom, Napoleon Hill, and the American dream of material success buoyed by spirituality have emerged, awash in positivism. However, there is a big difference between the resurgence of these themes today and their Horatio Alger antecedents. The difference lies in the unique emphasis on personal development within the dynamics of group consciousness and group success. What we are carrying out is a more basic proposition, identified by Marilyn Ferguson in The Aquarian Conspiracy and Alvin Toffler in The Third Wave, and by many others as a widespread social movement toward societal growth based on individual development.

Previously, external criteria for success were emphasized at the cost of internal factors. The need to experience and express inner enjoyment was not well articulated in any of the four most influential fields of endeavor today--business, politics, entertainment, or science. But now we are moving toward a more integrated vision of success, the kind that requires satisfaction on every level, that demands our full personal resources, that goes beyond success to greatness.

What this transformation involves is a completely new point of view. We used to believe in the zero-sum game--if one of us wins, the other loses; for you to succeed, I must fail. Now we are recognizing a new principle: the principle of mutual gain. If you succeed, I have a better chance of succeeding myself; if you fail, I may well fail, too. This is because, as we saw earlier, the laws of nature keep us all deeply connected. On the greatness journey, one person can't really profit at the expense of another. We are recognizing this principle by starting to create our own personal and mutual advancement, not by intimidation or contrivance, but by doing what is best not only for ourselves but for others, too. If we want to tap into our own greatest natural resources--the limitless potential of the human mind, imagination, and heart--we need to pyramid ourselves, to become one another's support system in order to become great.

It has been found that loving behavior is much more powerful than negative behavior. It automatically erases negativity. Lincoln understood this very well: The principle of how to "uncreate" an enemy. When asked by a woman acquaintance why he continued to speak kindly about his enemies instead of destroying them, he replied, "Madam, do I not destroy my enemies when I make them my friends?" Instead of wasting energy on defeating someone else to get to the top, we are learning that by bringing others along, we have a much better opportunity actually to gain the supportive environmental energy and power required for ultimate success. This is what "group consciousness" really means.

Becoming great is therefore not a luxury reserved for certain unique people; it is really a social necessity. We have to look to the great among us to see what each of us could become. People with great individual qualities pull the whole society along by enlivening those potential qualities in us all. And in this way, individual greatness has a survival value for the species.

It is a basic principle of sociobiology, according to Harvard professor Edward O. Wilson and others, that a small change in the behavior of the individual makes a huge change in the behavior of society. And if the amount of individual greatness in a given society could be increased by even 1 percent across the board, the beneficial effects on the entire society would be astonishing.

The Journey In

Many of the timeless myths and legends that we learn from child-hood on are allegories for a universal quest--the search for one's true inner self. This quest is what Jung called the "individuation process," a journey we all embark upon to find out about life from within. So the greatness journey is really a journey *inward*--toward that essence of human life which sustains not only the individual but the species.

It is clear that whatever we accomplish in society comes about because of our ability to organize ourselves inside first. The historian Arnold Toynbee has written, "It is through the inward development . . . that individual human beings are able to perform those creative acts, in the outward field of action, that cause the growth of human society."[28]

The inner life of a great person is always highly developed. This is what makes that person self-sufficient--able to be anywhere with only his or her thoughts and feelings as a source of activity. And because of their developed inner lives, great scientists, artists, busi-ness people, etc., even as they live "outward," may actually be creat-ing something else "inside." For example, DNA researcher James D. Watson was rarely physically in his laboratory. He played tennis, he partied, he spent endless evenings at the movies, but he continued to *think* during these external events and eventually thought out the structure of the double helix.

The Joyful Feeling of Greatness

One never learns to understand anything but what one loves.

GOETHE

The way you can tell if you are on the right track toward personal greatness is if you are feeling progressively good about your life, not necessarily successful, but necessarily right.

We all have frames into which we slip our own pictures. This is how we look at ourselves: They're our measuring stick of (in the words of New York City Mayor Ed Koch) "How am I doing?" Some of us expect the answer from others; we are validated, checked out, kept in line by the praise and criticism of our children, peers, parents, friends, colleagues, etc. For others of us, validation comes from inside, in the form of self-referral to an inner feeling of "How am I doing?", a sense of happiness and pleasure within oneself. No doubt we all fall in line somewhere between complete self-validation and complete "other" validation. Psychologists measure this as "field independence" and "field dependence"--you are either more likely to take your cues about life from inside or from outside.

But even if a hundred people tell you you're great, you may still feel not so great. This is because only *you* know what you're *really* capable of. And you will experience the pleasure of feeling great yourself only when you are using those parts of yourself that you love best. The performer can't wait for the audience response; he or she must feel it first. Composer Aaron Copland observed:

> The main thing is to be satisfied with your work yourself. It's useless to have an audience happy if you are not happy. It's nice to be confirmed, of course. If you think your work good and the audience agrees, that's a lovely situation.[29]

People who are enlivening greatness don't think in terms of output but in terms of a *feeling of inner pleasure* coming from the finest level of experience. Everyone has his or her own way of describing this feeling. Sculptor Louise Nevelson says: "Nothing in life has that vitality. You could be dancing on your head."

This profound level of feeling was identified by psychologist William James at the beginning of this century as "our deepest organ of communication":

> The deepest thing in our nature is this dumb region of the heart in which we dwell alone with our willingnesses and unwillingnesses, our faiths and fears. Here is our deepest organ of communication with the nature of things; and compared with these concrete movements of our soul, all abstract statements . . . sound to us like mere chatterings of the teeth.[30]

41

In analyzing interviews with creative people in many fields, researchers Stanley Rosner and Lawrence Abt found that creative work is generally accompanied by "feelings of excitement and pleasure," which come from finding new patterns. One scientist summed it up: "Those days when everything is hitting and you're seeing new relationships and each experiment works--this is a wonderful wild whole life."[31] No measures of success, no marks of fame are more compelling than this joy. Because they are aware of this form of pure pleasure, great scientists seem to do their work for the fun of it, the way an innocent child might. Nobel Prize-winning geneticist Barbara McClintock had no real chance to advance as a woman in a scientific career in the 1930s, but she recalls, "I did it because it was *fun*. I couldn't wait to get up in the morning! I never thought of it as 'science.' "[32]

The tendency we have sometimes to associate greatness with serious and somber drudgery--a holdover perhaps from the Puritan Ethic-- is quite the opposite of the truth. Runners run for the "inner high," performers perform for the "inner high," and thinkers think for the "inner high." According to mathematician Robin Ticciati, his colleagues are generally "only interested in those areas in which they can be joyously creative." They have the feeling that if they can't make a contribution to knowledge "in a way which is *personally* satisfying to them," no contribution is worth it.

When we discover something great in life, it has to be our own discovery, our personal "Aha!" not just something someone tells us is true or good. When this occurs, we get a feeling of happiness, a rising of the heart. Every five-year-old who learns to ride a two-wheel bike for the first time has this same joyous experience. No matter how many times we may have heard something, we don't enjoy it until we "own" it, until we experience it as an unfolding of our *own* thoughts and feelings. If one's inner appreciation of life is not developed, greatness has little chance to grow, even if outer success is achieved. The outer activity may satisfy some material or social need but it may not produce satisfaction inside. For example, there are people who seem to "have it all," but are miserable. It's always a surprise to hear that some famous, successful person is unhappy, but it is common. We are surprised because we assume that outer "success" has produced inner satisfaction.

Yet for some, no matter how much success they may have, if it is never *felt* as real success, it leaves only an empty feeling, with fulfillment continually sought after. It's like eating delicious food but being deprived of the capacity to taste and enjoy it. If success doesn't yield pleasure, it has surely failed in its primary objective.

You can't always finesse your feelings, slip them away when you're not looking. You can't pretend to enjoy what you don't enjoy. You can only use your feelings to help you decide what you love about life. No matter what you are about to do, whether a tiny or a large step in any direction, try to feel it out. Does it feel right? Are you happy heading out this way?

It's only natural to want to bring out the best in yourself. A 1980 Gallup study for the U.S. Department of Commerce showed that 88 percent of all working Americans are personally committed to doing their best on the job. Not because of an obligation to their company or to some external pressure, but simply for themselves. Similarly, a 1982 study for the Public Agenda Foundation stated that four out of five working Americans experienced the commitment to their work as "an inner need to do the very best job I can regardless of pay."

We all have very different internal requirements for personal happiness. One person may be happy with a little taste of a materially good life; another may need much more material success to be happy. One person living in squalor with lepers and other ill people may be quite miserable; Mother Teresa lives in bliss under these circumstances.

In order to achieve greatness, you need to find what gives you deep satisfaction--what you really enjoy doing. The secret of "doing" greatness is to do your best in what *you* enjoy--and not try to lead the life someone else has. Don't wish for what you don't have, but wish for what you *do* have to become fully realized. It's as basic as you always knew it would be. Feeling happy in your life and work is natural. Being unhappy is unnatural and can't possibly satisfy you. Says inventor Orlando Battista: "If you possibly can, do only what you enjoy doing best. Even if heaven is just as good as this, I don't want it. I'd rather stay here forever."[33]

The pieces for greatness are all there; all you need is the opportunity to fit them together; "fitting together" comes from a feeling of inner organization. And it seems that the sensation of things working out perfectly is what makes you happiest. You have a feeling of what you want--and that feeling materializes into reality.

❖ `

Greatness as a Field

Although it sounds farfetched at first, the feeling of everything fitting together, of how something materializes from within you, may be a reflection of how the physical universe operates at its most basic level. In fact, we may be able to explain some essential aspects of greatness in terms of the discoveries of quantum physics. We can suggest, for example, that greatness, although certainly recognizable, is really quite unbounded--not a characteristic of something else but whole within itself--more like what physics would call a "field" than a flower. "A field is like a perfume, a pervading influence," observed science writer K. C. Cole. Since fields are what the universe is made up of, endlessly interpenetrating and ultimately uniting, so thinking of greatness as a field would enable us to account for its universality.

A real psychology of greatness would thus require a picture of a field of greatness--and a means to measure the extent to which an individual is connected to it. And in this way we could argue that no matter what they do, great people succeed in being great because they are "well-connected," because they have tapped into a very real and infinite source of greatness--a field of life so basic that it transcends time and space and is perhaps identical to that field of wholeness which physicists describe as the "unified field" of all the universal laws of nature.

It is exciting to consider that the mysterious, elusive, and long-searched-for essence of greatness common to all those "peak experiences" great people have had could be simply identified as something tangible and accessible today by physicists attempting, as Einstein did, to locate the underlying unity amid all the diversity. So in the following chapter, we'll explore "the physics of greatness."

2

❖

THE PHYSICS OF GREATNESS: QUANTUM LIVING IN THE QUANTUM WORLD

❖

Our Natural Tendency to Enjoy Patterns

The element of all things, whatever their mode, observe an inner order. It is this form that makes the universe resemble God.

BEATRICE (to Dante), *The Divine Comedy*

This is a piece too fair to be the child of chance and not of care. No Atoms casually together hurl'd could e'er produce so beautiful a world.

JOHN DRYDEN

Something is great insofar as it pertains to an integrated world--an order of things. When you look through a magazine and see a picture of a beautiful house, you notice that it gives the impression of great orderliness. It is not haphazard; it is well thought out. It radiates an internal as well as an external order, almost as if the intelligence of the owner or the designer is visible in the "put-togetherness" of every room.

We often think of creative people as spontaneous, inventive, and fluid, rarely as methodical and orderly. But orderliness is essential, and it is typically found in great individuals. "The worth of the mind," wrote Montaigne, "consists not in going high, but in marching orderly."

In fact, internal orderliness is perhaps the most telling feature of all living systems. From cells to galaxies, all matter is arranged in an orderly way. Physicist Erwin Schrödinger identified orderliness as *the* essential ingredient that organisms require from the environment to help maintain their integrity. We on earth experience the benefits of this integrity, says biologist Lewis Thomas, because the energy from the sun in its steady flow to the earth and throughout the universe "is mathematically destined to cause the organization of matter into an increasingly ordered state. . . ."[1]

Orderliness in living systems is understood and appreciated by us humans in terms of *patterns*. Fewer than one hundred natural elements make up everything we know--all the insects, baseballs, cars, celestial stars, and movie stars--all decidedly different, yet all merely matter and energy from which each individual part of life is organized. Thanks to patterns, a small number of components can thus generate an infinity of new expressions. Recently, for example, physicist Peter Caruthers discovered the same statistical pattern in the structure of the atom and in the distribution of galaxies in the universe. Yet despite their sameness, patterns are in themselves capable of structuring endless variety. For example, every fingerprint of every person born is unique, yet each contains only three patterns--whorls, loops, and arches.

Since organized patterns are the basic characteristics of living systems, it is natural that the *recognition* of these patterns would be essential to our own human sense of orderliness. And in fact many researchers have demonstrated that all our knowledge about the world comes from the recognition of these patterns. Observed writer K. C. Cole: "Nature seems to be built on patterns, and looking for those patterns is the primary occupation of artists and scientists alike."[2] The eminent anthropologist-psychiatrist Gregory Bateson concluded that it is only because the patterns of mind are the reflection of the same patterns in nature that we can know anything at all.

Indeed, we are designed by nature to both recognize and create patterns. The reason the world we experience is most consistently "patterned" is because our human physiology *automatically* constructs orderliness out of disorder. This is what psychophysiologists call the need for "closure." If you've ever seen a moiré pattern in fabric, you've experienced how when many parallel lines cross, your eyes spontaneously search the field and tie together those points of inter-section that make the patterns. Patterns are thus created by our physiological need for them to emerge. In fact, so necessary are pat-terns that, author Anthony Campbell writes, we will "make a pat-tern even when no real pattern exists." He continues:

> Everyone must have lain in bed at some time and made up faces from marks on the wall. In much the same way, if one listens for some time to a conversation in a totally unknown language, such as Chinese, one will suddenly seem to hear, quite distinctly, a word or phrase in English. The brain is trying to make bricks without straw, finding non-existent patterns because any pattern is better than none.[3]

We all like things to be resolved or completed. Creative people also have this need, but seem to be able to hold out longer in order to pull more things together prior to "closure" time. Psychologist Frank X. Barron of the University of California postulated that most highly creative individuals have learned to integrate greater disorder because it gives them the opportunity to formulate "an elegant new order more satisfying than any that could be evoked by simple con-figurations."

According to creativity researcher Marghanita Laski, who has identified and collected creative experiences that bring about the feeling of what she calls "ecstasy," such ecstatic moments are linked to the experience of higher mental organization. The more complex patterns are found to bring greater pleasure, deeper satisfaction, and a sense of fulfillment to the human mind.

For this reason, to discover deeper levels of organization, order or pattern in their work, great people often spend years on their creative projects. This is also ·perhaps why many greats do their best work at the end of their lives. Milton envisioned his epic poem *Paradise Lost* during his youth, but did not complete it until his last years, when he felt his unifying powers were finally equal to the task. Walt Whitman continued to revise *Leaves of Grass* up to his death because he kept experiencing new connections, creating new patterns, having new inspirations for more beautiful and more "truthful" poetry beyond the original work.

If we keep wanting to integrate newer and bigger patterns in our lives, we start to sense that what we are really seeking is an ultimate pattern, some large picture of the whole universe that would resolve our need for order and bring the deepest pleasure, the ultimate satisfaction of the whole.

❖

Making Connections:
The Quest for Wholeness

We're here to see the universe. We represent the life force. We're here to know the gift.

RAY BRADBURY

To find greater wholeness in life provides us all with greater pleasure. This is not an illusion but a very real experience of a deeper connectedness to the world and to ourselves.

The continual integration of new experiences and thoughts into bigger and more complex patterns has actually been identified as the basic quest of all human life--what mythologists call *katabasis*, the quest for wholeness. No matter what our occupations or values, we all want to experience this complete connection. We all want to live our lives feeling both part of the whole and whole within. If we don't, we feel restricted in our ability to grow. In Evelyn Waugh's *Brideshead Revisited*, the central character, Charles Ryder, looks back wistfully at the results of an unfulfilling trip abroad and says, "I remained unchanged; still a small part of myself pretending to be whole."

Every child, said Emerson, is filled with a "desire for the whole; a desire raging, infinite." This desire for wholeness is also a description of greatness at work, which produces the ability to see and appreciate the Big Picture even in the most trying situations. We may have visited a friend lying in a hospital bed with needles in him everywhere, yet he makes a joke about his condition. His sense of himself, his self-worth, remains intact despite what he is going through because he can step back and observe his situation. In this way he appreciates the whole, not just the pieces of an experience, by putting everything into a broader perspective.

The need for wholeness seems to underlie every avenue of endeavor. According to former Secretary of State Henry Kissinger, a leader, to be great, must have the ability to grasp wholeness. The great leader uses insight, sees patterns, and envisions the future. Kissinger writes:

> The difference between great and ordinary leaders is rarely formal intellect but insight. The great man understands the essence of a problem--the ordinary leader grasps only the symptoms. The great man focuses on the relationship of events to each other-- the ordinary leader sees only a series of seemingly disconnected events. The great man has a vision of the future which enables him to place obstacles into perspective: the ordinary leader turns pebbles in the road to boulders.[4]

Wholeness is also understood as a key factor in business--but it is not often available, according to economist Chester Barnard. He observes: "A formal and orderly conception of the whole is rarely present, perhaps even rarely possible, except to a few men of executive genius, or a few executive organizations the personnel of which are comprehensively sensitive and well-integrated."[5]

In summary, if greatness is to be fully expressed, it seems it must be developed on the basis of wholeness. Otherwise, it is limited and partial and less than great. This is not only how we can experience it, but also how we might best picture it.

A scientific model of how the universe functions that has begun to prove most useful to this understanding of the value of wholeness in developing greatness comes from quantum physics. Using quantum theory to examine human greatness allows us to view the grand scale and open up our thinking so we really understand how greatness might emerge in each of us. If we don't take this larger look at our behavior, we may be missing the proverbial forest for the trees, thereby ignoring our own possibilities for becoming great. As economist George Gilder has pointed out: "While physicists begin to concede freedom for microscopic particles, social scientists still begrudge it to human beings."[6] The quantum world opens up a new way to think about the possibilities.

Entering the Quantum World: Becoming the Co-author of the Universe

All through the physical world runs that unknown content, which must surely be the stuff of our consciousness. Here is a hint of aspects deep within the world of physics, and yet unattainable by the methods of physics. And, moreover, we have found that where science has progressed the farthest, the mind has but regained from nature that which the mind has put into nature. We have found a strange footprint on the shores of the unknown. We have devised profound theories, one after another, to account for its origin. At last, we have succeeded in reconstructing the creature that made the footprint. And Lo! it is our own.

SIR ARTHUR STANLEY EDDINGTON

You never enjoy the world aright till the sea itself floweth in your veins, till you are clothed with the heavens and crowned with the stars; and perceive yourself to be the sole heir of the whole world, and more than so, because men are in it who are everyone sole heirs as well as you.

THOMAS TRAHERNE

Like the god Janus, science seems to be looking in two directions simultaneously--one direction leads to examining increasingly smaller and therefore presumably controllable pieces of the world. The other moves toward connecting what is already known with larger and larger pieces. In the latter direction, science is looking for greater integrity and the relationship of the parts to the whole.

But behind this dual movement in science lies a deeper issue: Is the reality being investigated inside us or outside us? It is an age-old debate. For centuries we in the West believed that the world existed only "outside" us--that an objective real world is out there, independent of our perception of it. However, according to the evidence from quantum physics, the world is not out there, separated from the observer. Rather, as Einstein first understood it, "physical concepts are free creations of the human mind and are not, however it may seem, uniquely determined by the external world."[7]

In fact, so pervasive is human consciousness that nowadays it is widely believed that no scientist can ever measure anything "objectively." Indeed, we have moved light years from the old principles of a classical objective world. Even the most innocuous experiments turn out to be subjective; the experimenter somehow always gets involved with the outcome of his experiments. P.C.W. Davies explains:

> Suppose we wish to measure the temperature of a cup of hot water, how is this to be accomplished? A good method is to immerse a thermometer in the water and read off the temperature. However, as likely as not, the thermometer itself is cold, and in heating up the water-temperature to give an accurate reading, it cools the liquid somewhat. . . . This example illustrates the general principle that *any* sort of observation necessarily involves some kind of disturbance to the system that we are trying to observe, and this is true whether the observation takes place through the intermediary of an instrument [thermometer] or by direct observation. . . .[8]

We do have an "out there" world, of course. We do have "things." However, these things really exist only because of the way nature's laws operate on earth--because of gravity and the other fundamental forces that hold matter together, and because of the way we humans are structured to perceive likenesses and patterns. As Bertrand Russell reminds us:

> "Things" have been invented by human beings for their own convenience. This is not obvious on the earth's surface because,

owing to the low temperature, there is a certain degree of apparent stability. But it would be obvious if one could live on the sun where there is nothing but perpetually changing whirlwinds of gas. If you lived on the sun, you would never have formed the idea of "things," and you would never have thought of counting because there would be nothing to count.[9]

So even though "things" exist, you can't always count them and you can't always count *on* them. They are in no way permanent. What *is* permanent, say the quantum physicists, is the underlying field that creates and structures things. As London University physicist David Bohm explains in *Wholeness and the Implicate Order*: "[We] need to look on the world as an *undivided whole*, in which all parts of the universe, including the observer and his instruments, merge and unite in one totality." Bohm calls this deeper reality "undivided wholeness in flowing movement" and points out that "flow is, in some sense, prior to that of the 'things' that can be seen to form and dissolve in this flow."[10]

However, while the quantum view asserts that *things* may not be stable, it confirms what we've already seen, that *patterns* are stable-- because the laws of nature are themselves universal and eternally stable. What quantum physics tells us, explains M.I.T. Professor Victor Weisskopf, is that "the *underlying pattern* of the world" (my italics) is unchanging. According to Weisskopf, the quantum view offers the scientific key to the laws of nature operating in the universe. "Before quantum theory," he says, "we could not account for the most obvious characteristic of nature; that all iron atoms are exactly alike; gold is gold wherever you find it; the same flowers bloom again every spring. . . ."[11]

❖

The Quantum Choice: Living in the Participatory Universe

Sir Alan Cottrell summarizes how quantum mechanics reveals our observer role in the physical world. He writes:

At root, we have only two notions--*particle* and *wave*--for visualizing material things. Both come from classical physics, where they stand entirely separate in the sense that a given thing is always either a particle or a wave. But in quantum physics the same things--electrons, for example, or pulses of light--can be observed to be either particles or waves, according to our choice of the form of our compulsory interaction with them. By changing this choice, we can change their observed nature from wavelike to particlelike, and vice versa, as often as we wish. The choice of how they shall appear is ours.[12]

So although in the classical world things are localized and observably constant, the quantum observer creates his own world by choice. And since a quantum view requires a major contribution from the observer and not much from the "object," it is, states author Peter Russell, "our being conscious of the world that forces it to adopt a particular reality."

As physicist John Wheeler describes it, we are really in a "participatory" universe where there are multiple potentialities and all possibilities available. Whatever we can think of, we can create. We each structure our own realities, based on the way our minds and bodies work.

But if each of us creates his or her own world, what then gives the impression of a stable world?

The reason our realities, our little worlds, are at all alike is because our nervous systems are alike, not because the material world around us is stable, but because we function in like manner as a species. If, however, someone is born without a certain function--let's say he's color-blind--the "red" of the world disappears for that individual. Since there is really no red color in the world anyway (only through human physiological functioning does the color appear), a color-blind person sees a real world, too--but his world is real without red. In other words, when we say we are learning about the world, what we are really doing is learning to use our own particular physiology to awaken our capabilities of experiencing.

Biologist C. H. Waddington says that there is no point in trying to achieve objectivity without realizing our dependence on our brain functioning: "We are a part of nature, and our mind is the only instrument we have, or can conceive of, for learning about nature or ourselves."[13] And since, according to the quantum view, the nature of the quantum wave function and its measurement are directly related to the consciousness of the observer, this suggests that by exploring our own minds, we can come to learn the secrets of the universe.

The human mind is thus identified as the key to the discovery of how the (human) universe functions. So, if we could discover the real nature of consciousness, we would also discover the laws or principles that structure the physical universe. This was why when two recent Nobel Prize winners in physics were asked what the Prize would be given for in their field twenty years hence, they responded, "For research in human consciousness."

To explore further this participatory universe, let's look now at how the quantum world is experienced. If we have a "quantum experience," what does it feel like? How do we "quantumthink"? What is the advantage to "Q thinking"?

❖

The Classical vs. the Quantum World: Linear vs. "Q Thinking"

Because we have learned to live comfortably with the classical view of the world, our style of thinking has of course become classical, that is, linear. We have learned to appreciate the world in a step-by-step, "right or wrong" way. Our expectations have also been linear; we never expected more than one right answer, nor did we even want one. But what has happened is that the world we live in has started to become a quantum world, a world of all possibilities.

We can find evidence of this transformation even in the simplest things. John Naisbitt points out in *Megatrends* that personal choice has expanded enormously as we have moved from an either/or to a multiple-option society. "Remember," he writes, "when bathtubs were white, telephones were black, and checks green?" He cites the infinite choices we now have in foods, pop music, architecture, as well as the 752 models of cars and trucks at last count. Those who can really maintain multiple choices are fortunate, for they can tune into the expansive nature of contemporary life far more than those whose "either/or" orientation restricts their choices. Without accompanying subjective growth, objective decision making becomes overwhelming.

But the quantum world offers a far more important opportunity for the development of greatness. The people who can enjoy the quantum world and benefit in it are those who can experience its multiple possibilities first within their own minds. For this, we need "Q thinking"--a new style of thinking that differs from linear step-by-step thought processes in that it gives the whole picture in every part just as a hologram does.

What Q thinking says about the world is that until an object is observed, it is infinite--understood to be all possibilities at once. So in Q thinking, there are multiple choices and no "always right" answers. The real pleasure of multiple choice is possible only when we can experience wholeness in everything. When everything feels connected, when more and more of life feels like one thing, then anything we choose feels and is right. How does this work?

❖

Thinking from the "Superposition"

There is a well-known psychological test--a picture of an unattractive woman and a beautiful woman that is drawn in such a way as to give a choice of observation. Depending on how you look at it, the drawing changes from one face to the other. At some moment you can see both faces right before the perceptual shift occurs. This way you can see the "potential" of each drawing just before you choose one. In a similar way, quantum physics represents the world as multiple possibilities, and until a choice is made, the world is a synchronous overlapping of all its alternatives, a combination known to physicists as a "superposition." Because everything is potential and not concrete, several opposing things can occur simultaneously. (What ultimately occurs is based on a principle of nature's perfect efficiency known as "the law of least action." What manifests is whatever requires the least amount of activity. Other things could happen but they are not as likely.) What is fascinating about this quantum reality is that there seem to be quantum processes operating in higher levels of human functioning that also give each of us the ability to experience opposing things "at once," independent of selection.

Psychologist Albert Rothenberg has postulated a construct called "Janusian thinking," which he describes as the ability to hold two opposing concepts in the mind simultaneously--"to look both ways at the same time." This integration of opposites does not require logical resolution, merely an acceptance of two seemingly paradoxical ideas from a greater vantage point.

In the Buddhist tradition, rhetorical questions called *koans* are used as teaching devices to wipe out logic and help the student let go of linear thought processes. Lewis Carroll used similar devices in his writings: "How is a raven like a writing desk?" asks the Mad Hatter of Alice, in the *koan* tradition. There is no right answer; what we have is the experience that the question itself produces--staging a way out of zero-sum, "right answer" thinking into quantum thought. There may be no objective similarity between a raven and a writing desk, but we feel subjectively enlivened by the question. Our creative juices are being called up to resolve the situation somehow.

The Unity Resolution

Opposites seem to be products of partial cognition and fade away with cognition of the whole.

ABRAHAM MASLOW

What happens when we experience opposition, imbalance or incongruity is that we automatically seek unity. We are forced in a sense to "go deeper," to experience reality at a level that includes and integrates. When this happens, we have an "insight." Many artists purposely set two unlikely events in motion together in order to experience this effect as a creative tool. Dancer and choreographer Merce Cunningham, for example, likes to watch football on TV while listening to classical music--to see the subtle movement revealed by the music.

Great artists have the ability not only to experience unifying patterns themselves but to create a unifying experience for others. In fact, this is the way many artists enliven our vision. Works of art that allow us to experience new connections are in a sense techniques for self-development. When we experience a shift in awareness toward more unity, we re-create the creative act in ourselves and may even experience the ecstasy of the artist in the creating. And when a work of art requires us to go to the limit--to the deepest patterns we are able to perceive in order to integrate the material-- we identify those works of art as great. Anthony Campbell illustrates this point:

> The reason we call one work of art "greater" than another is probably connected with the comprehensiveness of the pattern to which it gives rise in the mind of its audience. When we read *War and Peace,* or contemplate the Sistine Chapel, or listen to the *St. Matthew Passion,* we experience a sense of wholeness. For the moment, at least, many contraries have been resolved, and the mind is at peace. The depth of happiness which ensues seems to depend on the amount of material which has been unified. . . . A detective story may be, within its set limits, wholly satisfying, but the limits are very narrow and the sense of resolution comparatively trivial.[14]

Great unity thus seems to be the essential requirement for all great art. Even though a painter may use extremes in his or her work, from the palest to the most intense colors, from the most subtle to the most dynamic lines and forms, all the extremes must melt into one thing for a painting to become a work of art. If one part stands out and distracts us, then the satisfying unity of the work is lost. What great artists do is to bring together disparate elements and, through their unifying vision, compel us to accept them in a new way that creates a new unity within us.

Thus, to be life enhancing, wrote art critic Bernard Berenson, "visible things . . . must be presented in a way to make us feel that we are perceiving them more quickly, grasping them more deeply, than we do ordinarily." Picasso's "Guernica" is a good example of this, wherein shocking destruction has been structured in great creation. Art historian Leo Steinberg points to a similar effect in Leonardo da Vinci's work: "Leonardo does not give you events in succession, but in simultaneity."[15] The result is not merely the fusion or synthesis of two concepts but a unique way of experiencing, the way the great architect is able to envision both the inside and the outside of a building simultaneously, or the way James Watson finally pictured the double-helix structure of DNA--inside and outside together.

If we can look both ways at once, we can also, in quantum terms, have the ability to look in every direction at once.

This is what we call "Q thinking," seeing wholeness in each part, all equal. In this way, you can take any choice, any focus, and bring everything into it. This is how Emerson described the artistic function of bringing universality, "the totality of nature," to every work. He suggested that:

> Nothing is quite beautiful alone; nothing but is beautiful in the whole. A single object is only so far beautiful as it suggests this universal grace. The poet, the painter, the sculptor, the musician, the architect seek each to concentrate this radiance of the world on one point. . . .[16]

Therefore, when you have the capacity to enjoy and enliven wholeness, you can bring greatness to anything. The essence of being great may be having the ability to bring a sense of the eternal to any part. Said philosopher Immanuel Kant: "We call that sublime which is absolutely great. It includes anything in nature whose intention brings with it the idea of its own infinity."

❖

Applying the "Q": Becoming the Other

If we can bring a huge awareness to every little thing we do, or every little thought we have, then all activity starts to be incredibly enjoyable. And if we do in fact make what occurs in the world actually happen, then we are in the delightful position of being able to construct reality and live it any way we want. This is what great teachers and thinkers have been telling us for thousands of years--and what the Dale Carnegies, Napoleon Hills, and "success" motivators of today remind us of as well.

We can learn to rearrange reality by shifting from one level of understanding to another. Lincoln could "destroy" his enemies by making them his friends. If we operate from the "Q" field of "anything can happen," our attitude and attention can really serve to manifest all our desired goals.

Thus, living from the quantum perspective means living *inside* the universe--creating it, not observing it from the outside looking in. And this way we can get inside any part of the world and know it.

Scientists often use the Q technique to get inside the objects of their research. Dr. Jonas Salk recalls how he started to use this technique when researching the vaccine for polio: "When I had to deal with things that seemed paradoxical, I put myself in the place of the virus, and the immune system, and see how they would behave and why."[17] Similarly, Dr. Joshua Lederberg, the president of Rockefeller University, who won a Nobel Prize for discoveries that established the genetics of microorganisms, said recently:

> One needs the ability to strip to the essential attributes of some actor in a process, *the ability to imagine oneself inside a biological situation*; I literally had to be able to think, for example, "What would it be like if I were one of the chemical pieces in a bacterial chromosome?"--and try to understand what my environment was, try to know *where* I was, try to know when I was supposed to function in a certain way, and so forth.[18]

There was a book published some years ago whose main premise was: "If you want to catch a mouse, think like a cheese." Once you experience the characteristics of the "other," you will no longer be restricted by your own individual boundaries and you will become more "you" in the process. Pianist Lorin Hollander, in a television interview, recalled his experiences as a child prodigy: "When I would play a note, I would become that note. . . . At the keyboard I became fully myself."

When we use linear thought exclusively, it's almost impossible to see the other fellow's point of view. With Q thinking, all viewpoints become our own. In his film *E.T.*, Stephen Spielberg reminded us how the world looks to a child by capturing the "child's-eye view," with camera angles set three to four feet high. "Becoming the other" is a useful approach in almost any human endeavor. It has been said, for instance, that to marry happily, first you must become the kind of person you want to marry. So when that person comes along, you'll be just what he or she wants, too.

Using Q thinking you can basically structure yourself to become anything you desire: If you want to fly, you become the field of gravitation, the field of space in order to understand the laws of aerodynamics. It is the Q ability that allows for maximum creativity, maximum flexibility of thought, and maximum "tuning in."

With Q thinking, a great writer can genuinely enable a character to come alive from the inside. Eudora Welty explains:

> Characters take on life sometimes by luck, but I suspect it is when you can write most entirely out of yourself, inside the skin, heart, mind, and soul of a person who is not yourself, that a character becomes in his own right another human being on the page.[19]

To discover how the universe works, Einstein took the Q technique to its logical extreme by asking himself: "If I had been God, would I have made the universe in this way?" Einstein in a sense became the universe; he used his profound acquaintance with and trust in his own developed intuition and feeling for nature to predict what has only recently been confirmed by a new generation of physicists--that there must be a simple explanation for how the universe functions, a single source where all the laws of nature reside. It is in physics today where we find the scientific foundation to begin to confirm the experience of all great people; that indeed you can become anything you want, as long as it is O.K. with the laws of nature.

The Unified Field of Nature's Laws: Going Toward Unification

> Yes is a world
> And in this world
> of yes live
> (skillfully curled)
> All worlds.
>
> e. e. cummings

According to quantum physics, everything in nature is governed by four fundamental forces. The strong force is said to hold matter together ("May the Force be with you" is not just an idle request); the force of gravity keeps us on the earth and the earth near the sun;

the electromagnetic force gives us electricity; and the weak force organizes the decay of particular radioactive elements. However, the majority of scientists have always believed that there must be an underlying field from which all four forces arise and in which they are united.

If we look at some of the most significant theories in the history of physics, we can see a steady movement toward such unification, a search to explain more and more by less and less. It was apparent as far back as Newton, who observed that the motion of the planets, the phenomenon of the tides, and the movement of bodies on earth are all governed by the same law of gravity. This was a radical departure from the conventional wisdom of the day, and represented a triumph of simplicity and orderliness. Then, in the nineteenth century, James Clerk Maxwell came up with a theory that explained both electricity and magnetism at once, two forces that had been previously thought to be completely separate. In the twentieth century, Newton's theory was replaced by Einstein's more unifying general theory of relativity; and Maxwell's theory was translated into a more comprehensive quantum field theory called quantum electrodynamics.

In the past two decades, the pace toward unification has dramatically quickened: In 1967 the weak force was combined with electromagnetism, unifying two of the four forces of nature. Unification has subsequently been extended to include the strong force, leading to "grand unified theories" of the weak, electromagnetic, and strong interactions. Physicists are currently engaged in the task of formulating a theory of gravitation that would enable it to be unified with the other three forces. It is thought that when more energy is available to the field, then the boundaries of the four known forces of nature would be found to break down into aspects of a single unified field.

Until 1984, great hopes for such unification were placed upon a theory known as "extended supergravity" that appeared to pave the way for the concept of a "superfield." Theoretical physicist John Hagelin at Maharishi International University explains the theoretical model of a superfield as "a single field which embodies the grand totality of all the laws of nature as inseparable components of one self-sufficient, self-referral, infinitely dynamic field."

The concept of a superfield gave physicists an idea of what the universe might be like beyond what is called "Planck time," the shortest time and distance scale currently known. It seemed that the classical structure of time and space could be transformed into a completely different structure, an undivided continuum that combined perfect orderliness with unlimited energy and dynamism.

Despite the appeal of superfield theory, the mathematical problems associated with it proved insoluble. But such is the irresistible push toward unification that today an exciting new theory known as "superstring theory" has taken its place, and may turn out to resolve the ultimate goal of theoretical physics by providing a "Theory of Everything."

According to superstring theory, the universe at its most basic level is composed of infinitesimal "strings" of energy, spinning, curling, vibrating, and interacting with one another in a way that can represent any of the known particles of matter. And through the interaction of these particles, the four forces of nature become manifest. Although there are no experimental data as yet that prove the theory is correct, the current enthusiasm for superstrings is so great that according to a recent article in *The Chronicle of Higher Education*, nearly all graduate students in theoretical physics are writing theses on the topic. Because it seems to provide a long-awaited "real world" answer for the unification question, everyone *wants* superstring theory to be true. "What excites people," says physicist Stephen Shenker at the University of Chicago, "is that the theory, in a kind of broad-brush way, has a lot of the things that look like the real world. The inner coherence of it is really extraordinary. We see it as the true way to find out how the world works."[20]

Whether the unified field is made up of superstrings or not, perhaps we can most simply think of it in terms of the unifying patterns we considered earlier; in this light, the unified field would be the ultimate pattern--the largest, most complete, most coherent pattern of all. From this ultimate pattern would emerge all the smaller, localized patterns, all the laws of nature as we now know and experience them through the four forces. In this way we could understand our everyday world in all its great diversity as a series of fluctuations in an underlying field of perfect unity, orderliness, and symmetry.

Deepak Chopra, M.D., proposes that "the very nature of the anatomy and physiology of our sense apparatus limits our perception of the universe . . ." by freezing the vast potentialities of the unified field of fluctuating wave forms into "our familiar reality." He writes:

> It creates the illusion that mind, that realm of thoughts and images, is distinct from matter. But . . . they [thoughts and images] are composed of the same wave forms. . . . However, these wave forms resonate at a frequency not perceptible to . . . our ordinary waking state of consciousness. . . . The unified field . . . vibrating at a high frequency, creates mind and, resonating at a lower frequency, precipitates into matter. . . . We are, all of us and the objective world "out there," in essence the trinity of the unified field, mind and matter simultaneously.[21]

Unified-field theory is thus very compelling for everyone--not only for physicists and mathematicians--because it gives us a clue as to why at our most creative times, we are able to "break through" in a spontaneous way and experience the world transformed into "one thing," with no real boundaries to restrict us. Ultimately, if we could create from the level of the unified field, maintaining that universal breadth of awareness while focusing on anything we want to know or create, it would ensure our chances of becoming great.

Greatness from the Unified Field

> A hush of peace, a soundless calm descends. The struggle of distress and fierce impatience ends. . . . Then dawns the Invisible, the Unseen its truth reveals; my outward sense is gone, my inward essence feels.
>
> EMILY BRONTË

There have been a number of researchers who have collected and summarized the great experiential moments of many of the greats. Abraham Maslow used the expression "peak experiences" to describe them, Marghanita Laski called them "ecstatic moments," and William James called them "noetic experiences." There are now good indications that the unified field may be that field of silence which has been directly experienced throughout history by artists, poets, philosophers; by everyone who has ever had a "great moment." The unified field described by physicists today may be identical to the underlying source of creativity that great people feel they contact mentally when they receive a new idea. For if this field exists in all of nature, it must be locatable within the human nervous system, within our own human consciousness, and could thus be directly experienced as a state of awareness. This state, writes physicist Lawrence Domash, "may be a direct experience of the quantum level. . . . The 'enlightened man' may simply be the one who is able to experience a quantum mechanical world quantum mechanically."[22] We can suggest that human greatness is the ultimate result of being able to experience the unified field directly, to experience a quantum world in a quantum way.

We know from the descriptions of "great moments" that our nervous system is capable of functioning in a more coherent, more integrated manner than typically experienced. The unified-field model seems to be a useful approach to understanding these moments of greatness. Put another way, we could speculate that states of heightened organization in great people could best be described as functions of the unified field. And if we look at the subjective qualities of such momentary experiences, we can summarize them as follows:

- self-referral or self-referential--having within itself its own source of knowledge and validation or "rightness"
- self-sufficient--requiring nothing from the "outside"
- spontaneous
- silent
- infinitely dynamic--having its own unlimited energy
- eternal
- multilayered--everything happens "all at once"
- "superfluid"--a kind of frictionless flow
- defying logical or analytical thought
- coalescent, coherent, moving toward wholeness
- providing deeper levels of experience beyond the sensory

According to quantum physics, *each of these greatness characteristics is also a physical description of a quantum transformation within the unified field.* We could therefore say that during a typical "great moment," a quantum process goes on in one's mind and body much like that found in a quantum transformation: sudden expansion, zero friction, and zero entropy. Creativity researchers Paul Torrance and Laura K. Hall identify it as a "holistic" state of awareness, a state of "instant communication among all the parts." They describe how this transformation might work:

> The transcendence of consciousness from one mode of functioning to another is analogous to the transformation that certain fluids and metals go through when cooled to near absolute zero. Lead, for example, is transformed into a superconductor by cooling. In this state it becomes a perfect conductor; an electric current may flow forever, unrestricted, without friction. Electrons in this state form a single macroscopic coherent quantum wave indicating a transformation from multiplicity to wholeness.[23]

Both processes--the quantum and the creative--are described in terms of the sudden occurrence of inner change within the system and a resulting transition from one state to an entirely different state.

To summarize, we are suggesting that *creative quantum thought is to ordinary linear thought as a unified-field quantum process, such as superfluidity, is to an ordinary classical physics process.* Let's examine further some of these similarities.

Unified–Field-Based Experiences of Personal Greatness

At a creative moment . . . the poet has a sense of inexhaustible abundance. . . . This condition is one of joy. . . . In it the poet feels that his whole being is enlarged and that he is able to enjoy in an unprecedented completeness what in his ordinary life he enjoys only in fragments.

C. M. BOWRA

The real act of creation, contends Eudora Welty, comes from "all the connections that lie in wait for the writer"; all the "affinities," when they come together, form what she calls a kind of "confluence," a living field.

What Welty calls "confluence," mathematician Henri Poincaré called "coalescence." He was "fascinated by the way ideas coalesce in the mind to produce original thinking." He thought of all related ideas as "hooked atoms," which collide and give rise to new combinations. In a like manner, quantum systems are characterized by coherence, which causes their individual wave functions to coalesce into a collective state. Coalescence is thus the quantum equivalent of the "illumination" or "Aha!" experience with which we are familiar.

Mozart, for example, experienced first the melodies, then, within minutes of coalescence, he heard the whole symphony in polished form with all the parts individually discernible. He described his composition experiences in this way:

> Provided I am not disturbed, my subject enlarges itself, becomes methodized and defined, and though it be long, stands complete and finished in my mind, so that I can survey it like a fine picture or a beautiful statue at a glance. Nor do I hear in my imagination the parts successively, but I hear them, as it were *all at once*. What a delight this is I cannot tell! . . . When I proceed to write down my ideas . . . it is rarely different on paper than it was in my imagination.[24]

Along with coalescence, the ease of composition is similarly described by many great people--moments that are effortless and "right," which seem to occur in a natural and spontaneous way. "When I have those fantastic moments," says ballet dancer Edward Villella, "when all is happening right, it's so easy. I say to myself, my God, it's so easy."[25] Playwright Neil Simon also notices these unified–field-like experiences while he is working:

> It's hard to explain when things are going well. When I write something I like, I ask myself, "Who wrote that?" And I tell myself, "I didn't. I don't know where it came from." And yet I do know this. . . . It seems effortless.[26]

In addition to coalescence, effortlessness, and rightness, the unified-field model also serves to identify another "greatness" phenomenon, the experience of a continual, "frictionless flow." Actress Cicely Tyson recalls how a moment of greatness in the theater can feel like a flow: "When you push the button in a certain scene, it just flows.

There is no question how it will be, it just flows."[27]

Walking down Buckingham Palace Road, historian Arnold Toynbee had a great moment during which he "suddenly found himself in 'communion' not with just some particular episode of history, but with 'all that had been, and was, and was to come.' [He] was aware of the 'Passage of History' flowing through him in a mighty current, his own life 'welling like a wave in the flow of this vast tide.' " In Q terms Toynbee had such an experience because, as unified-field theorist John Hagelin explains: "With the quantum geometry of the unified field, there is no ability to distinguish past and future. Time, instead of flowing smoothly forward, can wrap around itself like a spring. And space can curl up on itself in such a way that to define distance in a classical sense seems impossible." This experience also evokes David Bohm's theory of "an implicate order," where the world is seen as an undivided whole in which everything, including human awareness, forms and dissolves, "like ripples, waves and vortices in a flowing stream."

This understanding further suggests the possibility that a "greatness transformation" could go on indefinitely, bringing a kind of self-referring, never-ending flow of creative experiences and ideas. Writer Virginia Woolf predicted this aspect of the quantum field when she speculated that "there may be some state of mind in which one could continue without effort because nothing is required to be held back."[28]

The condition of happiness during a creative moment is also a universal experience. When things were going well in his writing, lyricist Alan J. Lerner felt real joy: "Suddenly, you reach out and catch it in the air. . . . I get an exhilaration with a line, or a few verses, like no time else. At that moment, I'm probably as jubilant, as close to the real joy of living as I ever get."[29] And that joy feels expansive, says the perennial Bob Hope, describing his great moments in performing:

> When you turn the audience, that's sheer joy. . . . It's like
> being on the winning team, knowing you are doing the job.
> When you're floating free, when the laughs are coming in large,
> you regulate your timing in the great free-wheeling style. . . .
> Then timing is the rhythm of the world.[30]

A great moment can actually be so full as to bring to one's conscious awareness material and inspiration that last a lifetime. One day early in his career, during a walk in a park in Budapest, inventor Nikola Tesla experienced a burst of revelation that revealed scores of valuable inventions:

> As he gazed into the flaming orb of the setting sun, there had flashed into his mind, not only the marvelous invention of the rotary magnetic field and the many uses of multiple alternating currents, but also the grand generalization that everything in Nature operated on the principle of vibrations that corresponded to alternating currents. The host of inventions and discoveries which he made in all succeeding years had their roots in that sublime experience.[31]

Yet such a great moment is rarely "excited" in the sense of being overwhelming. Rather, it is usually described as utterly still, timeless, eternal. People who have experienced this timeless, spaceless realm appear both to themselves and others as having accessed some sort of "infinite data base," in which anything is possible, and in a sense they may have. They may have tuned into the laws of nature directly by experiencing the unified field itself within their awareness. Through such access, any of us could experience the dynamic source of our creativity.

Moreover, by being directly in contact with the unified field on the basis of one's own awareness, any individual could potentially function in a more orderly, more holistic way, thinking and living closer to the patterns and laws of nature. So, accessing the unified field could actually change us unconditionally in the direction of greatness. How would this work?

Quantum Expansion, Quantum Leaps

All great moments seem to bring with them some expansion of awareness. We could say essentially that quantum thought differs from ordinary thought by introducing an inner experience of new awareness. It is this expanding awareness that underlies the creative process--a process involving expansion, discovery, and the coming of new knowledge. It is also a unifying experience; a contacting of a deeper level of awareness and a subsequent revelation of a larger whole, a more complex pattern. And often it is the completion of a gap, long awaited, the fulfillment of what Laski calls "an intellectual want of long standing."

One of the clearest, most moving descriptions of such a great moment is Helen Keller's account of how she first discovered language under the guidance of her teacher Annie Sullivan:

> We walked down the path to the well house, attracted by the fragrance of the honeysuckle with which it was covered. Someone was drawing water and my teacher placed my hand under the spout. As the cool stream gushed over one hand, she spelled into the other the word water, first slowly, then rapidly. I stood still, my whole attention fixed upon the motions of her fingers. Suddenly I felt a misty consciousness as of something forgotten--a thrill of returning thought, and somehow the mystery of language was revealed to me. I knew then that w-a-t-e-r meant the wonderful cool something that was flowing over my hand. That living word awakened my soul, gave it light, hope, joy, set it free! There were barriers still, it is true, but barriers that could in time be swept away. I left the well house eager to learn. Everything had a name, and each name gave birth to a new thought. As we returned to the house, every object which I touched seemed to quiver with life. That was because I saw everything with the strange new sight that had come to me.[32]

Her description is so revealing because she is able to identify the precise mechanics of a deepened awareness locating new knowledge, what we are calling contact with the unified field within human consciousness. It starts with (1) contact with a field of *silence*: She "stood still"; (2) next comes the finest, most subtle feeling of *expanding awareness*, an intuition; then (3) there is a concrete *thought* that indicates the accessing of (4) some *knowledge*: "I knew then . . ." There is also (5) an accompanying feeling of pleasure, of the heart expanding, the description of *joy*; and finally (6) there is *unification*: first, an increase in wholeness on the level of the senses, then (7) *expansion*: "I left the well house eager to learn . . . because I saw everything with this strange new sight that had come to me."

This and other revelatory experiences can be broken down into the above sequence, but the steps are virtually simultaneous, occurring in a microquantum scale of time. The "all-at-once" feeling is more how it is experienced: The knower, the object of knowledge, and the process of knowing are actually one process, one experience that occurs all together. This is the subjective confirmation of the quantum physicist's explanation of how the observer, the object of observation, and the process of observation are really indivisible.

This is also what is meant by knowing something "directly." The result is an immediate expansion of consciousness. Philosopher Susanne Langer describes it as follows:

> . . . suddenly "seen" things that were always there. . . . [It] illuminates presences which simply had no form for us before the light went on. . . . We turn the light here, there, and everywhere and the limits of thought recede before it.[33]

Similarly, physicist Victor Weisskopf reminds us: "What's beautiful in science is the same thing that's beautiful in Beethoven. There's a fog of events and suddenly you see a connection. It expresses a complex of human concerns that goes deeply to you, that connects things that were always in you that were never put together before."[34]

Moreover, it does not appear to be a matter of trying, more just letting it happen. Then the answer comes. As the philosopher Nietzsche explained in *Ecce Homo*, "One hears--one does not seek; one takes--one does not ask who gives; a thought flashes out like lightning. . . . Everything occurs quite without volition." It may be that the unified field is doing it all.

We saw earlier that quantum theory explains how nature functions with perfect efficiency through the law of least action. Innumerable paths could be chosen, but the one in which the least amount of activity is required is automatically selected. Nature seems actually to consider all the possibilities in such a way that other paths, though not strictly forbidden, have a very small probability of occurrence. So, when we say that people who are great allow nature to flow through them unrestricted, we are saying that they are letting the best thing that could happen, happen.

Connecting the Moments

Obviously, greatness is quite tenuous and even elusive if it is only lived in moments. Yet unfortunately, most people don't experience their greatness consistently throughout their lives. And those geniuses who have had to rely on isolated moments of creative insight rather than sustained access to a field of creation often report feeling deprived and frustrated.

True, if you were to line up all the great moments of your life and compress them into one period of time, you would be leading a great (albeit perhaps short) life. But what about living this way all the time? How do we go from great moments to greatness as a permanent way of life?

What we have been considering is that the ability to sustain greatness may become a real possibility when we understand that greatness is connected to an underlying field that is always there, the unified field. This view is consistent with the theories of Plato, and Jung, along with many Eastern thinkers and others who have described a field of collective universal knowledge that the individual picks up on in a settled state of awareness.

Forty years ago, psychologist L. L. Thurstone hypothesized that individuals differ in their ability to be in rapport with what he called the "unconscious stages of the creative act." He suggested that an easy flow of ideas could be available at any time and regularly accessed by a mind that is in such a state of alertness at all times.

However, such alertness must require a developed physiology. It's possible that great individuals have had perfect spontaneous moments of contact with a field of creation because at the moment of expansion of awareness, their nervous systems were functioning perfectly; they were relaxed yet alert, stable yet open. Therefore, any of us may have either momentary experiences of greatness or lifetime ones, depending on our physiological ability to sustain this contact. Physiology seems to make a difference, because in an experience in which everything seems to occur all at once, very fine levels of focal discrimination are required to be maintained along with a corresponding awareness of the unified field.

What we are suggesting is that perhaps the reason we can have "peak" experiences among ordinary everyday experiences is because, as the physicists tell us, quantum coherent systems can coexist in the same material substance that simultaneously supports ordinary incoherent states of matter. In other words, order and disorder can occur at the same time in the same system. But because of its orderliness, even a minute amount of a superfluid in a quantum system can create order. This is how laser light is created, for example: A few coherent photons are lined up and all at once the whole system is transformed into a synchronous coherent light. By analogy, an "ordinary" person can have moments of perfection or of greatness--moments of "super-conductivity of creativity." At such times, one experiences one's mind as "laserlike," crystal clear, not just awake but what composer Johannes Brahms called "superconscious":

> I feel vibrations that thrill my whole being. . . . In this exalted state I see clearly what is obscure in my ordinary moods. . . . Those vibrations assume the forms of distinct mental images after I have formulated my desire and resolve in regard to what I want. . . . Straight away, the ideas flow upon me, directly. . . . Not only do I see distinct themes in my mind's eye, but they are clothed in the right forms, harmonies, and orchestrations. Measure by measure the finished product is revealed to me when I am in those rare, inspired moods. . . . I am still conscious but right on the border of losing consciousness. . . . The term subconscious is a very inadequate appellation for such an extraordinarily powerful state of mind. . . . Superconscious would be a better term.[35]

In the very near future, our understanding of neurobiology may be refined to the point where coherent quantum processes within the unified field are recognized as taking place in the human nervous system *all* the time in daily life. This would explain how we could always experience the parts and the whole together, to maintain the experience of unity, the feeling of being united with the universe within our own awareness while going about our daily routines.

It may be that these quantum processes normally occur in a very simple, natural way under all kinds of circumstances, but that the ability to focus attention consistently on these subtle levels of physiological functioning must be developed. Later on, in Chapter Five, we'll see how well some of the current research on human physiology supports such a possibility. But first let's take a different look at the way in which greatness grows in us individually.

3

———— ❖ ————

WHO IS GREAT?
LOCATING PERSONAL
GREATNESS BEYOND AGE,
GENDER,
AND OCCUPATION

We have proposed that greatness can be best thought of as a kind of field that any of us can access. We also want to consider how greatness manifests itself in our lives. In this chapter, we are going to see how the field of greatness can flow into even the most restrictive situations--if it's lively inside us.

❖

Beyond Biography

Great geniuses have the shortest biographies.

EMERSON

Many of us are avid lifelong readers of biography and we read the biographies of the greats with a definite eye toward learning their secrets. How did they live? What did they think or do to become great? We are interested in them not just because of their fame, but because of their *experiences*; they heard the music, led the nations, felt the movements of the planets--they were the ones who had the deepest experiences.

Very often, however, we find that the lives of the greats do not mirror their genius or our estimation of the kind of life we think they *ought* to have led. Freud understood this, and believed that "one ought to differentiate between greatness of achievement and greatness of personality." Looking at great people from the outside, it isn't clear that they have anything in common; some greats, like Beethoven, Van Gogh, and Galileo, led relatively unhappy lives, and some, like Bach, Haydn, and Picasso, led relatively happy lives. Moreover, many great individuals led mundane, uneventful lives: Some saints and holy men and women living in mountain caves, whose lives were silent and solitary, had almost nothing happen to them.

Ultimately, reading biographies really tells us only one thing: Greatness does not seem to be associated with a particular kind of life. Or, to put it another way, greatness has never had a strong sociological profile: We can't learn a great deal about greatness from the changing outer circumstances in which it occurs. The type of environment in which great individuals have been raised varies tremendously. Rich and poor, good families and bad families, all sorts of backgrounds have been represented. And even though the *kind* of lifetime achievement often relates to family background and education, many great people have been entirely uneducated and have had little traditional support. According to Eudora Welty, the creating comes from within anyway, and the life of the author is really secondary. She describes herself as having led a very sheltered life, which we know in no way hindered her ability to create huge worlds of fiction.

Overall, in looking at even the most unfortunate lives and personalities of the greats, we are once again reminded that greatness to be greatness is actually characterized by the *transcendence of limits or boundaries*. What we come to know is that many great people had gifts that did not always bring balance into their lives, but that human consciousness is so powerful, it can manifest greatness even in an imperfect nervous system or in a most limiting outer environment. So we could propose that greatness seems to happen regardless of the events of one's personal life.

Because ultimately, as Virginia Woolf reminds us, greatness lies in the ability to put oneself aside, to transcend the "I." This is the gift she finds in Emily Brontë's work, for example:

> . . . There is no "I" in Wuthering Heights. There are no governesses. There are no employers. There is love, but it is not the love of men and women. Emily was inspired by some more general conception. The impulse which urged her to create was not her own suffering or her own injuries. . . . It is this suggestion of power underlying the apparitions of human nature and lifting them up into the presence of greatness that gives the book its huge stature among other novels. . . .
>
> It is as if she could tear up all that we know human beings by, and fill these unrecognizable transparencies with such a gust of life that they transcend reality. Hers, then, is the rarest of all powers. She could free life from its dependence on facts. . . .[1]

Shakespeare and Jane Austen, observed Woolf, are two giants who had the kind of internal universality of awareness that prompted them to keep their egos and personalities out of their work and their personal grievances removed: "When people compare Shakespeare and Jane Austen, they may mean that the minds of both had consumed all impediments; and for that reason we do not know Jane Austen and we do not know Shakespeare, and for that reason Jane Austen pervades every word that she wrote, and so does Shakespeare."[2]

So, if greatness is a transcendent thing, keeping life events and personality at bay, how can we tell who is great?

Today, in our product-oriented society, we have a tendency to equate being great with achievements that are based on how much an individual has accomplished--how many plays produced on Broadway, how many franchises sold, how many titles or awards received. We may then deem someone great based on the sum total of their life accomplishments. Or we may believe that greatness lies all within a person, independent of what he or she has achieved. But even so, we may think of individual greatness in terms of some aspect of background or personality--or of what we do, our occupations.

As we are all too aware, our society is heavily focused on comparing personal data. We worry about how we are doing relative to weight, height, and hair color, not to mention age, gender, and occupation. No one would deny that any correlation between hair color and greatness, if such a connection were proven, is purely superficial. But how about age, gender, career? Is it really true--as history *seems* to indicate--that the great people are nearly all dead Caucasian men who primarily studied art, politics, science, and music? In reality, greatness to be greatness needs to be considered beyond all imposed limits, and therefore ought not to be specifically dependent upon *any* personal data. Therefore, in order truly to identify those people in whom greatness shows up, it seems we need to dispel a few more myths.

❖

The Grown-ups:
From Adolescence to Adult Development

If you don't live up to your greatest potential, then you are cheating God.

LOUISE NEVELSON

Elmo Zumwalt, Jr., former commander of the U.S. Navy, is said to have revolutionized the navy's practices in just a few years at the helm. He claims the reason for his success stemmed from his simple belief that people will respond well to being treated as grown-ups. But Zumwalt's attitude is unusual; most of us are used to living our adolescence even into old age because that is as far as our society demands that we grow.

Indeed, for centuries neurological development had been thought to peak around age twenty-five, shortly after adolescence. And because of this outlook, most of Western psychology--as represented in the work of Freud, Jean Piaget, and Erik Erikson--has focused more on child development than on adult development with regard to creativity, intelligence, and those abilities that manifest human greatness. Noteworthy exceptions have been Jung and Maslow, who each proposed that the healthiest, most fully developed individuals are the ones who keep growing beyond adolescence into adulthood, and are thus the ones most likely to become great. (Eastern thinkers, on the other hand, have long taught ways to effect the development of post adolescents and adults.)

Now, however, a new wave of research, some of which will be discussed in a later chapter, indicates that human physiology is really much more capable of adult change and growth than we ever knew, and that intellectual and creative development can (and should) continue onward throughout life into old age.

This research opens new directions for adult development that emphasize the reality of greatness from a much more broad-based perspective than the outdated "rare genius" view. It indicates that "ordinary" human experiences can be lived at much higher, more integrated levels of awareness and behavior than previously understood. For example, a recent theoretical description of adult development proposed by psychologist Charles Alexander at Maharishi International University identifies individuals in terms of their growth toward higher states of development. According to Alexander, most children "look ahead" developmentally. Although the six-year-old sees the world through six-year-old eyes, he also sees something good about being nine years old. In other words, he sees a stage of life toward which he knows he's moving and is starting to look toward that future time. "When I grow up," he thinks, "I'll be the best soccer player in my school." But do we think so clearly and project so optimistically into the future when we reach sixty? What the new research is suggesting is that indeed we should, because just as there are definite growth stages of childhood, puberty, and adolescence, there are also levels of development associated with adulthood, including old age, that enable us to become truly "grown up" at last, in mind and heart as well as in chronological age. As we shall see, adult development doesn't just mean behaving in a mature way during a divorce; it involves profound physiological and psychological growth.

These higher states of awareness available to us ought to be part of our normal developmental growth. We only have to understand them and do what is necessary to experience them. Unless we do, we "freeze" human development well before its prime. We give up, and by doing so, says Alexander, "we forego higher stages of evolution and end up living in an adolescent world." It's like having a 1,000-megabyte computer program and using it only to add up the grocery bill.

This may result in our having less than grown-up expectations of ourselves. Whereas both children and true grown-ups may think of rising to greatness, there is a kind of adolescent philosophy that may appear at any age which involves thinking, "Big deal!" "Why bother; life's like that--nobody's perfect." As a result, many of us never do grow up to become the great human beings we could be if we had the proper attitude and started living up to our better possibilities.

We can thus assume that the greats are the actual grown-ups; they see and experience the best, and seek to move themselves and others in that evolutionary direction. They have grown beyond the adolescent approach to life that often sees only limitations. They eliminate the gap between the open qualities of childhood and the greatness development of adulthood. Most important, they give a new meaning to the aging process.

❖

The Age of Greatness

Our creative faculty is the only one that can defy Father Time.

ALEX OSBORN

We may ask, How old is a great person? Or at what average age do great people become great? However, when we measure our lives in years and decades, we tend to develop a false psychology of "growing older" that is unrelated either to our physiological or mental capacities. We may then misperceive the totality of greatness. Mozart was young, seven, when his first composition was published; Golda Meir was old, seventy-one, when she became prime minister of Israel. It's hard to believe that the Reverend Dr. Martin Luther King, Jr., was only thirty-nine when he was killed; he left such a lasting impression of great maturity and wisdom. On the other hand, it may also be a surprise to learn that Michelangelo designed St. Peter's Church when he was almost ninety, because we generally associate such intensely dynamic creative activity with youth.

In reality, the greats among us may uphold the developmental values of all ages in themselves because, according to what is called "the theory of neoteny," there is a link between higher adult developmental stages and the retention into adulthood of traits associated with childhood. In other words, the qualities we often find in great people, such as flexibility, curiosity, energy, receptivity to new ideas, and lovingness, are first found in children and then maintained through adulthood. Anthropologist Ashley Montagu suggests that it is the unique capacity of the human being to continue its juvenile traits into old age. No other species seems to do this; the traits of youth die out in them. For example, although the juvenile human and the juvenile ape both display "the ability to play, the sense of humor, ability to learn . . . curiosity and inventiveness . . . imagination, the ability to make-believe . . . ," these traits disappear in fully grown apes, while they continue in humans. The eminent scientist Konrad Lorenz called this *"the unique human trait of always remaining in a state of development* (my italics)."[3]

Because highly creative adults have been found to retain these qualities of childhood as they age, it should come as no surprise that recent research indicates that the developmental trajectory of creativity, unlike other developmental trajectories, is "nonlinear": that is, both child and adult creativity resemble each other more than not, and both young children and creative adults have similar ways of processing knowledge. Says Harvard University researcher Howard Gardner, "Indeed, what may characterize the especially creative adult is precisely the capacity to gain access readily to earlier forms of knowing and understanding . . . which may prove of the essence in highly innovative work."[4] This implies that the greatness associated with developed creativity is not dependent upon one's age but upon one's inner experiences as one grows.

Of course, retaining the valuable traits of childhood during adulthood also requires an accompanying growth of integration and wisdom in order for us to rise to greatness. This combination of trait retention and ongoing development only occurs in adults. When we look at highly developed children, it's another matter.

As pointed out earlier, the child prodigies we hear of used to be a convincing factor in the argument that people are born great, with its implied corollary that greatness couldn't be developed or acquired. But not all child prodigies grow up to be great. And the truth is that most of them are born to families who devote themselves to the talents of their child at an earlier age and with a stronger dedication than most.

According to Montagu, "Educability is the outstanding species characteristic of humans." There is no doubt that those early environments that are well geared to a child's learning capacities have produced the great child prodigies. (John Stuart Mill, Mozart, and Julius Caesar were born into families that provided such education. By age three, Mill knew Greek, Mozart played the piano, and Caesar was riding with his uncle into battle.)

In addition, we can see from the results of such intensive early education in child prodigies, that these children often possess *adult* characteristics that distinguish them from their peers. They are generally brilliant learners with exceptional memories, are able to understand abstract thought at a young age, and they usually have a highly developed ability (uncommon in most children and many adults) to focus for long periods on the task at hand. In addition, they have an intense thirst for knowledge unusual for their age group. All of which makes them more adult. And so they become a blend of child and adult. (Because of this, we are often a little uncomfortable around them.)

But whereas adults benefit by retaining childhood qualities, child prodigies, not having had the depth of experience of adult life, generally lack several vital characteristics of greatness, such as innovation, wisdom, and depth. According to a recent *Nova* program, the fields in which such prodigies excel are musical performance (rarely composition), chess, gymnastics (before age ten), and math (after age 10). Each of these activities requires great focus but no great originality. We can think of violinist Yehudi Menuhin, gymnast Nadia Comaneci, chess player Bobby Fischer, and mathematician Norbert Wiener, all of whom began their startling accomplishments at a very young age. However, there are no child prodigies in nuclear physics or painting or literature, and one wouldn't want a surgeon who was three years old, even if she *had* memorized Grey's *Anatomy* cover to cover. Most qualities of greatness have to wait until we are adults to become fully enlivened and permanent in our lives. While we admire the works of the child Mozart, it is the adult Mozart who completely captures us. So although greatness is ageless in that it can start to appear at any age, it usually takes a certain amount of living to see it through to its maximum development, to acquire the depth of experience that brings the happiness and fulfillment that are also associated with greatness.

The Growth of Greatness
Through the Ages

For age is opportunity no less
Than youth itself, though in another dress,
And as the evening twilight fades away
The sky is filled with stars, invisible by day.

LONGFELLOW, "MORITURI SALUTAMUS"

If life begins at forty, greatness may actually hold out until eighty. In remembering Eubie Blake, pianist Billy Taylor commented: "One hundred years of creativity is something to aspire to. He played more as he got older." There are vast numbers of people throughout history whose most significant work was accomplished at the end of their lives--who seemed to have waited until their knowledge and experience were "big" enough, until they felt sure of what they wanted to do and how they wanted to be, and such integration occurred at seventy, or eighty or older. William O. Douglas, Louise Nevelson, Marian Anderson, George Balanchine, Georgia O'Keeffe, Alfred Hitchcock, Jacques Cousteau, Carl Jung, Rembrandt, Cezanne, Turner, Renoir, Chagall, Gauguin, Miró, Bach, Brahms, Haydn, and Tennyson are just a few of the greats who kept growing creatively as they got older.

The idea that great people live with such creative intensity that they burn out and die young is actually a myth. The reality is, our creative lives often *keep* us from dying young. The always-productive Picasso died at ninety-one; Michelangelo was close to ninety; Matisse's famous paper cutouts were a new art form he developed at age eighty-one; Henri Rousseau painted his most famous jungle pictures at sixty-five; Titian lived, it is thought, until at least ninety-nine, and painted his great "Venus and Adonis" while in his eighties. Goethe wrote *Faust*, Sophocles wrote *Oedipus,* and Verdi composed *Otello* and *Falstaff,* all when they were eighty or older. Playwright George Bernard Shaw's mind was said to be as sharp at ninety-four as it had been at age thirty. And these creators were not atypical.

According to Francis J. Braceland, M.D., writing in the *Journal of the National Association of Private Psychiatric Hospitals*, "Longitudinal studies--those that follow the same people over a long period of time--clearly show that intellectual abilities of healthy people grow greater through the years rather than less." In addition, it is obvious that the people who keep working are the ones whose minds keep working. The development of higher forms of intellect in humans is associated with complex symbol usage and more intense use of specialized areas within the brain. As we'll see in Chapter Five, the more we use the brain, the more it grows: Such brain growth continues into old age; therefore, new behavior constellations can develop at any time throughout life.

Of course, some older people do become rigid in their ways, especially if they believe their mental faculties will decrease with age--the expectation often produces such a decline. This rigidity is really based less on the infirmities of age than on years of established neurological patterns of functioning. What has been learned over the years can be always be modified. When a program is provided for changing to a more flexible, developmentally "healthy" state, older people respond extremely well and can actually reverse the aging process. For example, Harvard University researchers found that when elderly individuals (eighty years and older) were taught the technique of Transcendental Meditation, they showed enhanced learning capacity, improved cognitive and behavioral functioning, improved mental health, lowered blood pressure, and, as an overall effect, they lived longer than those who were not taught the technique.[5]

Among the groups of highest "well-being" people whom Gail Sheehy identified in her research on "pathfinders," the most fulfilled were over sixty-five. Integrative development continues into old age because thinking and feeling can continue to deepen even when the senses become less acute.

Impressionist painter Claude Monet had cataracts, which distorted his perception, but he used this distortion to paint his water lilies, and what we experience in his paintings is delicacy, lightness, beauty, and softness--coming not from perfect eyesight, but from perfect insight into the more subtle characteristics of nature. The mind can still be keen even when the body is less strong; creativity and love of life continue to flow even when physical activities are restricted.

There is also another myth--that people lose their drive and desire as they age and therefore can't keep up. True, when men and women grow old and retire, or slow the fast pace that society has required of them, they may feel a tremendous loss, both in self-esteem and in the channels of activity open to them. This could occur if they have become accustomed to a life of service to family, to friends, to coworkers, to a company, or to society. The paths of self-expression, of giving, seem to close, and it feels as if growth is ending. "Unemployment and retirement without a constructive purpose are unnatural," wrote Dr. Jonas Salk, because "as we age, we actually . . . handle our life situations with much more skill and satisfaction."[6]

But this is simply a limitation of our own culture. Under normal circumstances, there are several possible reasons why older people can finally come into their own greatness. Mythologist Joseph Campbell has said that young people often hesitate to act because they see the future structured by today's decisions. An older person, he says, has no fear of the future; "the whole world becomes plastic." Using our quantum model of greatness, we could say that as we age, we start living more in tune with the unified field. As an older man or woman begins to look beyond the cycle of life and death in order to overcome the fear of death, he or she may begin to sense that there is a deeper essence of life that has permanency and is untouched by death. This essence may be what the British poet Kathleen Raine identified when she wrote the following lines in "In My Seventieth Year":

It is enough, now I am old,
That everywhere, above, beneath,
About, within me, is the one
Presence, more intimate and near
Than mothering hands or love's embrace.

Old age seems to give one objectivity and a broadened awareness, an appreciation of an unbounded reality of life; as a result, older people may enjoy a certain ease they never experienced before. Psychologically, they often describe the feeling as a great *freedom to be themselves*--not to have to answer to anyone but themselves. But more significantly, they may find that they are breaking out of a restricted world view into a recognition of a bigger reality. They are thus, Campbell points out, attaching themselves to a more permanent state of life than politics or economics or social life. And once they become part of this larger reality, they seem to radiate wisdom. In the words of Sophocles: "The wise never grow old; their minds are nursed/ By living with the holy light of day."

This is where greatness really begins, right between the unbounded and the boundaries, between a big, unchanging reality and the restrictions of individual lives. In this way greatness almost has a life of its own. And nowhere has this been more evident than in the lives of women.

Where Were All the Great Women?

There is no mark on the wall to measure the precise height of women. There are no yard measures, neatly divided into the fractions of an inch, that one can lay against the qualities of a good mother or the devotion of a daughter, or the fidelity of a sister, or the capacity of a housekeeper.

VIRGINIA WOOLF

Why, in the history of greatness, do there seem to have been so few great women? Again it's a question of definition: If we equate great with well known, there were indeed only a few. But if unknown greats are acceptable, there were certainly many more. Researchers have recently begun to find some of the "lost women" of history, unearthing the names of those whose professional and creative work was purposely hidden, women who had to use male pseudonyms and names of male colleagues in order to bring their work to the public. We now know how many more women wrote, painted, performed surgery, invented, fought in wars, and generally contributed creativity and intelligence to society in what were then forbidden channels. And the acceptable channels--motherhood, teaching, religious life-- were never regarded in terms of greatness.

Of the great women we have heard of, the majority were writers because most educated women could at least afford pen and paper. Still, writing too was a difficult occupation under the social constraints. Even with family support, it was extremely challenging. Imagine Jane Austen, sitting quietly in the midst of a bustling, active drawing room, looking demure and ladylike while acutely observing and memorizing the most minute details of the subtle interactions between family and visitors. No possibility existed then for Austen to seek a private place to write down her observations. She had no "room of her own."

Yet Austen and the other great women writers were rare, as were all successful women in the traditional arts and sciences. For even if we eliminate "well-known" from the definition of greatness, women still seem to be erased from its history.

Perhaps no one has thought more deeply and insightfully about the issue of women's greatness than writer-critic Virginia Woolf, and it is to her insights we can turn. According to Woolf, the reasons for women's limited participation in the history of creative genius can be easily summed up:

When a woman was liable, as she was in the fifteenth century,
to be beaten and flung about the room if she did not marry
the man of her parents' choice, the spiritual atmosphere was not
favourable to the production of works of art.[7]

So, what happened to women's greatness if only a handful of women were able to express themselves and make their mark in history through the usual channels? How did their greatness express itself, if at all?

Melanie Brown

Women's Greatness: Life Products

Art is what men do. Crafts are what women and natives do.

GLORIA STEINEM

For centuries women were considered noncreative and noneducable. As with other uneducated groups, however, creativity always has a way of finding its own channels, irrespective of circumstance. And greatness, being an expression of the best of human nature, automatically springs up wherever consciousness is developed.

However, because creative opportunities were so limited for women, their greatness was rarely expressed in *products of a long-lasting nature*. Women may have propagated the species, but rarely the arts. They have represented nature, but not its "imitation." The artistic experiences we associate with the majority of great people had to be integrated into women's everyday lives, and not kept separate and distinct from ordinary work. The "products" are generally the useful ones-- the quilts, the baskets, the blankets, the pottery. Women's art has been more a social art, a living art, but not Art. As Woolf wrote, "Often nothing tangible remains of a woman's day. The food that has been cooked is eaten; the children that have been nursed have gone out into the world." Great paintings last; great dinners don't.

One interesting result of this situation is that women seem to have cultivated an ability over the centuries to be less ego involved with their art, less attached to the ownership of their work. In a contemporary study of men and women artists, researchers found that all other things being equal--money earned, critical acclaim, gallery representation, etc.--the one characteristic that distinguished men from women artists was orientation to the future. The men were consciously taking steps to ensure their future reputation; the women were not and, perhaps most significantly, *had no desire to do so*.

Thus, if we evaluate greatness as the legacy of lasting products, women have an insignificant quantity to show us. Therefore, we either have to assume that there were no great women or we have to rethink our definition of greatness. We have to move from external

86

parameters to internal ones. It's really a matter of what we're willing to attach value to. If we're willing to value a person as much as a product, if we can value the development of personal qualities as much as the making of things--the "being" aspect of greatness as much as the "doing" aspect--the greatness of women becomes more evident. And in this way we've enlarged our view of greatness to include inner quality as well as outer expression.

Let's see how this larger view of greatness has been manifested in the lives of women.

❖

The Permissible Avenues of Expression: The Supportive Professions

Women, as nurturers, use power to empower others.

JEAN BAKER MILLER

Even when they were educated, women had little opportunity for independent work; other than writing, there have been only a few acceptable channels of expression, and these have been service-oriented, mainly teaching and social services, both within and apart from religious life.

One channel, however, dominates all others as the way in which women have most consistently contributed to the history of greatness.

"All I am or ever hope to be I owe to my sainted mother," wrote Abraham Lincoln. Lincoln was not alone in this realization. The single and *only* consistent factor that great men and women identify as the basis for their life achievements is the positive influence of their mothers. This influence seems to coincide with the predominance of first-born children among history's eminents who are said to have received the most attention at home.

We know that many men who became high-powered leaders, like former Presidents Franklin D. Roosevelt, Harry S. Truman, and Lyndon B. Johnson, had noticeably close relationships with their mothers throughout their adult lives. Both L.B.J. and Truman had been taught to read by their mothers when very young, well before they entered school. And in there for the long haul, General Douglas MacArthur's mother, Pinky, stayed at a nearby hotel for four years to be present while he attended West Point. But although these mothers were often in full attendance, they apparently knew when to let go and encourage independence.

There are some who believe that great mothers are not really great, that their greatness is only "indirect," i.e., through the achievements of their children and are therefore not really significant. But is this another greatness myth? What these mothers learn to develop is the skill or art of eliciting greatness in others, of helping their children express their best qualities. This is exactly what great mentors and teachers do. No one would argue about the relative contribution of a Socrates to a Plato, or an Annie Sullivan to a Helen Keller, or about their true greatness in their own right.

When one mother began to study language development in her child using the methods child psychologist Jean Piaget used to study his own children, she validated a theory of the development of language at the same time her anthropologist husband was concluding his research on language development in a particular tribe. They both reached nearly identical conclusions about the origins of language and were able to contribute to each other's research as well as to the field of linguistics. But which of this woman's achievements was more significant? Should we value the more specialized channel of linguist more than the multifold channel of mother? Looking at the job of being a mother helps remind us of what greatness really is.

The outward activities of motherhood seem to comprise all the occupations of life in one: psychologist, teacher, linguist, musician, artist, lawyer, judge, decorator, nutritionist, doctor, mathematician, bookkeeper, hostess, diplomat, and, of course, politician. Throughout history, the job of being a woman required having to do everything and to do it well. Today we call her "superwoman," but there have always been "Renaissance women," even during the Renaissance (though we generally hear only about Renaissance men). If a woman had another career, she also had to run a perfect household, to be careful always to uphold all the social necessities of the day. To handle these multiple roles well requires a kind of personal integrity, a personality so integrated that it can finely tune in and adjust to every little change: Like a great artist attuned to nature's laws, when a woman maintains this balance, it is a sign of greatness.

Within their history of devotional service to others, whether as mothers or not, may lie the reasons why women have come to place greater emphasis on heart values over mind values. Despite educational reversals of the past century--a period that has seen women educated alongside men--women still put "people-caring" values first. Very few will give up the relationship-family aspect of their lives for their professions. Even very successful career women today place their relationships ahead of their high work achievements in identifying what really makes them happy. All values--social, professional, heart, and mind--are considered to contribute to the sum total of happiness. Women seem to require this totality in their lives and feel off-center if things are one-sided or unintegrated. Also, if a diminishing value is placed on the nurturing activities of women, the balance may be further thrown off.

The status of women is an index of the development of society. When women must band together to seek respect, society is obviously not balanced. Lack of greatness in women comes when there is a feeling of being alien and outside the most powerful currents of the culture. As Woolf describes it, "If one is a woman, one is often surprised by a sudden splitting off of consciousness, . . . when from being the natural inheritor of . . . civilisation, she becomes, on the contrary, outside of it, alien and critical."[8] Then personal and social integrity are lost.

When society is "on center," women are never second-class citizens, but emotional and spiritual mainstays sought for their power and wisdom. The way society has been structured in the large majority of cultures, the home is the center of daily life and the mother is the center of the home. Fortunately for civilization, home and motherhood have not always meant waxing the floors and driving the kids to school. Rather, "home" has been the inner basis for the development and progress of human life. And "mother" has meant not only the family mother, but also the symbolic, creative, and nurturing caretaker--the creator at the center of life--that represents silence, the inner life, the true home of humanity. In most cultures home has meant this inner self, and the journey home (like Ulysses' back to Penelope) means returning to the basic self--to the silence of one's inner nature.

Women have thus traditionally been the guardians of inner life, a life they have had ample opportunity to develop.

Women's Inner Education

> The especial genius of women I believe to be electrical in movement, intuitive in function, spiritual in tendency.
>
> MARGARET FULLER

On the journey inward, great people contact a deeper level of pure knowledge through their intuition. In the quantum model described earlier, all discovery is self-discovery, so nothing is required outside the self. And because it is self-sufficient, knowledge can be gained in isolation from the outside world, sometimes even more easily.

We might suggest that throughout the centuries, women, denied both an outer education and the opportunity to express their creative nature in "products," kept their creative energies turned inward in a kind of imposed withdrawal unknown to most men outside the clergy, and they developed the more abstract mental functioning we have come to associate with heightened intuition. Thus, not having been given a reasoning education, women educated themselves intuitively. Since intuition is developed through the ability to turn one's attention inward, it may have been better accessed without distractions from the environment.

Although there is no such thing as "woman's intuition" per se, it is commonly accepted that women do have more integrated intuitive skills than men. Deprived of ways to develop specialized analytical brain function, women no doubt relied on their intuitive abilities to gain knowledge of the world.

This intuitive mode of "knowing" is a dynamic aspect of the creative process and, interestingly, a very specific indication of the way women traditionally have "known" and lived greatness. For example, Saint Teresa of Ávila, the sixteenth-century founder of the Carmelite order, describes what she calls the experience of an intellectual vision--what we might term a direct cognition of knowledge without being "educated":

> It is as if a person who had never learned anything, nor yet was able to read, nor had ever studied, were suddenly to find himself in possession of all the data accumulated by science.[9]

Hers was an experience of the whole field of knowledge "at a glance," the kind of experience that only the very greatest thinkers share.

This extraction of pure knowledge from within has also been the hallmark of great women writers. As Virginia Woolf wrote about the Duchess of Newcastle, "It was from the plain of complete ignorance, the untilled field of her own consciousness, that she proposed to erect a philosophic system that was to oust all others." Similarly, Woolf describes the invalid Elizabeth Barrett Browning who "lived shut off, guessing at what was outside, and inevitably magnifying what was within." Going within, women brought "to the surface" what Woolf calls "trophies," which, "however we may dispute their size, are undoubtedly genuine."[10]

Perhaps as a result of the lack of education, women's writing in the past was marked by the beauty of its spontaneity, heartfulness, and directness. This directness of experience, which is apparent in all geniuses, is all the more apparent in the uneducated genius. Sir Walter Raleigh acknowledged how the works of poet Christina Rossetti touched him:

> I think she is the best poet alive . . . you cannot lecture on really pure poetry any more than you can talk about the ingredients of pure water--it is adulterated, methylated, sanded poetry that makes the best lectures. The only thing that Christina makes me want to do is cry, not lecture.[11]

Rossetti's intuition, writes Woolf, "was so sure, so direct, so intense that it produced poems that sing like music in one's ears--like a melody by Mozart or an air by Gluck." Like Mozart and other greats, "[Christina's] verses seem to have formed themselves whole and entire in her head, and she did not worry very much what was said of them because in her own mind she knew that they were good."[12] It is this ability to know what is artistically right and good, quite apart from societal reinforcement, that Woolf finds most admirable. She praises the genius of Jane Austen and Emily Brontë as "never more convincing than in their power . . . to hold on their way unperturbed by scorn or censure" but having, she concludes, "a very serene or a very powerful mind to resist the temptation to anger."[13]

This is what we can call the transcendence of greatness. From this view both men and women are great insofar as they are able to transcend environmental circumstance, societal roles or current intellectual fashion. This way genius can never be locked into dogma or polemics or any relative circumstances, including gender. Writes Woolf:

> They are not men when they write, nor are they women. They appeal to the large tract of the soul which is sexless; they excite no passions; they exalt, improve, instruct, and man or woman can profit equally by their pages, without indulging in the folly of affection or the fury of partisanship.[14]

Woolf's ideas are exceedingly contemporary. In *The Second Stage,* Betty Friedan emphasizes the direction of the women's movement toward a kind of wholeness beyond differences between men and women. She writes: "What's needed here is to transcend [polarized male and female sex roles], to transfuse the structure itself."[15]

Transcending gender roles means more than changing such roles. Art critic John Russell writes: "The creativity of women in the 1980's is one of the great incontrovertible facts of life--[it] operates on terrain, and in terms, that have until now been considered the preserve of men . . . [it] has nothing to do with what was once called 'feminine sensibility.' "[16] Nonetheless, in some ways it does. The challenge for women who are moving toward greatness today is to *retain* the intuitive, "heartful" values now that they receive the same education as men. Because although there are fundamental questions to which either gender may make contributions worthy to be called great, still there *are* very basic differences between the way men and women look at the world. And these differences are not all societally or culturally bound: Some are decidedly physiological.

Women and Wholeness:
The Origins of Psychophysiological Balance

Her discoveries are concerned with states of being and not with states of doing. Miriam is aware of "life itself," of the atmosphere of the table rather than of the table; of the silence rather than of the sound.

VIRGINIA WOOLF

As we saw earlier, Ashley Montagu has proposed that slower development into adulthood is what apparently enables humans,--unlike apes, for example--to "remain free to change as change is required by whatever environment they encounter." The retained development is both physical and psychological. Physically, skull growth is the most telling feature--the slower it grows, the greater the opportunity for development. It has been further suggested that women are better equipped for this prolonged development. According to Montagu, it is the female skull that "realizes the promise of the species rather more fully than the male," in that female features remain flexible, soft, and childlike developmentally longer than males--a sign of higher evolution according to Montagu's theory of neoteny.[17] This theory is perhaps most interesting in the light of other scientific studies.

We know, for example, that there are differences in the way men and women take in information--not differences in intelligence and brain capacity, but in the way each uses the brain. Recent brain research indicates that there seems to be a more complete integration of hemispheric function in females. It has long been known that females recover more quickly from strokes than males. The *corpus callosum*--that section of the brain which connects the left and right hemispheres--provides cross-communication in the brain and its size may account for variations in neural flexibility. Researchers Christine de LaCoste-Utamsing and Ralph Holloway found that the *corpus callosum* is as much as 40 percent larger in women than in men. It is possible that because of the greater number of neurons in the *corpus callosum*, the female brain has greater "plasticity": That is, when a

93

part of either hemisphere is damaged, women have noticeably less serious deterioration in function than men and regenerate lost functions more quickly.

Specialization of each hemisphere has its own advantages, but the greater opportunity for integration in the female brain may explain why women have a more developed ability to integrate and identify "wholeness in the parts." Women are found to be good "abstracters": According to the results of cognitive tests conducted by the Johnson O'Connor Research Foundation laboratories on a quarter of a million women and men, it was found that women scored higher than men on aptitude for grasping the abstract. Men, on the other hand, excel in spatial reasoning and seem to have more developed right-hemispheric functioning.

How this "wholeness" capacity appears can be explored in connection with a study done at Stanford Research Institute (SRI) that identified male and female styles of leadership. Male style is called "alpha" and is characterized by a direct, aggressive, linear, one-task-at-a-time, zero-sum, win-or-lose orientation. Female style is called "beta" and is considered more fluid, more synthesizing, intuitive, contextual, and relational. It is unclear whether these styles are really innate to each sex or have been polarized by role expectations. It may be that women's physiology has developed to be a better vehicle for beta-style leadership.

The SRI researchers believe that a balance between these two styles is essential for good leadership. In a time of great change, however, they conclude that the beta style may be more useful. In fact, the research indicates that beta thinking gets the job done more effectively. In a group of beta thinkers, everyone has an opportunity to be a leader. The emphasis is more on group function, wholeness, interdynamics, and the abstract subtleties of interaction.[18] The beta style is most apparent when Gloria Steinem lectures: She generally turns her talks into opportunities for organizing a group within the audience; a "we're all in this together" attitude thus prevails.

Women have had a long history of social cooperation which is manifest in various cultures and social organizations, and also in the "living" arts. These arts don't demand individuality as much as they require cooperation. Quilting is a perfect example of this cooperative style of functioning. According to quilt historian Julie Silber, "Quilts . . . grew out of the lives of the people who made them and are the precious repositories of those lives. They represent the women who were able to harmonize their individuality for the greater good." In these group creations, there must be a certain egoless maturity, a willingness to work as part of a group without personal acknowledgment, with the belief that the group result is more unifying and more powerful than each individual contribution.

This attitude is also apparent in other areas. In her research on women's morality, Dr. Carol Gilligan of Harvard University identified women as "the scientists of interpersonal relationships," who base their moral decisions on the effect they will have on others, on a personal system of caring and responsibility. According to Gilligan, morality requires dependability. She found that little girls consider "dependency" a positive word, as in "you can depend on someone." She concluded that women's moral decisions are based on relative judgments structured in this caring nature--they act on feelings relative to circumstance, rather than on some absolute principle of right and wrong.[19] It is a relativism based upon pure subjectivity, not unlike our quantum model.

When we examined the quantum world, we saw how one thing can be "right" and another seemingly contradictory thing can also be "right." It depends on who is doing the looking and how they choose to look. "Rightness" therefore is directly related to the awareness of the observer and is also dependent on each situation. It is possible that women are thus more in tune with the quantum world, and their morality more a "start from anywhere" sense of right and wrong, whereas Gilligan and other researchers have found that men operate from more of a hierarchical, linear, absolutist viewpoint.

Gilligan's research also lends itself to speculation that women's behavior may come from a more integrated level of awareness. We know that intuition accesses a greater wholeness than logical thinking. Intuition also operates closer to the heart, and by acting from the heart, as it were, perhaps one upholds a more harmonizing life-supportive influence. This may be why women have a very special contribution to make to world greatness.

The "Peace Personality"

I did learn that truly great people are always kind.
BROOKE ASTOR

If we agree that to become great, heart development is as important as mind development, the desire for other people's happiness and fulfillment is not a martyr's negation of self--it is a real principle of greatness. It is responsibility for the well-being of others. Kindness, support, and love are not antifeminist principles, they are the essence of feminism, as Betty Friedan and others have pointed out. Love and kindness encourage transcendence--and counter opposition by eradicating the boundaries. Poet Louise Bogan counsels that "from now on, no woman should be shamefaced in attempting, through her work, to give back to the world a portion of its lost heart."

Now that we realize that greatness can no longer be thought of only in terms of a painting, a book, or a well-prepared dinner, we can give it a far more all-encompassing definition: *Greatness is the ability to express our own nature fully in every thought, gesture, and activity.* And because over the centuries women seem to have developed the ability to perceive wholeness in the parts, a more integrative brain function, a greater reliance on intuitive functioning, a moral behavior based on concern for others, and a tradition of working cooperatively in groups, it may be that they have had an education for the greatness needed in the world today.

It has been suggested that the deepest level of woman's nature is to preserve human life. Psychology has found no force greater than a mother's impulse to protect her child, and that protectiveness encompasses a greater and greater territory as she develops. In addition, a woman who is a great mother, like a great teacher, learns to be evenly disposed toward each of her children to the best of her abilities by virtue of her desire to harmonize and balance.

Harvard psychologist David McClelland's research on "war psychology" demonstrates that the people who are most warlike have a high need for power and low empathy. We may suppose that a "peace personality" would have a low need for power and high empathy. Despite the fact that women's territory of influence has traditionally been limited to family and community, her preparation for a peacekeeping role is quite extensive, and it should come as no surprise that women are often leaders in the peace movements. Says Helen Caldicott, M.D., "Women understand the genesis of life innately. It's our responsibility."

The harmonizing qualities of greatness required for a transformed society are a key to a peaceful world, but are also an endangered species, more valuable now in their possible absence than ever before. The concern, of course, as voiced by writer Phyllis Rose, is that women will lose their "lovableness" as they move into powerful positions alongside men. But this seems unlikely to occur because the nurturing, life-supporting qualities--primarily because they *are* life supporting--are far more likely to be retained than any psychological style created by cultural conditions.

According to the Lamarckian view of evolution--wherein useful characteristics are acquired and passed on--what is retained in the collective consciousness of the society is information that is most evolutionary for the growth of the species. As we have seen, women seem to have developed and maintained within their *physiology* the very qualities most needed in the world today: kindness, love, nurturance, and cooperation, which will outlast competition, opposition, and destructive tactics. As the greats have always known through experience, real power comes from getting nature on one's side; the laws of nature are the ultimate power base.

Trying to operate from limits is the old linear way of achieving; the quantum way requires expanding, gaining wholeness, forming new connections inside and out in order to grow. Women intuitively understand what it means to win through the integrating force of love. In the words of an Indian woman saint: "If you want peace of mind, do not find fault with others. Learn to make the whole world your own; no one is a stranger, my child, the whole world is your own."[20]

Having seen how greatness has manifested itself in the psychological, physiological, and social development of women beyond what may have seemed like limits, let's explore now how greatness becomes "occupied."

"Occupying" the Boundaries: Channels of Greatness

A song for occupations!
In the labor of engines and trades and the labor of fields
                                    I find the developments,
And find the eternal meanings.

<small>WALT WHITMAN</small>

Garson Kanin, in *Hollywood*, describes how a young songwriter was putting down Irving Berlin as overrated. " 'Hell,' he said. ' "All alone. By the telephone." What's that? Anybody could write that.' 'Yes,' said Oscar Hammerstein, 'anybody could, but Irving did.' "

We're all geniuses, but some people get things done. Plenty of us have good ideas that fall away like dreams in the morning sunlight. But doing is doing *something*. And unless we are enlightened saints whose every thought is an impulse of nature's desire, most of us express our greatness through activity. This means that, in general, greatness likes to have a channel through which to grow and become localized--through a particular activity--be it molecular biology or soybean farming or dancing or reading a book to a child.

Essentially, the channels of greatness--whether science, art, sports, or parenting--all require the same basic capabilities. Yet although all channels are available, the specific endeavors we choose will vary according to personality, educational opportunity, background, cultural demands based on the needs of the time, and a variety of other factors. When she was an eight-year-old TV star, Tina Yothers was asked what she would like to be if she weren't in show business. She replied, "I'd like to be a checker at a supermarket." To her, at that age, the two occupations were equally fascinating.

"Valued" occupations change as we grow and also as societies evolve. It's interesting to look at the changing list of the "most acceptable" or "most valued" occupations and the weight assigned to them. For example, nowadays science seems more important than art--more significant and worthy--while art seems somewhat idiosyncratic and a little self-indulgent. As a result, we expect a great deal from scientists in the way of responsibility and not very much from artists. However, two centuries ago art was considered the proper course of study for the well educated, and science was considered a waste of time.

With the same sense of it being the thing to do as any parents today who send their child to college to become a scientist, William Herschel was sent from Germany by his father to study music in England; instead, William did the unacceptable--he spent every spare moment learning the science of astronomy and eventually became a great astronomer. It was the eighteenth-century equivalent of today's physics student dropping out of school to become a famous rock star.

Perceived values also change *within* particular occupations: Actor Alan Alda recalled when he first gave up the dream of his youth--to play Oedipus Rex. "I think in that moment . . . I decided to accept doing as well as I could with what was before me. . . . And I really haven't minded not playing Oedipus since then." The character of Hawkeye may not have had the range and depth of Oedipus, and Alda might or might not have succeeded at playing the latter, but there is no question that he has touched many millions more people in *M.A.S.H.* and in subsequent roles than he could ever have playing Oedipus today.

In reality, the actual means one uses to express one's greatness is far less significant than the ability to experience happiness and satisfaction from whatever channel one has chosen. But because of perceived values, we may be convinced that certain occupations cannot serve as such channels, and consequently devalue the greatness potential of the people who do choose them, forgetting that a great individual can bring greatness to any occupation.

The Great "Occupiers": The Democratization of Greatness

A painter is a person who paints.

Van Gogh

Melanie Brown

An artist is not a special kind of man--
but every man is a special kind of artist.

ANANDA COOMARASWAMY

Some years ago, a typical undergraduate question was going around
a college dormitory: "Can a shoe salesman be great?" After much
discussion, the eventual collective answer was "No." But it wasn't a
terrific answer. What the students failed to understand is that a great
shoe salesman is a great person who sells shoes. As long as a given
occupation "occupies" you--and you occupy it--then you can become
great in it. Salvatore Ferragamo became an international shoe salesman after starting as a shoemaker, apprenticed at a young age (despite the protests of his family). During his subsequent career, he
invented the "wedge" (a pump with a cork heel), and used materials
that had never been associated with shoes before--raffia, snail shells,
and seaweed. But his major contribution was in constructing shoes
that were both glamorous *and* well fitting--with such features as arch
supports in every shoe. His wife recalls how she succumbed to his
charm and married him after trying on a pair of shoes he had made
for her: "I had never worn anything so comfortable. I thought I could
fly." Not only did Ferragamo make shoes, he learned to sell them
well on an international scale, and indeed became a great shoe
salesman.

Just as a great artist raises the object he paints to the status of
greatness by painting it, we, too, can become great in any field as
long as we bring our own reservoir of creativity and a sense of universality to it. We can glorify even our everyday acts in this way. It
is for this reason that great individuals tend to express their greatness
in everything they do and why we find them charismatic even "off-
stage" . . . or "off the field." Said television reporter Bill Moyers
about poet Maya Angelou, "Her entire life is an artistic expression--
a process connecting her with the world in the most creative way."

There is really nothing uncreative about any activity as long as it
uses your full abilities. Underuse of one's abilities is the primary cause
for job dissatisfaction. However, some people bring the best to whatever they do, even if the field isn't what they would ultimately choose.
"A creative person will be creative in any field," says art teacher

Victor Lowenfeld. It does seem to depend on the inner liveliness of the person.

Usually, however, because of the specialized nature of our own uniquely developed abilities, we prefer certain channels over others. Philosopher Mortimer Adler has said that he enjoys literature and prose far more than paintings. Not surprisingly, his whole life having been focused on the written and spoken word, he is very much at ease with words, and his intelligence is thus most deeply connected to literature and not as open and responsive to subtleties of color and form.

The truth is, you don't need to be a great ARTIST to be great at what you do as long as it taps your deepest resources. The highly successful and long-lived *Peanuts* cartoon characters are the work of a man who recognizes what he's good at and thereby does what he most enjoys. Charles Schultz says: "The comic strip is just right for someone of my talent. I can't write that well and I can't draw that well but I've found my medium to express myself."

Yet for another kind of artist, a fine artist, for example, who might also require depth, color, and abstraction to express herself, cartooning would feel wrong and unfulfilling.

If you are an inventor, you might invent a Hula Hoop or you might invent an entire universe, like the astronomers, physicists, and science fiction writers do, depending on what size abstraction you enjoy working with. What you invent, however, will depend ultimately on three factors: what you know--knowledge; how you know it--intelligence; and what you do with what you know--creativity. If you know mechanics, you invent machines. If you enjoy words, you invent poems, novels, or crossword puzzles. And if your creativity and intelligence are developed, you invent good ones.

Defining Your Territory

A first-rate soup is worth more than a second-rate painting.
ABRAHAM MASLOW

It's not what I do, honey, it's the way that I do it.
MAE WEST

Greatness in any field comes on the basis of operating in your own territory. If you don't know and feel enough about something to represent it deeply, you won't enliven it so others can benefit.

By operating in your own territory, it may only take a very small amount of input from which to grow to greatness. For material for her writings, Jane Austen found that "three or four country families are enough." Out of her observations, based solely on the people coming in and out of her father's home, she wrote her first masterpiece, *Pride and Prejudice*, at age twenty-one.

Great parents may not win a Tchaikovsky competition, but they, too, are maximizing their greatness capabilities, perhaps even more rigorously than in many other fields. Laura Huxley, wife of Aldous Huxley, said: "I have done a little bit of everything, but never have I known of anything that demands the exceptional qualities it takes to bring up a child."

It's definitely the qualities we bring to it, not the occupation per se, which makes us happy in ourselves. Although one might assume that a big thinker like Einstein would have hated the daily drudgery of a patent office during the seven years he worked there, that was not the case. Einstein looked back on this period as one of the happiest in his life: "The work on satisfactory formulation of technical patents was a true blessing to me. It compelled me to be many-sided in thought, and also offered important stimulation for thought about physics. Following a practical profession is a blessing for people of my type."

Interestingly, it is often in the most restricted areas that creativity is most challenged and therefore most called upon. This is because limits force a transcendence of the intrinsic boundaries of that activity in order to bring enjoyment and growth. Take housework. Observes TV host Phil Donahue:

> When I think of the countless women in this country who get up
> in the morning, make breakfast, see that the kids are dressed
> properly, send them off to school, dress, go to work, come home,
> make dinner, speak to the emotional needs of the children, do
> the wash, retire, and get up in the morning only to do it over
> again, I don't know how . . . they manage.[21]

Naturally, those who do anything as a mindless chore may well suffer from boredom. But for others, doing any activity for people they love is perhaps one of the greatest pleasures in life. And that love becomes the energy force of a creative mind. Given even the obvious limits of housework, creativity finds its way to expression. There is the couple, for example, who play the military march music of John Philip Sousa while they are cleaning house--to enhance the speed and efficiency of getting the work done, while they march around in time to the music, unavoidably laughing at themselves. Or there's the talented woman who creates meals in which the aesthetic experience is as important as the cooking and the eating. She will, for example, serve an all-white or all-orange dinner where color unifies the food, table covering, plates, flowers, and so forth, or serve only foods starting with the letter C, just to challenge her own imagination. She brings pleasure to all who know her, for she complies with one of the basic rules for creativity: to experience the ordinary in an extraordinary way.

Once you realize that your activity or your job or your profession is *yourself*--there's no separation between being a great person and doing a great job--because you're always doing it for the ultimate boss: *you*. Egypt's late president Anwar Sadat discovered that outward recognition was not as important to him as his own "real" self: "I have," he said, "realized that my real self is a greater entity than any possible post or title." And if "yourself" is a big self, you bring that huge awareness to everything you do, in a natural way, without restriction. In a newspaper interview, Otis Coles, for thirty-two years the bathroom attendant at New York's Club "21," said, "I make the bathroom a happy place. That sounds funny, I know, but it is God working through me." He created that environment as skillfully as any artist.

Thus, it is those individuals who bring themselves fully to their jobs, who seem to slip past the restrictions of background, age, gender or the countless other excuses the rest of us offer, who are the greats. They are the ones who have realized their own value *apart* from what they do; they are the ones who grew up after all.

Once we know that greatness has a life beyond any particular occupations, we can look more toward their suitability to our development. Obviously, monthly bills need to be paid; our aim is not to avoid responsibility but to embrace it fervently while doing something we enjoy. We know whether we feel happier in a lively office environment that stimulates our social and organizational skills, or doing a construction job that demands our alertness and strength. The thing to remember is that *nothing we do is more important than who we are*. And if we want to be great, we have to accept that the outside career track may jump around. As you grow, you may need to do first one thing, then another. Because greatness isn't a career, some people move toward greatness through a variety of occupations in a lifetime.

❖

Changing Lanes, Not Cars:
The Leonardo Factor

Enjoy more things. Grow, develop. Don't just do one thing well. Live fully. Attend to music, art, nature.

Roger Baldwin

Since most creative people try more than one technique for self-expression, we may not be surprised to learn that actors Henry Fonda and Anthony Quinn and musicians Bob Dylan, Joni Mitchell, Cat Stevens, and John Lennon were also artists. What is more telling is the genuine diversity of occupational changes by so many of the greats.

Prior to his literary career, Joseph Conrad was a sailor for sixteen years; poet Wallace Stevens was vice-president of a large insurance company; Sir Arthur Conan Doyle was a physician whose Sherlock Holmes books were a hobby. Justice Oliver Wendell Holmes also was a physician before embarking on his monumental legal career. Similarly, inventors often develop products that seem to have little to do with their original careers. For example, an actor invented the first corn reaper, an Irish schoolmaster invented the first useful submarine, a Scottish veterinarian invented the pneumatic tire, a French priest invented the hydrofoil, and astronomer Edmund Halley, of comet fame, modified the invention of the diving bell.

Even within their own professions, great people are often freer from the confines of specialization. Flutist James Galway thinks of himself as "an actor on the flute" and does not feel he has to limit himself to one kind of music. For him the music is more important than what it represents. He plays classical, country, pop, and traditional folk tunes, all with the same degree of investment and pleasure.

Sometimes, career changes are very dramatic. After climaxing her figure-skating career with an Olympic gold medal, Dr. Tenley Albright wènt on to medical school and became a surgeon. Economist Alan Greenspan, former chairman of the Council of Economic Advisers, was a musician, a Juilliard graduate who played the clarinet in a dance band in the 1940s. After a year or two, he felt he wasn't good enough to have a career in music; he began to study economics between sets, and eventually he received a graduate degree and started a career where he felt he could succeed maximally.

As unique as they were, Albright's and Greenspan's occupational shifts aren't so unusual today. What is unusual is how *many* people are seeking second or third careers. Willy Loman is on the wane. Having realized that personal happiness is a first priority, career changing is becoming the norm for a large number of us. And although the U.S. Bureau of Labor Statistics reports that as many as twenty-four million Americans (one fourth of the labor force) don't like their jobs, they also report that one third of American workers in a recent year's time (except farmers, farm workers, and household workers) changed careers.

According to a *Newsweek* magazine article, a large number of people today have what is called an "entitlement mentality": They feel they ought to be able to do what will please them. As a result of this sentiment, "lawyers are becoming teachers, teachers are becoming accountants, doctors and dentists are going into real estate."[22] These changes reflect the growth of a society that is better able to uphold developmental opportunity for all in that the freedom to make these changes has been extended to a greater majority than before. They also reflect an increasing awareness that careers are not always linear. According to University of Geneva psychologist Howard Gruber, the most useful way to think about real achievement in the context of adult development is as an ongoing large-scale network of enterprises over an extended period of time, even an entire lifetime.

To carry on a wide variety of activities to achieve a complex goal may require a person's involvement in *seemingly unrelated fields*. To the outsider, such a person may look as if he is at loose ends, floundering around, trying to "find himself." But what may actually be happening is the formation of an elaborate series of interconnections that will finally meet the individual's own specifications--those inner visions that may only be half acknowledged. This inner life is the secret life that greatness ultimately leads. And it explains why sometimes we have to wait nearly our whole lives to satisfy it. Or go all over the career map to integrate it, perhaps becoming a Renaissance person in the process.

In the Renaissance it was considered the hallmark of genius to express one's greatness in a variety of fields. Leonardo da Vinci was the outstanding representative of the age--a man who excelled in over forty occupations. As a result of his remarkably prodigious life, Leonardo has become the universal model of human creativity and intelligence in action. No channel of expression was too elusive for him. Although we may remember him primarily for his art, in which we see most dramatically the depth of his refined awareness, above all he was a lifelong experimenter. He was an anatomist, caricaturist, naturalist, architect, musical inventor, theatrical designer and producer, engineer, philosopher, mathematician, mapmaker, and bridge designer. His designs included ideas for the printing press, the still camera, the slide projector, the parachute, shrapnel, the machinegun, the revolving stage, hydraulic power devices, the grandfather clock, water turbines, the automobile transmission, the first accurate anatomical drawings of the spine, the wrist, and hand--and the "Mona Lisa."

Like many other great people, Da Vinci's work was so extensive, he could rarely do one thing at a time, and he left many projects undone; they had been thought out but never put down on paper or built or painted. Sadly, because there was so much left to do at the end of his life, he felt defeated by time. He described the feeling of not having used "all the resources of my spirit and my art," and on his deathbed he asked God's forgiveness for this omission. He felt deeply the responsibility that comes with the territory of greatness. Yet it wasn't any one occupation in which he became great; his genius transcended all fields, and his greatness ultimately lay in his willingness to use every avenue to give something of himself, to give what he felt he had personally been given.

We all know individuals who seem to be going everywhere at once. It's obviously not easy to be all over the map--but we need to look at the totality of their lives before we reprimand them for not sticking to one thing. They may be pursuing an inner career track that we can't readily see.

On the other hand, whereas some of us are hopeful followers of Da Vinci, exploring life in many fields, others seem to know from Day One what they are supposed to do to be happy. They are the enviable group that feels chosen.

❖

Accepting the Right Channels for Yourself

The secret of living is to find people who will pay you money to do what you would pay to do if you had the money.

SARAH CALDWELL

An aim in life is the only fortune worth finding; and it is not to be found in foreign lands, but in the heart itself.

ROBERT LOUIS STEVENSON

For composer Aaron Copland there was no choice: "My entry into music was instinctive. I wasn't choosing anything, I was chosen. I didn't have the choice of Shall I be a mathematician, or an instrumentalist, or a teacher? That never occurred to me."[23]

In the ancient Indian Vedic tradition, there is a concept called *dharma*, which means one's rightful path of action. When one is in one's *dharma*, then life is full and simple and maximally evolutionary. Often people with long-lasting lifetime careers are those who have found their *dharma*. Actress Carol Burnett is one of them. She says: "I absolutely know I'm a fortunate woman. Being able to get up in the morning and go out and do what I enjoy."[24] Similarly, newscaster Walter Cronkite said, before his retirement, "I still get the greatest pleasure out of what I am doing. The greatest pleasure I get is from what seems the routine; going out to the [news] desk every day to decide what goes in and how much to give each piece of news."[25]

While being in your *dharma* feels very natural, not being in it can sometimes lead to unhappiness, and trying to be in someone else's is worse. There are the "grass is always greener" people who, unable or unwilling to accept their own gifts, chase after other people's rainbows, generally to no avail. In an interview in *Arabian Horse World*, Sheila Varian, a horse trainer from a family of great horse trainers, recalls her mother's advice to stay within her *dharma*: "You may sit with the most influential people. You may travel with the wealthiest of people. You may have opportunities in this business that are extraordinary. But you must remember who you are so that when you go back to your own little area of contentment you do not wish for something that is not yours to have."

What the Vedic tradition calls *dharma*, the Buddhists call "right action." This concept is deeply ingrained in Western traditions as well. We may experience it as a "calling." In explaining this feeling, Dag Hammarskjöld, the former UN Secretary General, wrote: "For someone whose job so obviously mirrors man's extraordinary possibilities and responsibilities, there is no excuse if he loses his sense of 'having been called.' So long as he keeps that, everything he can do has a meaning."[26] In this way you remember how lucky you are to have been called.

In its *dharma* mode, work becomes not merely a means of achieving success in something, but a way to achieve maximum growth within oneself. As the nineteenth-century philosopher John Ruskin observed: "When men are rightly occupied, their amusement grows out of their work, as the color petals out of a fruitful flower; when they are faithfully helpful and compassionate, all their emotions are steady, deep, perpetual and vivifying to the soul as is the natural pulse to the body."

When we are rightly occupied, we feel "at home." Actress Kate Nelligan remembers this at-home feeling when she first stepped onto a stage. We experience this degree of comfort when we best express who we really are. In this way, all great people are rightly occupied and in their *dharma*. This is the essence of being occupied, to find *one's self* within one's activity.

Here are a few suggestions for thinking about what will lead you to this:

How to Decide What to Do

1. *Listen to nature.* Nature gives us inside clues to our own life and to what society will allow for us. Notice where your breaks come. Some things are easy--doors open, everything feels right. Other things are burdensome and awkward. Be willing to accept that nature may have a better idea for you than you might at this time.

2. *Evaluate your own desires and abilities.* If you are good at something, you will enjoy a deeper experience of life in that channel. The better you are at it, provided it is not too small and doesn't bore you, the more likely you will feel your greatness emerging when you do it.

3. *Do that by which you can give the most.* Establish priorities based on the most universally beneficial thing you could do. Want the best for your life--don't settle. But don't worry about a late beginning. It's never too late to give.

4. *Become the captain of your own ship.* Zero in on your destiny. You are your own responsibility. Recall the words of Saint Bernard: "Nothing can work me damage except myself."

5. *Be simple.* Nature does not easily reward calculation and complexity. Don't do what you know is wrong to get to "right." Real success depends upon the purity of your life. As you sow, so shall you reap. As Dag Hammarskjöld observed:

   > You cannot play with the animal in you without becoming wholly animal, play with falsehood without forfeiting your right to truth, play with cruelty without losing your sensitivity of mind. He who wants to keep his garden tidy doesn't reserve a plot for weeds.[27]

6. *Live your own life.* Let yourself be inspired by others, but don't try to live other people's lives or live through someone else.

7. *Exit at your destination but not before.* Don't sell yourself short. Says Walter Hagen, "Don't hurry, don't worry, and don't forget to smell the roses."

8. *Find your tradition.* Look at great traditions, and at the lives of great people, especially older and wiser people whose experiences can teach you. Find long-lasting values and uphold them in your life, even if you're living in the fast lane. Since it's the most life-supporting influences that form our traditions, you'll gain maximum personal support from them.

We've explored greatness from the perspective of limits and have seen how it can stretch to its larger stature with regard to age, gender, and occupation. We've also seen how greatness is really that field which is attached more to what we are inside than what we are outside, that goes beyond the local and the temporal events of life. So, it would be helpful to look at the *inner qualities* of great people, to identify those personal characteristics that are most associated with the growth to greatness.

4

❖

THE PERSONAL CHARACTERISTICS OF GREATNESS: SEVEN QUALITIES OF GREAT PEOPLE

❖

Naturally Great

The more I try and think of the essentials of music, the more they seem to depend on general human values. It's all very well to be a genius, but the intrinsic value . . . depends on what you are.

NADIA BOULANGER

So far as personal appearance goes, no one can look upon him without feeling his force . . . when he talks you listen. You do not know what he is saying, but it enthralls you. You feel the importance without understanding the meaning. . . . Yet he has a keen sense of humor and the most beautiful manners. He is the most genuinely modest of men. He knows no jealousy. He has never decried the accomplishments of another, never refused

credit. . . . He lives inside himself. He takes a profound interest
in his own work. He has that supply of self-love and self-
confidence which usually goes with success. . . . Never was a
human being filled with loftier ideals. Never did a man labor so
unceasingly, so earnestly, so unselfishly for the benefit of the
race. Tesla is not rich. He does not trouble himself about money.
Had he chosen to follow in the footsteps of Edison he could be,
perhaps the richest man in the world . . .

A DESCRIPTION OF THE INVENTOR
NIKOLA TESLA BY HIS BIOGRAPHER

We can all identify, using whatever terms appeal to us, the way
certain individuals affect us. K. C. Cole speculates whether "a force-
ful or attractive or repulsive person is surrounded by a kind of 'field'
of influence . . ." We can observe, she notes, "the dark cloud that
seems to hover over some people, while a sunny streak lights the
path of others . . ."[1]

The greats have specific qualities that attract us to them, qualities
that are either quietly communicated on a "being" level or are actively communicated, expressed through gestures, speech, works, and
deeds. However, those individuals who represent the deepest qualities of life, whether silently or overtly, are generally those whom we
identify as great. Therefore, to understand greatness better, we ought
to look more closely at these qualities. First, let's consider where
they come from.

In general, if you read through their diaries and journals, you begin to see that the ideas and works that the greats believe to be their
best are frequently closest to the basic patterns of nature itself. This
is because these patterns are not only there outside of us, they are
the patterns of our minds, our self-created social systems, the structured rhythms of our daily lives. They are the patterns with which
we create. Said the artist Georges Rouault: "I have painted by opening my eyes day and night on the perceptible world and also by
closing them from time to time that I might see the vision blossom
and submit itself to orderly arrangement." As such, the study of human greatness is actually the study of nature's perfection. By living
and creating in accord with these natural laws, we become great.

For example, there is an elegant proportion in nature known as
"the golden section," which is found everywhere--in eggs, for ex-

ample, and in seashells, and in those human faces where the eyes are located equidistant from the forehead and the chin. Architects throughout the centuries have used this proportion to good advantage, as a guarantee of structural beauty. The Great Pyramid, the façade of the Parthenon, and Chartres Cathedral are just a few examples of great architecture based on the golden section.

In this way the personal characteristics of greatness can be understood as the characteristics of nature, colored and shaped by human needs and aspirations. The same properties that determine how a tree will grow best, ultimately determine how each of us will grow best, and the people who express nature's laws as precisely and completely as trees do are generally the great ones. (Although, observed G. B. Shaw, "No man manages his affairs as well as a tree does.")

The laws of nature thus give us all the information we need to be great. The order, intelligence, purposefulness, and beauty that we see in nature is our possession, too, not separate from nature but coextensive with it. As E. S. Russell points out:

> [We should] regard human purposive activities . . . and modes of thought as being a specialized development of the fundamental "purposiveness" or, as I prefer to call it, the directiveness and creativeness of life.[2]

And because they are the qualities of nature, the personal qualities of greatness are constant and found everywhere. In their universality they cross cultures and eras. They are lively in those works of art that touch the deepest feelings of people everywhere, regardless of time or place. We can think of the qualities of greatness as the agents of nature within ourselves--inherent motivators that bring us to the best part of ourselves. And once we embrace them within, they give us the opportunity to become great--to take the raw materials of life and refine them--much in the way gold ore is refined from its crude natural form into exquisite jewelry.

The essential characteristics that great people express most vividly are of course not limited to just a few; they are present within us all, at least to some degree. Yet not every great person has every great quality; sometimes, even one or two outstanding ones are enough to uphold greatness.

So, now let's look at seven qualities that show up consistently in the greats, and perhaps a little more intermittently in the rest of us. We can identify them as: (1) integrity; (2) commitment; (3) happiness; (4) an ability to "maximize" or create good luck; (5) a "let it happen" or "surrender" orientation; (6) a sense of compassionate responsibility; and (7) boundary breaking, or transcendence.

Integrity

Great people "stand for something." Essentially, they stand for the best of themselves. Playwright Garson Kanin wrote about Katherine Hepburn: "[Her] popularity has never waned because people . . . recognize that in a time of dangerous conformity, and the fear of being different, here is one who stands up gallantly . . ."[3]

Integrity means integration and it means truthfulness. With great people there is an integration that keeps growing during their lives--an integration between what they desire for themselves and what their minds, hearts, and bodies cooperate to give them. Because great genius demands more of everything, it cannot remain lopsided. Along with a brilliant mathematical mind must come a developed heart, enormous vitality, and high morality. All parts of your life have to be developed to the same degree of perfection as you grow--this is what is meant by the integration that leads to integrity.

It takes integrity to "be all that you can be." Everything you think, feel, and do has to connect; otherwise you feel scattered, unsettled, unbalanced. "Your every separate action should contribute towards an integrative life," wrote the ancient philosopher Marcus Aurelius. Actor Alan Alda, reports his wife Arlene, most values the qualities of being rational, fair, and cheerful and, she says, "He has been integrating them his whole life." Integrity is a leading characteristic of greatness because it automatically brings many qualities together within us.

In addition, integrity is both the cause and the result of a kind of balanced behavioral integration through which all conflicts are resolved. This results in the most economical and beneficial course of action in daily life. People who have a high degree of integrity don't have to make uncomfortable choices. Their behavior is spontaneously "right." As we saw in our discussion of quantum physics, nature automatically acts by choosing the best path possible. Similarly, in human behavior, concludes psychologist Frank Barron, "The more fully developed and finely articulated we become, the less possibility [there is] of alternative integration."

Thus, when we are truly integrated, what we become is the resolution of all the aspirations, desires, and conflicts of our lives. We don't give up the family we long for in order to have a better career unless the career choice is ultimately going to make us feel more fulfilled. By trusting ourselves, we naturally choose the most evolutionary way to integrate all our desires. Like nature, we find the perfect path where the least amount of effort is required to bring about the most joy. Integrity thus depends on the ability to be self-reliant, to trust one's own thinking, never to compromise one's own inner values, never to stop seeking deeper integration.

Integrity is a group motivator as well. Peters and Waterman report that "owing to good luck, or maybe even good sense, those companies that emphasize quality, reliability, and service have chosen the *only* area where it is readily possible to generate excitement in the average down-the-line employee. They give people pride in what they do. They make it possible to love the product." They name Willard Marriott, Ray Kroc, Levi Strauss, James Cash Penney, Robert Wood Johnson, Bill Hewlett, and Dave Packard as examples of those founders of excellent companies who were able to stick to their values and uphold integrity in their employees, customers, and product quality. They identify the quality of integrity in business as a generative force. "When people have *integrity* in the precise sense of the word in a manufacturing system, they generate a feeling of integrity, in a broader sense, all around them."[4]

The Integration of Opposites

Integrity generally also grows when we put opposites together to form a new integrity. In fact, it is usually those things which are most opposed that provide the most satisfying integration. Business people talk about "loose-tight leadership," what Peters and Waterman describe as "the coexistence of firm central direction and maximum individual autonomy."

The ability to integrate opposites is what creative individuals have been found to do best: Singer Dolly Parton draws our attention because, as she herself observes, "I *look* one way and I *am* another." In addition, psychologists have found that as people become more psychologically healthy, they become more tolerant of opposites in themselves, more able to integrate diverse personality variables. For example, people who are what we call "centered"--internally stable-- generally have the greatest flexibility. These two properties, although opposites, are very natural together. Picture a big palm tree in the Bahamas battered by the 80-mph winds of a hurricane. It bends and moves, always graceful, anchored in its well-tested, stable root system. Similarly, human physiology maintains a very precise form of internal stability--a body temperature of 98.6°F under a variety of environmental circumstances.

Greatness upholds this automatic internal stability in the face of continual change. Great people thus often face challenges with equanimity. When asked by a young reporter about her "long-range plans," Eleanor Roosevelt--that great model of integrity--replied, "My dear boy, I have no long-range plans. I just do what comes first to hand."

What has been identified as "risk-taking" in our culture may thus well be a kind of flexibility that strong, stable individuals have. When you feel stable inside, nothing feels like a risk. When you feel sure of yourself, when you know you have, for instance, the skills needed to place your feet in the tiny crevices along the side of an icy wall, climbing a mountain becomes less a risk than a precise and significant use of your developed abilities.

Let's take another example of the integration of opposites: humility and confidence. In speaking to a colleague, Israeli Prime Minister Golda Meir advised, "Don't be so humble; you're not that great." We respect humility when we see it connected to a genuine comfortableness in the world. Humility is usually unattractive in a weak person and breathtaking in a strong individual. Great people feel humble because they have experienced the larger measure of life. It is this personal knowledge of nature's gifts that produces humility. According to a Sanskrit proverb: "It's only the tree barren of fruit that raises its proud head to the sky. The tree heavy with fruit bends low to the ground." At the same time, humility requires self-acceptance and self-confidence. One needs the confidence to go, as Thoreau said, in "the direction of one's dreams," despite obstacles. This is what produces that sense of destiny which we associate with greatness. And when one learns to get the ego out of the way, to become a channel for nature, greatness is usually ready to emerge.

"Artistic" Integrity: The Search for Truth

Great art exists to increase men's happiness by presenting ennobling truth.

WALTER PATER

An artist is not someone who works with art media. It is someone who recognizes his most positive feelings and longs to represent them accurately and concretely so that they can be recognized by others.

AGNES MARTIN

Being great has to mean being true to yourself. Real integrity comes with living this truthfulness in everyday life. Even in the most mundane enterprise, anyone with integrity brings the best of himself to the work.

Great people want very much to "tell the truth," to write it, to paint it, or to express it in their behavior, always remaining true to themselves above all. Emerson believed that anyone who is sincerely true to his or her own self will become great. Louis Danz wrote: "Great men cling to the truth as if their hearts had teeth." When they locate it, they are capable of penetrating truth and conveying it to others.

Composer Leonard Bernstein relates how his teacher Serge Koussevitzky spoke about commitment to truth by using the phrase "The Central Line." By that, Koussevitzky meant "the line to be followed by the artist at any cost, the line leading to perpetual discovery, a mystical line to truth as it is revealed in the musical art."[5]

First and foremost, great people seek this central line to truth. Of course, what is true is different for different people. This is "subjective" truth, truth as we each have experienced it. However, as we know, truth, even for oneself, changes with new knowledge and experience. What doesn't change in great people is their commitment to seeking an ultimate truth. And as composer Aaron Copland concluded, the central line leads ultimately to oneself: "I must create in order to know myself, and since self-knowledge is a never-ending search, each new work is only a part answer to the question, 'Who am I?' "

At the same time that they look to satisfy themselves, great people are looking for an all-time truth about life to satisfy everyone else, an objective truth. And we are beginning to see a very real possibility that self-knowledge and universal knowledge may ultimately be the same, or at least have something very fundamental in common. But before it becomes publicly "true," it must first be true for the creator.

The critics called Beethoven's Second Symphony a "filthy monster." However, he held fast; he was an explorer, eager to reinvent music for himself. Fame and success were not what motivated him. Today his music is considered, in the words of violinist Yehudi Menuhin, "the very incarnation of truth . . . [music] which joins us to the cosmos."

"Integrity," observed Virginia Woolf, ". . . has nothing to do with paying one's bills or behaving honourably in an emergency. What one means by integrity, in the case of the novelist, is the conviction that he gives one that this is the truth. Yes, one feels, I should never have thought that this could be so; I have never known people behaving like that. But you have convinced me that so it is, so it happens."[6]

Perhaps the best sense we have of integrity is the never-ending desire to be and do the best we can. It is a sense of choosing "the highest first," going for the highest-quality life. To do so, we rely on another characteristic of greatness--the ability to make a wholehearted commitment to what we have chosen for ourselves.

Commitment

How far both from muscular heroism and from the soulfully tragic spirit of unselfishness . . . is the plain simple fact that a man has given himself completely to something he finds worth living for.

DAG HAMMARSKJÖLD

On the road to greatness, commitment is essential and requires three things: (1) something to be committed to; (2) the ability to be wholly absorbed and focused on it; and (3) the ability to accomplish it with the least effort.

First, one needs something to be committed to. "Effective leaders" concluded Warren Bennis in his study of business leadership, "are committed and persistent . . . able to hang in there."[7] And knowing from the start where you're going certainly helps you get there. When Alice asks directions of the Cheshire Cat, it asks her in turn where she is going. When she isn't sure, he quickly lets her know that if she doesn't know where she is going, ". . . then it doesn't matter which way you go."

Generally, commitment begins as the desire to see a goal accomplished. "My goals," wrote educator Mary McLeod Bethune, in *A Spiritual Autobiography*, "were the unifying ideas of my life, and I was willing to go through whatever life brought me in order to reach my goals." It is this goal orientation that "success" experts try to awaken in their clients. The goal can be small or large, take a week or a lifetime to accomplish, but it is a requirement if the dynamic movement toward achievement and fulfillment is to be set in motion.

Still, there is more to commitment than goal-setting. Even knowing where you want to go, you may be easily distracted unless you are really absorbed in what you are doing.

According to recent studies, people work not for the money but "to feel useful," "to have a sense of accomplishment," or "to lead a productive life." They want to work and do it well, not because of an obligation to their company or to some external pressure, but for themselves. Consequently, as researcher Edward Deci at the University of Rochester has demonstrated, lasting commitment to a task is engendered only by fostering conditions that build intrinsic motivations and rewards. Deci found that people must believe that a task is inherently worthwhile if they are really to be committed to it.

Similarly, despite the focus of many self-help books on becoming rich, research shows that the vast majority of rich people have become rich because they were profoundly absorbed in their work. The idea is that if one's daily business activity is compelling and absorbing enough, riches will automatically accrue. For Texas billionaire H. L. Hunt, wealth was really a by-product of his vast energy and personal commitment to his daily business life. Nothing intervened to draw him away.

The Mozart Factor

To achieve great things, what we need is a kind of total involvement in our creation. Because his focusing power was so good, Bertrand Russell was able to write a book in twenty days, dictating three thousand words a day. Wherever such a single-mindedness is found, we can call it "The Mozart Factor."

Mozart was well known for his lifelong gift of becoming fully absorbed in his music. He could sit on a train and compose an entire symphony in his head, hear it played mentally, and conduct it without a written note in front of him. Without his incredible ability to focus, the various problems he faced throughout his life could easily have intervened and taken his attention away from his music. Even a little problem could have done it. Suppose he had run out of music paper one day, gone to the store, met a friend, decided to get a pizza and go to a show. We might never have heard *The Magic Flute*.

Becoming truly committed seems to require precisely this "one-pointedness." As John D. Rockefeller, Jr., observed, "Singleness of purpose is one of the chief essentials for success in life, no matter what may be one's aim." One-pointedness is the spontaneous ability to go toward a goal without looking back. Such purposeful absorption eliminates doubts and fears. It clarifies the central reality of one's life at any given time to the point where other realities can't intrude. It relies on an inner push, not on external circumstances. The greats understand that even a single doubt can do you in. According to Philippe Petit, the French high-wire aerialist, "Every thought on the wire leads to a fall." Similarly, "doubtful" thinking can create defeat in any endeavor. To counteract it, greatness relies on full focusing. Says ballet dancer Edward Villella, "To me the ultimate idea is total concentration, to eliminate all impeding outside ideas and thoughts. So the moment I step onstage, I have a straight line of concentration. From then on, everything is spontaneous . . ."

Today, with all the options playing for our attention, this ability to be wholly absorbed is more necessary than ever before. Anyone who succeeds in a big way has to be a highly focused individual. Actress Jane Fonda, for example, could never have accomplished half of what she has in so many fields without the one-pointed self-discipline she brings to every undertaking.

Plato recounts how his great teacher, Socrates, could focus, fully absorbed:

> A problem occurred to him early one day, and he stood still on the spot to consider it. When he couldn't solve it, he didn't give up but stood there ruminating. By the time it was midday people noticed him, and remarked to one another with wonder that Socrates had been standing wrapped in thought since early morning. Finally in the evening after dinner, some Ionians brought their bedding outside--it was summertime--where they could take their rest in the cool and at the same time keep their eye on Socrates to see if he would stand there all night as well. He remained standing until it was dawn and the sun rose. Then he made a prayer to the sun and went away.[8]

This focusing ability is not limited only to the greatest thinkers. Srully Blotnick, in his research on millionaires, found that all of them were as deeply absorbed in their lives' work as any genius would be. He writes: "Business executives who shook their heads in mock puzzlement at Einstein's deep involvement in his work were no less involved in theirs. These people had been seized and were held tightly in the grip of their work to an extent which is difficult for anyone-- including themselves--to imagine. 'Consumed,' as a description, barely does the situation justice."[9]

Real Commitment Is Effortless

The things that are really pleasurable in life, whether it's playing softball or working on your stamp collection, really require no effort.

Woody Allen

> No great intellectual thing was ever done by great effort; a great thing can only be done by a great man and he does it without effort.
>
> JOHN RUSKIN

No one has to try to be great. Although hard work and careful practice are absolutely essential, they have nothing to do with effort. For more than two centuries in America, the Puritan Ethic--the ultimate model of Hard Work--was thought to be the key to real success, whether or not it brought personal reward. Wrote Longfellow:

> The heights by great men reached and kept
> Were not attained by sudden flight,
> But they, while their companions slept,
> Were toiling upward in the night.

But was it really "toil" or something else that kept these great individuals going "while their companions slept"? Might there not be something more like an "ease ethic"? Let's look at this possibility more closely.

One of the most telling signs of commitment in great people is their ability to stay with a project, never losing interest or enthusiasm even after many years. As psychologist Howard Gardner reports, the "fully developed adult at the height of his powers" works "with an enhanced intensity, extending over a wider body of knowledge, and with a more pervasive goal in mind than most of us can realize or even envision in our everyday workings."

Great achievement is thus almost always accompanied by a commitment that extends for years, even for a lifetime, and sometimes without real recognition or support. Einstein spent eleven years working on the general theory of relativity and a lifetime on a unified-field theory that he never resolved. And he fully appreciated others who were as purposeful as himself. He wrote:

> What a deep conviction of the rationality of the universe and what a yearning to understand . . . Kepler and Newton must have had to enable them to spend years of solitary labour in disentangling the principles of celestial mechanics. . . . Only one who has devoted his life to similar ends can have a vivid

realization of what has inspired these men to remain true to their purpose in spite of countless failures.[10]

So what's the secret? How do people maintain a long-term commitment? The answer is that they find the commitment to be a deeply pleasurable and joyful experience. And when the commitment and therefore the joy are deep enough, it seems that all the necessary energy miraculously becomes available, and then every action needed for accomplishment is effortless.

We may call it perseverance, which has the sound of something endlessly forced. But when your attention is fully absorbed, your mind is easily engaged in the task, never forced. Perseverance, therefore, isn't a strain when it's simply a series of smaller steps, each one pleasurable in itself, moving toward a goal. The little accomplishments along the way to Wimbledon, to the Pillsbury Bake-off, to the presidency are the only steps one *can* take; all giant steps for mankind are merely the accumulated result of millions of little steps. What's important is that it doesn't *feel* like a trek--each step feels more and more pleasurable as you approach your goal. When you are deeply involved in what makes you happy inside, it feels completely natural--not at all like a struggle or "hard work."

This often leads automatically to what we know as greatness. Wrote professor and writer George E. Woodberry:

> I think the wisest men and often the greatest--have come to their powers of great service somewhat by accident and the place they found themselves in; but one condition of their power in the end was they had the habit of doing little things day by day and always as well as they could, and so their greatness came on them almost unobserved. They didn't think about greatness but grew up to it.[11]

Clara Hale, the founder of Hale House in Harlem, a home for children of drug addicts, was recently awarded an honorary Doctor of Laws degree from St. John's University. At the ceremony, she recalled that "all along, I was only thinking about getting from one day to the next, taking care of the children. I never dreamed it would go so far."

The bottom line lies in the *degree* of commitment one makes to what one wants. Many successful people report that it is not until all your bridges are burned and you are completely committed that the environment supports you. In other words, when you can't go anywhere else, nature pulls out of you the most remarkable faculties you didn't know you had and wouldn't have been able to generate any other way. It seems that nature, God, or whatever you want to call it will help you only if you are absolutely committed. You go out on a limb, but only on *one* limb, not crawling from limb to limb around the whole tree. If there is any kind of wavering about whether you want to do it or not, then nature wavers, too.

The German poet Goethe described this process of absolute commitment:

> Until one is committed, there is hesitating, the chance to draw back, always ineffectiveness. Concerning all acts of initiative (and creation), there is one elementary truth, the ignorance of which kills countless ideas and splendid plans: that the moment one definitely commits oneself, the Providence moves too. All sorts of things occur to help one that would never otherwise have occurred. A whole stream of events issues from the decision, raising in one's favor all manner of unforeseen incidents and meetings and material assistance which no man could have dreamed would have come his way.

A full commitment must of course absorb our hearts as well and move us in the direction of the growth of our own happiness.

Happiness

> Do you not see, O my brothers and sisters? It is not chaos or death . . . it is form and union and plan . . . it is eternal life . . . it is happiness.
>
> WALT WHITMAN

> I'm trying to do everything I'm capable of doing and have a perfect balance in my life--to be successful at my work, and at being a wife and a sister and a friend. I have to have all those things in their proper place. I don't want to be a star if I have no life. . . . I think one of the big mistakes celebrities make is that they think because they are so popular, it sets them apart and

makes them like gods instead of just extremely lucky people.
. . . The important thing is that I am happy with myself.

DOLLY PARTON

. . . And then my heart with pleasure fills And dances with the daffodils.

WILLIAM WORDSWORTH

It may sound unusual to consider happiness an essential quality of greatness, especially when we are used to thinking of greatness as a solemn undertaking. But on the inner journey to greatness, increasing happiness is a highly significant landmark--a sign that you are indeed going in the direction of your dreams. More than any other characteristic of greatness, happiness is the most intimate, the most personal inasmuch as only *you* can know what makes you happy. No one else can.

Yet, like the qualities of integrity and commitment, happiness also requires constant attention. We are all faced every moment of our lives with the decision whether to be happy or not. We tend not to think of this as a matter in which we have a choice, but we do. Happiness does not just arrive--we have to know and think and do and be the things we want to have happiness come to us. When actress Helen Hayes was asked during an interview about the secret of her joyous nature, she indicated that it had been a conscious choice: "I made my *decision* to be happy."

Not only does happiness *result* from having good things happen, it often *causes* them to happen. Remember how you feel on your birthday? It seems to give you a boost, no matter how concerned you may be about your advancing years. It's a magical day, and the magic tends to show up in whatever you're doing. For example, baseball statistician Bill James noticed an impressive performance by first baseman Keith Hernandez on Hernandez's birthday during the last game of a World Series play-off. Curious, he ran a "birthday" check and found that there is a "definite birthday effect" on better hitting-- a very high average of .337. When you feel happy, you feel integrated in mind and body and you play better.

At some time or other, we all experience the feeling that "life is great," or say to ourselves, "I am great and I can do anything." This feeling is so close to the deepest aspect of our being that it is often too abstract to put into words.

However, if we could perceive this feeling more clearly and watch closely as it builds upon itself to form an idea, a thought, a plan, or an action, we would actually be watching an impulse of nature un-fold in us, that very creative process which all great people describe as their most thrilling experience. This is how, as creativity moves within us, happiness rises in our hearts.

Indeed, there are research findings that indicate that happiness and greatness are positively correlated. Psychologist Lewis Terman and, later, creativity researcher Paul Torrance found that creativity is significantly related to happiness as well as to compassion and em-pathy. This correlation occurs because being happy and doing what makes you happy are always closer to your real self. And if a major factor in becoming great is becoming happy--not just okay, not get-ting by, but *deeply happy*--then perfect greatness would equate with an inner state of perfect bliss.

When you are doing what makes you happy, you have the best chance to be fully in tune with your own greatness. Writes former race-car driver Patrick Bedard:

> For me there's no terror. Only joy. Nothing focuses the mind like 750 horsepower at your foot and a license to use it. Nothing else demands that level of concentration. Or commitment. . . . You're the force that makes it work. Without the driver, a racing car is just like a tool, dumb as a hammer. The driver transforms it into kinetic art, makes it waltz with physics. And the dance makes the spirits soar.[12]

For aerialist Philippe Petit, who has walked between the towers of Manhattan's World Trade Center and between the spires of Notre Dame Cathedral in Paris, it is the stillness on the wire that gives him joy: "The feeling of a second of immobility--if the wire grants it to you--is an ultimate happiness."

In general, however, we don't have to do flashy things to experi-ence happiness, or even run all over the place to find it. By just settling down to enjoy the deepening experiences of growth, life can get better and better, not just newer and newer, but more and more rewarding. In fact, it is in *pursuing it* that happiness is experienced.

Happiness: The Pursuit

Any experience can produce happiness--whether it is climbing a mountain or straightening out the checkbook at long last--when it allows us to experience steps of progress, a sense of ongoing accomplishment and some awakening of latent capacities. The pursuit of happiness is active and purposeful. Action that is not purposeful does not tend to bring happiness, either during the process or at its end.

Most of us know that when we are truly absorbed in a task, time ceases; we feel relaxed and not at all fatigued. Sometimes, we even feel let down at the end of a project we've been working on, not because we're displeased with the results but because the actual enjoyment came with the doing, not, as we might have been expecting, with the final product.

This is the feeling that Charles Lindbergh described at the end of his 1927 solo flight across the Atlantic:

> Within the hour I'll land, and strangely enough I'm in no hurry to have it pass. I haven't the slightest desire to sleep. There's not an ache in my body. The night is cool and safe. I want to sit quietly in this cockpit and let the realization of my completed flight sink in. . . . It's like struggling up a mountain after a rare flower, and then, when you have it within arm's reach, realizing that satisfaction and happiness lie more in the finding than the plucking. Plucking and withering are inseparable. . . . I almost wish Paris were a few more hours away. It's a shame to land with the night so clear and so much fuel in my tanks.[13]

We may think our forefathers cheated a little by upholding the right to the *pursuit* of happiness rather than guaranteeing us the right to happiness itself. But they wisely knew that happiness exists only in its own pursuit, that the process is what brings waves of satisfaction and pleasure; the achievement of the goal is just one more step in the process. This is how greatness is manifested through the pursuit of happiness, as we experience the delight of "baby achievements"--the steps of progress day by day, leading to minor or major accomplishments.

This understanding of achievement is common in Eastern cultures. The *Bhagavad Gita* counsels its readers to be concerned with the "doing" and not mind the results, which are embedded in the doing. And if you do the job well, and give it all your attention, you'll do a better job than if you worry about the outcome.

The process is entirely effortless and unconscious as we move in the direction of more and more happiness. A favorite book holds our attention, but if a favorite person walks into the room, our attention may be automatically drawn to him instead. We are drawn to that which we love most. What happens is that you fall in love with what you are committed to and thus become more committed. Scientist Michael Polyani describes how the true scientist emerges when, throughout all the facts and theories, experiments and research, a *passion* wells up--a belief in what is being sought, a belief in knowledge, in science as a way to know truth. Without this passion, you could never write a great symphony, or raise a happy child, or paint a house to perfection, or continually search for a cure for any disease.

The process of increasing happiness leading to greatness also has another dimension. It requires a future as well as a present orientation.

An Optimistic Future Orientation

No matter how well you've succeeded in the past, it is only your present activities that let you experience the pleasure of progress. Carol Heiss, 1960 Olympic gold medal figure-skating champion, observed: "The gold medal doesn't make you happy the rest of your life. It doesn't wash the kitchen floor and it doesn't change the children's diapers . . ."

To maintain happiness, you have to keep growing and exploring further. An artist who continues to repeat his past successes may be able to maintain his reputation and popularity, but he will ultimately be bored and unfulfilled. It's easy to see why retirement is such a blow to many people who find that it cuts them off from continuing personal growth. Despite her great success in the most glamorous of professions, actress Claire Bloom reminds us of its drawbacks:

> I can imagine being much happier now in some profession that offers increasingly greater satisfactions as you get older, rather than the reverse. In acting, as you get older the parts get fewer--films die out for nearly every actress after forty and you can count on your fingers the number of important stage roles there are for mature women.
>
> I would have liked to be in a profession where, when you reach your full maturity and are at the height of your powers, everything is there for you to do, rather than it all going away.[14]

Because the desire for happiness motivates them, great people have a strong and optimistic sense of the future; they look forward to each new stage of accomplishment. They not only have a sense of happiness in the present, they also anticipate future happiness. They have what psychologists call "an optimistic future orientation." Research psychologist George Vaillant identified "preparing for the future" as one of the strategies employed by healthy persons. We could add that creating a *happy* future is the optimistic strategy employed by the greats--and it works.

The celebrated actress Ruth Gordon, for example, began structuring her great future at age four: "That was in 1900 and I got organized. I knew I was going to have the damndest great things happen to me." And when at age seventy-three she won an Oscar for *Rosemary's Baby*, she remarked, "I can't tell you how encouraging a thing like this is."[15] No resting on laurels, but an ever-moving thrust into the future epitomizes this characteristic of greatness.

Because of its dynamic energy, many thinkers have proposed that happiness is *the* essential fuel of life; through the growth of every individual's happiness, the whole purpose of creation is served. Perhaps no one has elucidated this observation more beautifully than Goethe:

> When the sound and wholesome nature of man acts as an entirety, when he feels himself in the world as in a grand, beautiful, worthy and worthwhile whole, when this harmonious comfort affords him a pure, untrammeled delight: Then the universe, if it could be sensible of itself, would shout for joy at

having attained its goal and wonder at the pinnacle of its own essence and evolution.

For what end is served by all the expenditure of sun and planets and moons, of stars and Milky Ways, of comets and nebulae, of worlds evolving and passing away, if at last a happy man does not involuntarily rejoice in his existence?[16]

It seems likely that greatness would not arise within any of us without this feeling of joyful happiness at what we are experiencing, thinking, feeling, and knowing about the world and ourselves. All of us have the feeling, but not all of us, not even the majority of the greats, have it every minute. We do however recognize that it is perhaps our deepest connection to everything around us. And once we feel this connection, we recognize that we have some choice in the matter of our own lives. Based on this feeling, we can *choose* to have wonderful things happen to us. This is what we can call "maximizing" or making good luck for ourselves.

Maximizing: Creating Your Own Good Luck

If a man be lucky there is no foretelling the possible extent of his good fortune. Pitch him into the Euphrates and like as not he will swim out with a pearl in his hand.

BABYLONIAN PROVERB

The Support System

Archaeologist Froelich Rainey reports how, as a graduate student in the West Indies, he made his first significant discovery. He was supposed to tell the site foreman to quit digging at a certain level. But after a big lunch, he fell asleep. When he was awakened, he was told his crew had continued to dig and had come upon some painted pottery no one had seen before in that part of the world. Rainey's career was launched.[17]

This is the support we sometimes get from nature. We usually call it good luck. With it, an artist doesn't draw a line he has to erase. A father, wondering how he is going to handle the issue of an allowance with his six-year-old, opens the morning paper and sees a well-written article entitled "Children and Allowances." Or a meteorologist starts to investigate the effect of climate on creativity, and from then on, in every magazine or book she picks up, on every TV or radio show she turns on, some pertinent factor of climate and creativity is mentioned.

In abundance, this is the kind of support that enables our life to be "mistake-proof." We could say that at those times when we are innocently putting ourselves in a position to allow nature to help us make choices, such actions become maximally effective; we don't make errors. Of course, "mistake-free" living doesn't really mean a problem disappears. It's our perception of the problem and how to overcome it that's changeable. One day, it's a mountain; another, a molehill.

When you experience this support, somehow everything starts to go your way. Johnny Carson observed: "When you're performing and everything comes together, you can almost do no wrong." But is it going your way or are you yourself at last going the way you're supposed to? You are, at any given moment, either swimming with or against the tides. If you are open to being flexible, and are able to respond to inner and outer cues, you can gain the allegiance of the environment by putting yourself in the right place at the right moment. Jonas Salk calls this "the error-correcting process of evolution . . . an orientation toward fulfillment."

Emerson observed that the wise worker "hitches his wagon to a star, and sees his chore done by the gods themselves." According to one sportswriter, gymnast Mitchell Gaylord's 1984 Olympic performance on the high bar "was made to look effortless, as though all the power had come from someplace other than the gymnast's body."[18] When someone has access to this support system, we often look at that individual and think "Boy, is she lucky!" But what do we mean by that observation?

❖

Making Luck

It is often said that successful people are lucky risk-takers. But it may be more accurate to call them "maximizers" or "advantage-takers."

Nature gives them an opportunity and they take good advantage of it.

Having a lucky day is commonplace for great people--because they have prepared for it. They know how to create their own favorable circumstances. This is what George Bernard Shaw contended in *Mrs. Warren's Profession*:

> People are always blaming their circumstances for what they are. I don't believe in circumstances. The people who get on in this world are the people who get up and look for the circumstances they want and, if they can't find them, make them.

What Shaw is describing is something great people do easily. They make the best events happen. They "maximize" life; they seem to have a flawless organizing ability. This does not simply mean that they can manage time and people effectively; it means that they can organize *circumstances* to their benefit.

In 1972 in a research study entitled "Inequality," which looked at factors of financial success, Christopher Jencks and his colleagues at Harvard's Center for Educational Policy Research concluded that "luck has as much effect as competence on income." In a later book, *Who Gets Ahead?*, Jencks and associates put a little less emphasis on luck and more on personality characteristics. But luck was still the unpredictable variable, especially early in the career and especially for those individuals with fewer advantages. In a survey of over seven hundred CEOs conducted by the American Management Association, these business leaders themselves considered luck to be one of the top five factors in their success and regarded it as more important than risk-taking or talent.

Similarly, in a recent article Daniel Seligman observed that the role of luck is far more significant in the distinguished careers of the top successful people than we might think. Among others, he describes the luck-filled career of Harry Truman who at thirty-eight in 1922 was "out of work and in debt." By 1945 he was the leader of the free world.[19]

So what do we mean by luck or chance? It might be fortunate meetings with people who eventually help us rise to the top or generally "being at the right place at the right time." But it is likely that the "right connections" occur at a much more subtle level of human interaction.

Economist George Gilder argues that the "luck" theory that Jencks as well as fellow economist Lester Thurow propose is really much more an issue of profound creativity:

> Critics of capitalism often imagine that they have discovered some great scandal of the system when they reveal its crucial reliance on luck; its distribution of benefits and attainment of riches by unpredictable and irrational processes--its resemblance, at some level, to a lottery. Chance, to many economists, is something bad, arbitrary, haphazard--a descent to aimlessness or chaos and a domain for the remedies of government.
>
> Chance, however, is not the realm of the anarchic and haphazard but the area of freedom and the condition of creativity. It taps the underlying and transcendent order of the universe. We call it chance because it is beyond the ken of ordered rational processes, part of the "mysterious" realm that Einstein called "the cradle of true art and true science." The domain of chance is our access to futurity and to providence.[20]

Perhaps we can describe luck as the narrow picture of what, if we had a broad vision of life, we would see as our just reward. When we are extremely lucky, we have somehow tuned into the precise laws of nature that guide all creation--at least our own lives--and are cruising on *full.* Luck happens to us when nature operates with us in mind, almost as if it had "adopted" us. Ignorant of its workings, we ascribe it to chance.

Accidents Will Happen

A surprising number of discoveries by great people have been called "accidents"--that is, they seemed to have happened by chance. But the greats know better.

A story is told about Louis Pasteur. He was the guest of honor at a reception, and one of his colleagues came up to him and exclaimed, "Isn't it extraordinary how many scientific achievements of our century are arrived at by accident?" Pasteur replied, "Yes, it really is quite remarkable when you think about it, and furthermore, did you ever observe to whom the accidents happen?"

Film director Sidney Lumet had this to say about so-called accidents:

> When you are right, when you are functioning well, all the accidents happen *for* you--you get better accidents and none of them work against you. At the times when you're at your full creative juice, when there's nothing wrong with the piece, when you attack it properly you get all the breaks. On *Seagull* I needed six days of sun and ten days of clouds: I got six days of sun and ten days of clouds. It was exact. Other times on a picture called *The Fugitive Kind,* in which something had never become resolved in the script and it only became more aggravated, the hole kept opening up bigger and bigger and the accidents were against us. There is a kind of mystique about it; or maybe when you are functioning well you can make almost anything work for you.[21]

The Vedic *Upanishads* describe how great, fully realized people live supported by all nature. *Upanishad* means "to sit near." When everything "sits near you," nothing is out of reach. This is the luck over which we preside as masters of our own universe. It's never out of reach.

And how do you create fortunate circumstances for yourself? By acting as nature does, by spontaneously favoring that which is good and useful. Just as a healthy cell membrane lets in only those molecular substances that support its growth (amino acids, glucose, vitamins, etc.), people adjust to the various inputs of the environment. Great people may have a better ability to filter out nonuseful influences and automatically seek and create useful ones.

Maximizing thus means making the most of things. In making decisions, the maximizing person always chooses that which is better for his or her life: real food over junk food, true friends rather than superficial ones, the beautiful rather than the horrible. And in this way, maximizing people always pull you up with them, never put you down.

Maximizing produces an evolutionary growth toward gaining greater intelligence, creativity, and happiness. It also means "going for it" in the highest and best sense, favoring your deepest desires over your lesser expectations. In explaining her yearning to continue her artistic growth as a serious actress, Barbra Streisand quoted the medieval Jewish philosopher Maimonides: "If I do not rouse my soul to higher things, who will rouse it?"

Today, when we talk about "going for it," we think of an aggressive, all-out push to get at what we want. However, when we look closely at what "going for it" entails, it might be more accurate to describe the process as *letting go for it.*" This willingness to put yourself in nature's hands is a highly significant aspect of greatness. The greats describe it as a feeling of "surrender."

Surrender: The "Let It Happen" Orientation

But at some moment I did answer "Yes" to Someone or Something--and from that hour I was certain that existence is meaningful and that, therefore, my life, in self-surrender, had a goal.

DAG HAMMARSKJÖLD

When Nature has a job to be done, she creates a genius to do it.

EMERSON

If nature, as Emerson believed, chooses great people to express her best work, how do you get to be chosen? It happens, it seems, when you learn to get out of the way, when you adopt a "let it happen" orientation even in the midst of the most committed activity.

❖

Getting Out of Nature's Way

Have you ever been in an argument with a friend and realize there's one angle that you know would convince him you're right, but you can't get the idea out . . . it's on "the tip of your mind"? Your frustration is getting in the way of clear thinking. Later on, just as you're about to fall asleep, the right tactic comes to you easily, and you wish you had had that clarity during the argument.

135

We call this phenomenon "getting in your own way." It can often occur when a performer is mentally and therefore physically blocked and even "freezes" completely. Freezing simply means a stoppage of flow. It happens to many of us in sports, on the stage, at meetings. The opposite happens when performance flows freely, and the player, performer, or speaker simply allows it to continue. Film director John Huston has said that a good director can never force a scene; he or she must just let it happen and wait for it to be "solved."

"Getting out of the way" seems to be an important aspect of succeeding at whatever one does. In Blotnick's study of millionaires, most attributed their success to something other than themselves. "It wasn't any of my own doing," they typically responded. Blotnick concluded that those who had succeeded had gotten their egos out of the way. As such, "they unwittingly generated more harmony and cohesion." Similarly, Warren Bennis and Burt Nanus, in a four-year study of ninety successful business leaders, found that these leaders "trust themselves without letting their ego or image get in the way."

We like to think that adventuring, pathfinding, and risk taking are the dominant traits of greatness. But are they? It may be instead that the truly great are not really pathfinders at all, but excellent *path followers*--and that the only requirement is loss of the ego.

There are numerous descriptions given by the greats who have experienced how useless it is to interfere in the process of creation. Madame George Sand, for example, revealed Chopin's lack of trust in the gift given him and his struggle to free his music from "himself":

> His creation was spontaneous and miraculous. He found it without seeking it, without foreseeing it. It came on his piano suddenly, complete, sublime, or it sang in his head during a walk, and he was impatient to play it to himself. . . . He shuts himself up in his room for whole days, weeping, walking, breaking his pens, repeating and altering a bar a hundred times, writing and effacing it as many times, and recommencing the next day with a minute and desperate perseverance. He spent six weeks over a single page--to write it last as he had noted it down at the very first.[22]

A writer may have to let go of a particular angle he cherishes in order for a story to be perfectly developed and free from any intrusion. As Virginia Woolf observed, "The desire to plead some personal cause or grievance always has a distressing effect, as if the spot at which the reader's attention is directed were suddenly two-fold instead of single."

Selden Rodman describes how Walt Whitman, in his most profound poems, is able to "just let the world and what he saw of it . . . operate, producing a work of such great magical intensity as 'Song of Myself.' " But once Whitman becomes conscious of his role as a theorist of poetry, he loses his innocence and becomes obsessed with ideology. Says Rodman, "In 'Song of Myself,' he was happy, and he expressed it without any of this probing into his own subconscious mind. It just welled out of his subconscious mind, if you like, because it was there. It's there for a great work of art, in the same sense that the Sistine Ceiling is."[23]

The seemingly effortless creations and discoveries that result when the ego is held in abeyance often occur at unlikely times and places, like the one described by mathematician Henri Poincaré, who was "given" a mathematical solution to a problem he had long been working on, as he boarded a bus: "At the moment when I put my foot on the step, the idea came to me, without anything in my former thoughts seeming to have paved the way for it . . . and later, for conscience's sake, I verified the result at my leisure."[24]

Psychologist William James studied this universal phenomenon of surrender in creation and concluded: "This feeling is so strong that the creator may consider himself passive, as if the solution were not really his to come to him."

According to the Indian Vedic tradition, such experiences offer an initial awareness of a permanent state of enlightenment coming from the continual connection to a basic source of creativity--wherein "one who is in Union with the Divine and who knows the Truth will maintain: 'I do not act at all.' "

Soetsu Yanagi, a Japanese folk-art historian, describes the process as one of "forgetting," used by the great Japanese artists as they drew the same designs over and over again, hundreds of times a day: "They forgot themselves as they worked . . . or perhaps it would be more correct to say that they worked in a world so free they were able to forget themselves."[25] This process of surrender is identical to the surrender in romantic love or to that which a devoted student feels for a great teacher. When the sculptor surrenders to the inherent forms in the marble or clay, she leaves herself open to the possibilities she might have missed by imposing a single preconceived idea. Surrender is thus a kind of technique to allow the best to emerge.

In actuality, you are surrendering only to yourself--to your greatest self perhaps--when you act according to what is best, or, we could say, according to what nature wants for you. In this way surrender is like getting into a taxi with a great driver. You tell him where you want to go, and he takes you by the best route possible.

Many distinguished people have described how this inner flow of creativity feels as if God or some other divine force had chosen them as a vehicle. "They do not consider themselves the prime movers," write creativity researchers Stanley Rosner and Lawrence E. Abt, "but simply the instruments through which certain operations take place." J. S. Bach is reported to have said, "I play the notes in order, as they are written. It is God who makes the music." Many of the greats have explained that they don't consciously have the thought, "Oh, what is the will of God? If I only knew, I would do what is wanted." It just happens. The feeling creates its own response: "Let Thy will be done." They just allow nature to act *through* them. And that surrendered attitude often facilitates a powerful experience.

In his novel *The Search*, C. P. Snow describes the moment of discovery of what he understands to be "God," after years of scientific work:

> Then I was carried beyond pleasure. . . . My own triumph and delight and success were there, but they seemed insignificant beside this tranquil ecstasy. It was as though I had looked for a truth outside myself, and finding it had become for a moment a part of the truth I sought; as though all the world, the atoms and the stars, were wonderfully clear and close to me, and I to them . . . I had never known that such a moment could exist. . . . When I was young, I used to sneer at the mystics who have described the experience of being at one with God and part of the unity of things. After that afternoon, I did not want to laugh again; for though I should have interpreted the experience differently, I thought I knew what they meant.[26]

Almost all great individuals have experienced a sense of union with God, or some greater power. It does not always require a belief in God, but it does seem to require a sense of God, or something, believing in them. Real greatness is generally associated with a feeling of a gift, *a presence within* to which one surrenders. Believing in something outside yourself or in yourself may be different sides of the same coin. Whether you call it becoming a channel for God or nature or a vehicle for your own gift, in every case you step aside. You allow whatever is there to be expressed without your controlling it.

Over time, this surrender to a greater power can become devotion-- and devotion serves as an essential ingredient in human development. The feeling of devotion is often expressed as love; it binds us to the loved one as a source of knowledge and growth. It is only the people we love from whom we really learn.

In the development of great people, devotion comes from a continual uniting of total commitment and total surrender. It is necessary to one's craft, to a work of art, to another person, to one's heart's desire in any aspect of life. It involves a kind of constant all-out surrender to one's own best self, to one's greatest thoughts. And then, in that state of surrender, our behavior becomes simple.

❖

Simplicity: The Behavior of Surrender

I have a philosophy which is "play the melody." It means don't overarrange, don't make life difficult. Just play the melody; do it the simplest way possible.

JACKIE GLEASON

Nothing is more simple than greatness; indeed to be simple is to be great.

EMERSON

Great people are often admired for their childlike innocence, their openness to life, their continual ability to be simple, never contrived. Simplicity of heart, according to Alma Wright, Frank Lloyd Wright's mother, "is just as necessary for an architect as for a farmer or a minister if the architect is going to build great buildings."

When we have surrendered and become devoted, and have learned not to interfere in our natural growth process, we can start to move without complication and division: Simplicity happens when we let go, when we allow greatness just to *be there.*

In a complicated world, the expression "simpleminded" has come to mean unintelligent. But the truth is that simplicity is non-interference, nature's own "no-frills" plan, something that we equate with elegance, basic and perfect in itself. Physicist Richard Feynman found that "in physics, when you discover new things, it's really simpler. We have these integrations where everything is simpler than before." Feynman recalls how physics needed a more true, more condensed way of identifying the patterns among particles; "quarks" were the answer, the elegant truth, the most concise description of the events. "That is common to all our laws; they all turn out to be simple things. . . . You can recognize truth," he wrote, "by its beauty and simplicity."[27]

British Prime Minister Margaret Thatcher recalls:

> The simplest lectures at University were from the most brilliant professor whose mind was totally lucid, who had total comprehension and understanding and therefore could put it simply. . . . In the end, if you really understand things, you are able to make them simple.[28]

Yet even though nature at its source is always simple, we may still find that our own ability to let go, to be simple, is not so easy to come by. As the authors of *In Search of Excellence* realized, the great companies "worked hard to keep things simple in a complex world." We almost have to *learn* to be simple, to do less, to let the essentials have the spotlight. And as we experience the "letting go," we find ourselves supported. Actor Jack Lemmon recounts how he mastered this lesson:

> In my first movie with Judy Holliday, George Cukor drove me crazy. I'd come in every day with five thousand ideas and he'd just say, "Less, less, less, Jack. Less is more." Finally I blew up and yelled, "Are you trying to tell me *not* to act" and he said, "Oh, God, *yes!*" And I never forgot it. I've learned my craft from that advice. . . . It's the hardest thing in the world to be simple and the easiest thing to act your brains out. . . . I've spent my life trying to get down to the basic truth without the frills . . ."[29]

Once the greats have experienced this level of simplicity and sur-render, they start to live their greatness easily and comfortably. And then they look around and see that they want everyone else to live this way as well.

Compassionate Responsibility

> As each of us improves himself, he helps the world just that much. As he neglects to improve himself, he holds the world back just that much.
>
> ALAN BOONE

> A succinct definition of love is that it is the ability, by demonstrative acts, to confer survival benefits on others in a creatively enlarging manner. This means that by one's acts one not only enables the other to live but to live more fully realized than he would otherwise have been.
>
> ASHLEY MONTAGU

Recently, ecologists at the University of Washington found that wil-low trees transmit a warning to other willows from as far away as two hundred feet. When caterpillars are attacking, the trees emit a chemical signal that travels on the wind. This enables distant trees to prepare their protection--phenol in the leaves--which is distasteful to the caterpillars. This advance warning of an attack amazes scientists: The individual trees have the ability to behave in a way that benefits not just themselves but the whole species. So, if the trees can do it, why can't we?

According to Ashley Montagu, we humans have become compet-itive when we are actually meant to be cooperative:

> We have tended to make egotists of creatures who are biologically organized to function most efficiently as altruists. The evidence indicates that from birth onward the direction of the human being's drives is toward cooperation. . . . It appears then that whatever contributes toward personal and social health and happiness is good and desirable for human beings.[30]

Compassionate responsibility for others is a natural by-product of greatness. If you are in tune with the natural world, you understand that your own growth is intimately associated with the advancement of others. "No true and permanent fame can be found except in labors which promote the happiness of mankind," wrote Charles Sumner. Many wealthy men and women become philanthropists once they have achieved their own success, because they discover a basic truth--success demands greater responsibility for others in order to maintain satisfaction in oneself. Once a person is successful, said Buckminster Fuller, "he's going to see that he can't enjoy his success until everyone else is fixed up."

First, we must become self-sufficient. Real philanthrophy comes from fullness. You can't give away what you barely have--only what you have in abundance. If I give you fire from my candle to light yours, it does not diminish mine and cause a loss for me. I don't need it back. In fact, if I want more light for myself, I need you to have light also. Based on our own success, or as a result of it, we begin to take responsibility for others, which ensures that our success continues to grow. Then it can only be a pleasure to take on the responsibility.

"I am used," said actress and politician Melina Mercouri, "to bring out the best in others." This sense of responsibility is described as a sweet delight to those who partake of it. It brings deep happiness. It unfolds new levels of greatness within. In addition, according to Harvard Professor David McClelland, it establishes a level of social maturity that is characteristic of great leaders. McClelland suggests that taking responsibility for others is also a means "to avoid the stress and illness associated with a strong power drive."[31] Thus, it's a healthy way for highly energetic people to turn their extra energy to good use.

The Territory of Greatness

I know very well that many others might, in this matter, as in others, do better than I can; and . . . though I believe that I have not so much of the confidence of the people as I had some time since, I do not know that, all things considered, any other person has more; and, however this may be, there is no way in which I can have any other man put where I am. I am here. I must do the best I can, and bear the responsibility of taking the course which I feel I ought to take.

ABRAHAM LINCOLN

The extent of one's territory of influence is based on the extent of one's knowledge, both of oneself and of the world. As Lao-tzu wrote many centuries ago, "He who grasps the ultimate structure of reality draws everyone to him. They approach him without being harmed and find security, satisfaction and contentment."

We expect a lot from great people. And they expect a lot from themselves. Because of this, a sure sign of greatness is the recognition of the responsibility for the gifts one has been given. At age fifteen, Beth Vigoda became the youngest student at Princeton University. She had learned to read by age three, learned Latin by eight, calculus by eleven. But she was also well aware of the future awaiting her. Said Beth, "I haven't done anything big yet. I have this gift and I don't want to waste it. I want to contribute it." By knowing the value of your own potential contribution, you learn to act in its service. According to singer-actress Bette Midler, "People are not the best because they work hard. They work hard because they are the best. It's a matter of responsibility to your talent." "In a great discovery," wrote C. P. Snow, "the scientist must satisfy two criteria: He must know what the discovery is and he must know how important it is."

What you ultimately take on as your responsibility results in your territory of influence. Observed the Indian poet Tagore:

It is difficult to achieve greatness of mind or character where our responsibility is diminutive and fragmentary, where our whole life occupies and affects an extremely limited area.

Thus, a hero's greatness is determined by the size of his or her victory; that is, it is most heroic, most worthy, most great if it is a victory for all humanity. If it is a victory for some but a defeat for others, it is less great. "We measure a great idea," says Norman Cousins, "by its ability to fit not the needs of the few but of the many."

To cultivate greatness, one puts oneself in charge of great ideas, great territories, and great issues. Then the territory itself demands that we rise to it. Washington felt the responsibility of his office to be so all-encompassing that it was reflected in his smallest gesture, even for generations to come: "I walk on untrodden ground. There is scarcely any part of my conduct which may not hereafter be drawn into precedent."

Having a large territory of influence does not of itself imply greatness. Hitler was very influential, but led his people and millions of others *into* misery, not out of it. The responsibility of greatness thus must include a profound sense of morality.

The Moral Imperative of Greatness

> Whatsoever a great man does, the very same is also done by other men. Whatever the standard he sets, the world follows it.
>
> BHAGAVAD GITA

Not only do great people behave responsibly, their behavior is also highly moral--not in a strained or contrived manner but spontaneously so. They invariably seem to recognize their moral responsibility.

C. P. Snow wrote that Einstein "was as certain of his moral . . . as of his physical insight. He wanted to do his best for his fellow humans, but he was the least sentimental of men. He recognized no collective loyalties except to the human race." Einstein himself wrote:

> Humanity has every reason to place the proclaimers of high moral standards and values above the discoverers of objective truths. What humanity owes to personalities like Buddha, Moses, and Jesus ranks for me higher than all the achievements of the inquiring and constructive mind.[32]

What all these personalities have in common is an unwavering territory of moral influence. It is often said that politicians can't legislate morality; rather, it is a by-product of individual awareness within every society. Similarly, corporations cannot be made to be moral. Only individuals can be uncompromising in the values they uphold.

Great people will always naturally create great things, but they can never guarantee the consequences of their creation. Generally, because they are functioning in tune with the laws of nature, what they create may be socially beneficial, but how their creation is valued depends on others. Society colors it with shades of better or worse, depending on the level of collective appreciation.

When questioned about his responsibilities as a scientist, the Nobel Prize-winning physicist Brian Josephson replied:

> I don't know whether the fact that you are the creator of a new idea gives you much influence over the way society uses it. I can't quite see what effect it would have if I were to tell IBM that it should stop developing high-speed Josephson junction computers because these machines might be used by the military.
>
> I'm more concerned with expanding public acceptance of higher states of consciousness, which may help to produce a more peaceful world.[33]

We cannot hold the physicists who discovered the properties of atomic energy responsible for atomic warfare. In itself, atomic energy is potentially one of the most life-supporting discoveries, one that can make every nation in the world entirely self-sufficient. But collective consciousness determines its use. Perhaps because Einstein recognized this vital truth, he considered morality to be the "most important matter in the human sphere."

Morality is an individual matter, but every individual both produces and is the product of a collective moral influence. We are all obviously responsible for each other whether consciously aware of it or not. Since greatness is inherently moral within the individual, its territory of influence includes a moral component. And because greatness is the result of more than individual behavior, its influence is also collective and as catching as laughter. (Crying, on the other hand, does not tend to be catching--it is individual and personal, not collective.)

In this way, through its harmonizing influence, greatness stirs greatness. It seeks its own level in everything and everyone. When Einstein said, "Everyone ought to become directly acquainted with the best," he was speaking of the effect of this contact. This is the responsibility of greatness. To create a better world, we start with individuals who experience the best of themselves. Then everything falls into place from there.

And the most direct way to stir greatness in oneself is to transcend all the boundaries, all the limits, and tap the most powerful field of influence within ourselves.

Transcending: Breaking the Boundaries

> A man that looks on glass
> On it may stay his eye;
> Or if he pleaseth, through it passe,
> And then the heav'n espie.
>
> GEORGE HERBERT

When I found I had crossed that line, I looked at my hands to see if I was the same person. There was such a glory over everything.

HARRIET TUBMAN (*on her first escape from slavery*)

❖

Boundary "Braking"

Boundaries, it seems, can be many things; they can be physical, psychological, emotional, or intellectual. They can be spiritual or social; they can be very subtle or very obvious. They are the structures through which we lead our lives. And if boundaries are restrictive, so life will be. Life will always be here; it's a matter of how much of it we use. When some people come to a boundary, they just stop. They "brake" for boundaries instead of breaking them.

If you live in a house, you can choose to be anywhere in it you feel at home. We all know people who never use the "good rooms"-- they save them for company. But isn't this a rather restricted use of the house?

The same applies to the house of the mind, which really has an infinite number of rooms. Yet so often we live in only a few of them, and not necessarily the best ones. Then periodically, because life is expansive and restriction unnatural, the desire arises to expand the boundaries to include all possibilities, to begin to live in the whole house. When this expansion occurs, we feel huge and wonderful, and more and more fully at home.

A recent TV program reported a story about a group of tough New York City kids spending three days in upstate New York with rural teenagers. The viewer was given a close look at the dissolving boundaries: Even after three days, a tremendous change took place. The city kids began giving up their hard edges and were obviously gaining a deeper appreciation of themselves as they learned to appreciate those "cow" kids. Even their speech softened. The country children lost some parochialness--their belief in a mythology about city kids dissolved as they opened up their homes and hearts. Both groups seemed to wake up. You could feel their excitement, their liveliness, their self-discovery as they entered new territories of experience.

This dissolving of boundaries is also a typical experience of those of us who joined the Peace Corps, or who travel to other parts of the world. Of course, if we spend enough time in any new place, the barriers start to erode and some integration with the environment starts to take place. And we may begin to see our own country and ourselves in a larger perspective. But there's always a point at which the expansion process stops. Once you've been to Tahiti several times or lived for a while in another culture, it no longer has the same expansive effect. The first time you may experience a contrast, a breaking of a boundary; later on you don't. Generally, even when we travel, we bring our inner constraints with us. And we may erect new boundaries often as rigid as the old.

The need therefore is to break boundaries continually, inside as well as outside. This is a major characteristic of and condition for greatness in all fields of life, because it means we are growing beyond yesterday's habits and limits and are free to reach for the proverbial stars. For example, if we don't break boundaries in love, if, with our loved ones we only go so far--a safe distance--and remain there, we won't experience satisfaction in our relationships. There is no such thing as a permanent relationship that doesn't change. Instead of seeking new levels within the relationship, we may seek another partner and just reexperience the old levels with that new person. We may also find that this situation is not very rewarding because we keep remaining within the same boundaries--our perfectly "safe" level of depth of intimacy. Then when we return to the stage in the relationship where we must risk breaking a few internal boundaries, and we move away again, we are creating a cycle of "no risk, no growth, no glory."

So, what is the real key to boundary-breaking and how does it occur?

Inner Heroics

We are inspired by people when we see them break internal boundaries. What great people help us do is to let go of rigid mental habits and limited thinking. "Creation," said Picasso, "is destruction of the known." If you have one idea about a situation and then something intrudes to alter that idea radically, a boundary is broken and you can never go back again to the old way of thinking. If you do go back, it is in retreat.

If, for example, a physician witnesses the "miraculous" healing of a terminal patient, her thinking about the practice of medicine has to be forever changed. If she does not allow that experience to expand her awareness of the possibilities of extending human life because it is "not statistically significant"--then something that has opened is shut, and her knowledge of medicine remains static and restricted.

Franklin Roosevelt transcended the image of a weak man sitting helplessly in a wheelchair by structuring another image of a great, courageous man rising above his circumstances. Norman Cousins recalls this latter image:

> I remember thinking that I'd never seen a healthier human
> being. There was also the look of greatness. It was inevitable.
> Anyone who could come back out of retirement after having
> been afflicted with a dreadful disease that shrank his limbs and
> that made it impossible for him to walk unaided would be great
> for that reason alone. You could see his braces where they
> entered his shoes, huge pieces of steel that seemed to reach
> inside you as well. It did things to you because one hundred and
> thirty million people were leaning on this man and the weight, if
> anything, was making him stronger and bigger.[34]

One often grows bigger and better through negative circumstances by creating a new structure and leaving an old one behind, much in the way a caterpillar becomes a butterfly. Whether mental or physical, this is what it means to transcend, to break boundaries.

Each of us is infinitely more capable of great accomplishments than we tend to allow ourselves to believe. When a mother lifts a 2,500-pound car off her child and saves his life (yes, this has really happened), we wonder how such a thing could occur. An "impossible" boundary has been broken--not only physically but mentally. The mother may not think she can lift the car: She just doesn't see its impossibility. She has only one intense, focused thought: "I must save my child." By her desire, the mother draws on some force inside that she uses to become "superhuman"--or, according to some researchers, merely fully human--using what she has available but had never needed until then.

Overcoming specific physical limitations is a very clear indication of boundary-breaking and easily captures our admiration. Indeed, of the "Heroes of the Year" chosen some years ago by *Quest* magazine, more than one third achieved that status through overcoming physical disabilities.

We admire not only physical but also emotional courage; the boundary one has to overcome may be more psychological than physical or both. And when the boundary-breaking drama is played out in a forced-choice, life-and-death situation in which the person must risk all or die, we are deeply inspired. Traditionally, soldiers have been this kind of hero in history, but these days, soldiering is not entirely a hero's profession. Instead, we look for soldierlike heroics. Civilian hostages, fighting psychological and emotional battles within themselves, become great heroes for us. And if they are released, even without a fight, we have the definite feeling that they have "won".

However, most of us face a more nebulous area of boundary-breaking. Since every day life generally involves some compromise, our "inner heroics" may not be so well and concretely defined. Perhaps this is why some of us try to create clear situations to challenge us; racing cars, skydiving thrills, events where the boundaries to be broken are precise and exact.

Or to break boundaries a little more safely, we watch others. In our culture sports have been popularly analyzed as a means for fans to let off aggression, violence, and the more primitive side of their supposedly dualistic nature. However, we are perhaps more strongly drawn, and in greater numbers, to nonviolent sports like baseball, golf, and tennis. We watch them because we feel great when we see great events created on the field. We can almost feel the movement of growth, the progress of society, as sports records get broken by our representatives, the great athletes, year after year.

To break these records, however, sportsmen and women first have to break boundaries inside, and all of them are well aware of the internal changes. According to a number of sports reporters, for example, golfer Jack Nicklaus has the ability to *will* the ball into the hole, to concentrate so perfectly as to create a field of influence between the ball and the hole. Like many exceptional athletes, he organizes the outcome mentally and it occurs physically. To accomplish such feats, great athletes know they transcend. Most have had what they call a "moment of eternity"--the unbounded moment--when anything is mentally and physically possible for them. This is what O. J. Simpson experienced in his sixty-four-yard come-from-behind victory run in the legendary USC versus UCLA Pacific Eight title game. He remembers: "Somehow I knew it was going to happen, even though it was a spontaneous thing. . . . But I'd made that run a million times before in my mind." During a game, a transcending athlete is said to be "in the zone"--acting and playing in another state of consciousness--where the feeling of playing the game is the feeling, says O. J., of being in a "sweet dream." We, the audience, can feel it, too, and we also have similar experiences at other events.

Artist and Audience: Bound to Be Boundless

Along with athletes, great artists serve to pull the audience completely into their "sweet dreams," their works of art. Their desire is to include us, bring us into another level of awareness, help us transcend. The pianist Arthur Rubinstein was entranced with experiencing his "music rising through the audience." The audience became part of his creation as well.

In Jane Wagner's play *The Search for Signs of Intelligent Life in the Universe*, Lily Tomlin's character Trudy takes several little aliens from outer space to the theater in order to give them "the goose-bump experience." When they later report to her, they have indeed gotten goose bumps, but didn't know they were supposed to have watched the play; they had been watching the audience.

A great performer can put each member of the audience in touch with his or her own personal greatness and enable them to experience a dissolution of boundaries. Singer Barbara Cook describes how a performer breaks the performer-audience boundary:

> I think mainly what I'm trying to do is to be there, to really be there. I'm trying to let the event happen and to pull people into it, to help them participate. There's no way I can do it alone. Unless people come with a certain vulnerability, unless they're willing to participate emotionally, the evening can't fully happen.[35]

Magician Doug Henning explains how he projects his illusions to dissolve the boundaries:

> People who do tricks can do the mechanics to make it work, but the audience can always see how it's done. That's because they're thinking about the method, not the effect. If I produce a coin from the air, I don't think "Now I'm putting the coin from this hand to the other, etc." If I think that, the audience will know how it's done.
>
> Instead, the magician must transcend his technique. His attention is on the level of feeling and intuition. When I do magic, I'm manipulating the *feeling* of the audience. Everything a magician does must emphasize the *effect* and deemphasize the method, including the magician's thought. This is the key to magic.[36]

With every great performer, something is set in motion that breaks boundaries and creates a new outlook on life for everyone listening and watching. To be at a Louis Armstrong performance was to experience not just the greatness of the music, but the happiness he felt within himself spilling over. His joy in his performance created waves of joy throughout the audience. In this way, the great performer reexperiences his or her own greatness reflected by the audience.

❖

The Transcending Experience

Psychologist Abraham Maslow, in his final work, distinguished two types of "self-actualizers": those whom he termed healthy but who had few or no "transcending experiences," and those for whom transcendence occurred regularly. The ability to transcend means the ability to grow continually beyond your current level of awareness or consciousness to a more and more inclusive and unifying level. Transcendence, wrote Maslow:

> . . . refers to the very highest and most inclusive or holistic levels of human consciousness, behaving and relating as ends rather than as means, to oneself, to significant others, to human beings in general, to other species, to nature and to the cosmos.[37]

According to Maslow's preliminary observations, transcenders have more and better peak experiences. In addition, he found that they themselves are "awe-inspiring, producing the subjective response in others . . ." And he concluded they are the great people and are found everywhere, in all walks of life:

> Because it will be so difficult for so many to believe, I must state explicitly that I have found approximately as many transcenders among businessmen, industrialists, managers, educators, political people as I have among the professionally "religious," the poets, intellectuals, musicians, and others who are *supposed* to be transcenders and are officially labeled so.[38]

Transcending experiences can be understood when you realize that your mind really has no boundaries; like the unified field of which it is no doubt an intimate part, it can go anywhere in space and time.

When we draw boundaries to live inside of, it's really just for convenience and out of habit; they aren't entirely real; at least they aren't the most fundamental reality. Caught up in the localized boundaries of experience, it's easy for all of us to forget that the underlying *unity* is what is most real and most permanent. It helps to remember what Einstein observed during a few precious moments of insight:

> The true rock of the self, the happy rock sheers up out of the muck of the soul. . . . This is not the self about which books are written, but the ageless self. . . . Just as the slightest breeze can set a vast forest in motion so, by some unfathomable impulse from within, the rocklike self can begin to grow, and in this growth nothing can prevail against it.[39]

Einstein's real gift was to be never entirely captured by the smaller, localized values in life, but always to transcend to the wholeness underlying these values. This simply means that he was moving, like all great people do, in the direction of using the "whole house," using the totality of the human mind.

However, you don't have to be an Einstein to transcend. We all can experience moments when we feel an indescribable happiness and connectedness, a feeling that we are not so much *apart* from the rest of the universe, but a real *part* of it. It is a complete reversal of our typical everyday way of experiencing the world.

Normally, when we stand on the shore and look at the incoming ocean, we often see only the waves and in so doing we may forget the unbounded magnitude of the whole ocean. Its size and beauty become lost in the boundaries of our limited perception of each wave as it rolls in. Or when we look at a piece of sculpture, we often forget the surrounding space. But to really see the parts, we have to be able to view them against a background. When we are captured by our limited boundaries, we forget there are unbounded limits of cosmic space and time onto which the universe and our lives have been painted.

But what if we could see the bounded and the boundless not only separately but together, experience each wave and the ocean simultaneously, the sculpture and its spatial environment together, the manifest universe and also its underlying, unmanifest, unbounded value? This is the ability we described earlier as "Q thinking"--the ability to enjoy several or all realities at once.

To do this, you have to transcend. By transcending, you go beyond one reality to another even more real, even more connected, even more joyous. Whether we are artists or not, we all have the ability to coordinate the boundaries with the boundless. We can learn to maintain our experience of the ocean along with the waves, the big picture along with all the little ones, the underlying field of greatness along with all our daily activities. And when we can do this continually, we are living our own inherent greatness fully.

Now that we've seen what greatness is and how it is expressed, in the following chapters we'll explore how actually to structure it for ourselves.

5

❖

THE PHYSIOLOGY OF GREATNESS: BEAUTIFUL BRAINS HAVE A MIND OF THEIR OWN

❖

The Physical Characteristics of Greatness

If it is to be at all reasonable to apply the ideas of modern science to discussion of our creative behavior, we need to assume that all intellectual accomplishments of which we, as biological systems, are capable are determined by purely physical-chemical interactions between our bodies (including our nervous systems) and the environment in which they seek to survive.

N. E. GOLOVIN

Every state of mind is supported and/or caused by a particular state of the nervous system; in this way the evolution of consciousness is based on the evolution of our physiological structures. So, every experience in human development ought to be directly correlated with

155

specific mental and physical parameters in every individual. These experiences, however, will differ for each of us depending upon what we put out attention on and how our bodies respond. For example, both Marcel Marceau and Bill Irwin, two of the greatest mimes of our era, are unable to wear a watch because watches stop on them. Irwin speculates that it is his magnetic field that causes this; he may be right. The physical sensitivity of mimes to the space around them may be enlivening certain electrical responses otherwise dormant in the rest of us.

Science is currently opening all doors into the "mystery" of individual greatness by verifying, quantifying, and physically measuring human capacities that up until now were unmeasurable. Electrical patterns in the brain, neurological responses, blood chemistry, and other biological considerations are presently being used in researching greatness. These physiological findings are then correlated with psychological tests of creativity and intelligence that have long been used exclusively to evaluate higher human functioning. Says psychologist Stanley Milgram: "[There is] the essential unity within psychology--the understanding that all psychological events rest on a biological substrate . . ."

EEG coherence, for example, is a measure of the synchronous function of electrical brain waves, and is considered an excellent measure of one's overall state of conscious awareness. An EEG reading can assess how brain functioning differs both within the individual and between individuals. We can now also measure consciousness through blood analysis. Dr. Jonas Salk has suggested that creative people produce chemical reactions within themselves, "internal opiates--particularly the endorphins," which show up in blood chemistry.

Maslow predicted this direction of research thirty years ago when he wrote, "It seems to me that we are on the edge of a new leap into correlating our subjective lives with external objective indicators. I expect a tremendous leap forward in the study of the nervous system because of these new indications [preliminary research showing mind-body correlation]."

In his later years, in addition to his research on the behavioral and perceptual characteristics of self-actualizers, Maslow became intrigued by the observation that all desirable mental, emotional, and physical traits in human beings seem to be positively correlated. As a result, he proposed that psychologically "healthy" individuals also be examined as potential specimens of excellent physical health. He wrote: "It has been my experience through a long line of exploratory investigations . . . that the healthiest people (or the most creative, or the strongest, or the wisest, or the saintliest) can be used as biological assays . . ."[1]

From this viewpoint, no matter what era or what field, greatness is based on the developed physiology of the individual. The myth that great genius is equated with physical weakness probably comes from the same thinking that suggests that creativity requires suffering. True, a number of great people have had to overcome physical handicaps as well as psycho-emotional ones; however, they were not great *because* of these weaknesses but *despite* them. (It is also possible that any extensive unhappiness and depression in creative people has to do with their inability to maintain the kind of a stress-free constitution that would enable them to express their gifts easily.) Because of the intimate relationship between mind and body, in order for intelligence and perception to be both highly developed and maintained over time, the biological functioning of a great individual would have to be as highly developed. And the evidence suggests that this is indeed true.

The first studies of the relationship between the mental and physical characteristics of greatness were conducted by Stanford University researcher Lewis Terman and his colleagues in the 1920s, 30s, and 40s. They found that gifted children as a group were physically stronger and healthier than average children. In addition, the gifted children were highly versatile, "good at everything." Genius, then, began to be understood as broad, not narrow, in range, and to involve physical as well as mental fitness.

We may think of great geniuses as burning out early, but greatness is often surprisingly long-lived. In Terman's longitudinal follow-up studies of the same gifted and average children in their adult years, it was found that the former were living significantly longer and were less suicidal than the average.[2] Another study of over one thousand of the most eminent men of the past several centuries showed that more than 50 percent were still living at the age of seventy, a proportion several times larger than the general population.[3]

So, it is not unusual that many of the great individuals we admire for their mental and artistic accomplishments were also physically very well-developed. Composer Richard Wagner, for example, was an excellent acrobat as a youngster, a courageous mountain climber, and could stand on his head at age seventy. At age fifty-seven novelist Leo Tolstoi walked 130 miles in three days, and at sixty-five was an excellent swimmer. At sixty-six he learned to ride a bicycle. Historian Charles Lamb could "walk all day" without fatigue. And despite his club foot, the English poet Lord Byron swam the Hellespont to prove that the mythical hero Leander could have done it.

George Washington is another example of a great mind in a great body. Along with his military, political, and artistic skills (he served as the principal architect in the design of Mount Vernon), he is reported to have been a sensational athlete. Once he jumped twenty-two feet, a jump not one man in ten thousand is able to make even today in our far more athletically trained society.

Perhaps the most telling argument for the mind-body parallel was the amazing physiological development of Leonardo da Vinci, arguably the world's greatest artistic and scientific genius. Art historian Kenneth Clark says of him:

> The steadiness of his hand was almost inhuman . . . and [his] eye was preternaturally fast; he could grasp and isolate fractions of movement in time with a precision that would only be confirmed more than four centuries later, by strobe photography. . . . Living on a diet of mostly fruit and water, shunning doctors, the steadiness of his coordination continued into his sixties while he was still producing tiny, postage-stamp size drawings which the ordinary human eye still has difficulty deciphering.[4]

The Great Athlete

The science of physiology gives us insight into the development of human greatness by allowing us to see how human beings change in dramatic ways over time. The notion that we can all be great is based in part upon our collective developing physiology as a species.

Whereas in the past it was the rule for only a few people to be exceptional, we can now expect the exceptional to be the rule. We can ask far more of ourselves and each other when we recognize just what degree of potentiality we're working with.

Perhaps the most obvious group of individuals in which to observe the changing physiology of greatness is great athletes. These athletes can tell their bodies to do things at will that other people simply can't.

Athletics research, like all research, requires a base line of possibilities against which to measure individual achievement. When we identify athletic skills, we try to see the limits of possibilities in order to predict future events. Sometimes the limits seem almost infinite. For example, the current records for pitching a baseball stand around 100 mph--set by Nolan Ryan and Goose Gossage. If we ask, "How fast *could* a pitcher throw, assuming he has all the necessary physical attributes and had received proper training?" predictions can be pushed right to the limit. Dr. Gideon Ariel, a former Olympic discus thrower who operates computerized sports labs considers a pitch delivered at 140 mph not unreasonable. At that speed, the ball would arrive in 0.295 seconds, and, declares Dr. Ariel, "a batter's decision whether to swing and the sound of the ball hitting the catcher's mitt would be roughly simultaneous events."[5]

But often predictions are made without accounting for the factor of individual greatness. The great athletes themselves don't consider limits. They defy predictions. Says neurologist Dr. Ernst Jokl:

> The wonderful thing about sport is that it is unpredictable. The arrival of geniuses like Bach and Mozart in the world of music could never have been predicted. And the same is true for genius in athletics. Unpredictability is an element of sport at its best.[6]

Generally once the predictions are made, then the moment of greatness is awaited, not in the labs but on the playing fields. The four-minute mile run by Roger Bannister in 1954 is the classic example. Until that time, it was assumed that *no one* could run a mile in under four minutes, that it was physically impossible. Now, the mile is run regularly in 3:45 minutes. And the record-breaking free-style swimming of multiple-gold-medal winner Mark Spitz in the 1972

Olympics would not be fast enough to bring him even one medal today. In fact, modern athletes have actually created entirely different golf, tennis, and football games than those of earlier years. Says Don Peters, 1984 coach of the Women's Olympic gymnastics team: "I don't think anyone on the '76 team, doing the same kind of work they were doing then, would have even been able to *make* this last team. The level of performance has gotten that much higher."[7]

Sometimes an athlete will perform a prodigious feat, one that sends all predictions out the window. Such was Bob Beamon's famous long jump.

In the 1968 Olympics in Mexico City, Beamon took his first jump in the finals and achieved a distance of 29 feet 2 ½ inches, beating the previous record by 2 feet. Commented Dr. Jokl to the American Association for the Advancement of Science: "It is impossible that [Beamon's mark] will ever be improved by the same margin by which he surpassed the world record." According to Jokl, a thirty-one-foot jump "is beyond the range of the . . . potentialities of man." He called it a "mutation" performance because, according to the predictions of increases in sports capabilities, Beamon's jump *should not have occurred* until the twenty-first century. Despite the help of the thinner air and lower gravitational pull over mile-high Mexico City, Beamon's jump is said to be the greatest single feat in the recorded history of athletics. But observed Beamon, "It felt just like a regular jump . . . I don't think that that was my limit."

Greatness as Sustained Achievement:
The Field and Stream of Consciousness

Someone should be able to sneak up and drag you out at midnight and push you out on some strange floor, and you should be able to do your entire routine sound asleep in your pajamas. Without one mistake. That's the secret. It's got to be a natural reaction.

MARY LOU RETTON

Beyond an outstanding single performance now and then, great athletes as well as most great individuals in every field live greatness as

160

sustained achievement. If you go into your house and toss your hat, and it lands on the hook twenty feet away, is that considered "great"? Well, it definitely was a "great" moment, but doing it once doesn't make you a great hat tosser. Anybody can do it once. What is valuable is continuous greatness. What this means is that you're in contact with a continuous field of greatness built into your physiology, enabling you to have perfect mind-body cooperation pretty much when you want it. Anyone can drive a car around a corner at the maximum possible speed, but Mario Andretti can do it for ten hours at a time without mistakes.

To achieve and maintain perfection, it may be that great people have universally well-developed physiology that gives them the ability to maintain fine attention to and fine coordination with their work. Tennis star Bjorn Borg is said to have such an even, efficient physiology that his resting heart rate is only thirty-five beats a minute, whereas the norm is about eighty. Various technologies account for the continuing maintenance and improvement in athletic performance--training and nutrition are two of the most well-established key interventions. But however it is achieved, a strong physiology combining mind and body development is essential.

Sustained achievement on the mental level also demands a stable, highly developed physiology. Great ideas become fragmented and lost if your attention swings from one thing to another because you can't focus clearly. If you lose your mind-body coordination in any field, you lose. "Mental," "musical," and "artistic" Olympics are just as rigorous in their physiological demands as are sports Olympics. Just as the latter call for powerful thinking to set the stage for the best physical performances, mental Olympics require the development of a strong physiology that operates with "all systems go." How does this development get established?

Rest and Activity: The Basic Principle of Physiological Greatness

The movement of withdrawal and return is not a peculiarity of human life which is only to be observed in the relations of human beings with their fellows. It is something that is characteristic of life in general.

ARNOLD TOYNBEE

> From Nature doth emotion come, and moods
> Of calmness equally are Nature's gift:
> This is her glory; these two attributes
> Are sister horns that constitute her strength.
> Hence Genius, born to thrive by interchange
> Of Peace and excitation, finds in her
> His best and purest friend; from her receives
> That energy by which he seeks the truth,
> From her that happy stillness of the mind
> Which fits him to receive it when unsought.

WILLIAM WORDSWORTH, *The Prelude, Book 13*

The creative lives of great people give us a clue to the need for a balance between withdrawal and activity. There is a period of inwardness and withdrawal from the outer world that seems to precede most of the major accomplishments of the greats. And because the cycle of rest and activity is obviously a basic law of nature, perhaps the most important rule for structuring greatness in all fields is a simple program of rest before activity.

Even during the first few hours following birth, researchers have noticed this need for alteration between rest and activity. The newborn infant has been observed to experience what pediatrician T. Berry Brazelton calls "a state of quiet alert." During these first hours, a delicate balance between rest and activity is maintained. The infant interacts with the mother, then takes a rest, and thus avoids either being overwhelmed or not being stimulated enough.

In adult life there seems to be a physiological reason for the need for mental rest as well. You may have noticed that once you relax after a big project on which you've been heavily focused, you can't recapture your earlier mental alertness immediately. According to physiologists, this happens because the brain has both inhibiting systems and activating systems, and requires a resting period before it can resume production of the stimulating neurotransmitters. We experience this need for an inward or a settling-down period in almost all areas of life, especially during our most creative times.

In order to create, educator Harold Rugg writes, both artists and scientists benefit from "a relaxed condition of body and mind." Most ideas emerge effortlessly when we are rested. In fact, the "moment of insight" invariably occurs when one's attention is relaxed or entirely "off the problem." The two essential steps of the creative process outlined more than half a century ago by G. Wallas are deep rest ("incubation"), followed by highly dynamic activity ("illumination").

Neurosurgeon Wilder Penfield explains that the creative moment occurs not because the brain is working on the problem during the incubation stage, but because the brain is *resting*. Once you get rid of the fatigue that is blocking your ability to see a solution clearly, says Penfield, you recollect the problem and "You see it suddenly simplified. . . . What seemed difficult is easy." This is also the experience of artist Oppi Untracht: "Feeling either rested or tired has a great effect on the work. It is basically a question of being physically alert or not, and one functions better when in top physical condition."[8]

In addition, intuition, that basic tool of creativity, has been found to occur most often when a relaxed state of mind provides the basis for a quick learning response. For this reason, creativity researcher Paul Torrance suggests there is a need for "both active and quiet periods" in structuring creative learning.

To carry out everyday activities, we obviously all require rest; but, depending on our differing physiologies, we require different amounts of rest. Dr. William Dement's well-documented sleep research conducted at Stanford University indicates that even after eight hours of sleep, many people are sleepy during the day when they should be awake. On the other hand, great creators are often awake when they're supposed to be asleep. Thomas Edison was famous for needing little sleep, perhaps three hours a night. He kept a cot in his office on which he used to lie to solve problems. He didn't need sleep--but he needed rest even while he remained awake. His contemporary, Nikola Tesla, had an even more remarkable physiology and slept even less, no more than two hours a night, remaining awake without fatigue sometimes three or four days at a time. If he became fatigued, however, he reported that his ability to visualize inventions--his main means of research--would leave entirely. Once he gained the rest he required, the visualizations would return in an unusual way: "By re-peating events of earliest childhood and successively re-enacting later events, until it brought him to the actual moment and then . . . [he would experience] a visualization of an event that had not yet taken place."[9]

Dreaming too is a form of resting, but it has a somewhat different function. According to recent studies, dreams are the mind's way of unclogging itself or of unlearning, of getting rid of useless or even harmful neural pathways, of relieving itself of mental stress. Because of this, using dreams as a key to personality development as did Freud, Jung, and others may not always be beneficial. Nobel Laureate Francis Crick and his colleague Graeme Mitchison suggest that "attempting to remember one's dreams should perhaps not be encouraged, because such remembering may help to retain patterns of thought which are better forgotten."[10]

Optimal Physiologies

In the previous chapter, we considered the heroic mother who lifted a car off her child to save his life. It's fascinating to learn that we all have this capacity; there is a simple physical explanation for her outstanding act. Geneticist James Roberts of Columbia University has recently reported that the body normally uses only 1 percent of its endurance capacity, but under demanding environmental conditions, usually dormant cells in the pituitary gland will increase their hormone production a hundredfold. As a result of this and other research, we are beginning to see that human physiology holds tremendous possibilities for growth even on the cellular level.

It is likely that among the greatest individuals, there are those who function with maximum efficiency in *every* cell of their bodies at all times and are thus realizing the true physical and mental capabilities of human greatness. Such a level of integrated growth is said to accompany a distinct style of functioning of the nervous system, a state of optimum neurophysiological development that in the East has been termed "enlightenment."

This state of development is described as combined alertness and rest--a seeming paradox. How can anyone be both deeply at rest and perfectly alert at the same time? In physiological terms, how can the brain be simultaneously excited and "de-excited"? Researchers have found that such a state is characterized by a lively EEG reading (the mind is alert) and a metabolically at-rest physical system that demonstrates very faint breathing, lowered blood pressure, a resting heart rate, and other characteristics of physiological rest. The researchers call this the "hypometabolic" state of consciousness, which is considered a valuable physiological basis for creativity, and, as we'll discuss in a later chapter, it is achieved most easily through meditation. It is also described as a state of stress-free functioning of mind and body.

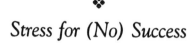

Stress for (No) Success

O God, I could be bounded in a nutshell and count myself a king of infinite space, were it not that I have bad dreams.

SHAKESPEARE, *Hamlet*

Stress is the term that best describes the impediments to perfect psychophysical functioning. For years within the Western medical profession, all illnesses were considered separate and distinct in cause and condition. Dr. Hans Selye, who originated the concept of stress, recalls when he was a young medical student, making rounds of the different parts of a hospital: "I saw people who were sick with this disease and sick with that disease. There was something about it that was in the back of my mind and I couldn't quite place it. They had something in common that nobody had identified." As he was walking down the hospital corridor, he thought, "Of course, they're all sick and they all *look* sick. And there's something they share--some kind of 'stress' that goes beyond the particulars of what they're sick with." [11]

Dr. Selye's great discovery was that stress underlies all illness, an important scientific contribution that showed there was something that transcends the distinctions of human illness and refers to an overall (lack of) functioning. What Selye discovered was that when stress is added to human life, it can produce all sorts of illnesses.

If stress is defined as an overload on the system that acts as a generalized basis for illness, can *lack of stress* be considered the basis for health? And if so, could a person who was functioning relatively free of stress then be a candidate for greatness? Let's examine how stress affects our greatness potential.

The Physiological Blocks of Creating

We have learned that stress takes up a lot of energy and may be very damaging, even genetically. Some scientists have recently hypothesized that our growth is "coded" for much higher levels of development than we may have imagined. It is known, for instance, that chemical changes occur in the body from birth and that the schedule of change is programmed in DNA, the blueprint of the genes. But stress can arrest this development and the schedule of growth is then thrown off. By eliminating stress, we may be able to achieve our rightful growth, which would result in a much higher level of neurophysiological development.

The effects of stress are obviously not limited to physical conditions but to mental and creative ones, too. Stress does not benefit our creative efforts. Quite the opposite. What seems to happen is that by being exposed to a stressful environment, we become "overhabituated" in our thinking. As a result, little of our physiology is used for new responses. Creativity expert W. S. Ray described this as "functional fixedness"--a characteristic result of stress that inhibits freedom of perception and prevents originality. Stress can cause functional fixedness and thus interfere with problem solving. In his experiments, he found that "above a minimal level necessary to produce work at the problem, further increase of [stress] would produce increasing inhibition of problem solving, the effect being greater with complex problems."[12]

Functional fixedness is also found in organized groups. Within a business organization, overall success is significantly diminished if, as Peters and Waterman found, "there is a tendency toward over-organization, producing a rigidity that is intolerable in an era of rap-idly accelerating change." Then the flexibility associated with great companies is unable to be maintained.

The Brain Has a Mind of Its Own

Our nervous system, according to psychologist Jerome Bruner, is not "a one-way street," as had long been believed. Rather, the brain "prioritizes"--it controls the information coming in from sensory sources and permits only certain information to be perceived. It has, we can say, a mind of its own.

Perception is adaptive, or what is called "selective." We learn per-ceptually what to look for. At a conference on creativity, engineer N. E. Golovin defined perception as "editorial": "It is the function of sensory systems, by their physiological design, to reduce the amount of 'useless and irrelevant' information reaching us and to serve as selection systems." Golovin further described the procedure of scan-ning, whereby coded information stored in the central nervous sys-tem is brought into conscious awareness. However, in some of us, the system can be blocked under certain conditions:

> If past experiences have induced patterns in the nervous system which make certain of the storage areas partly or wholly inaccessible either to conscious or to unconscious scanning, [then] the available material for securing suggestive patterns by random search will be diminished. The effect of conventions and inhibitions, if they are involved in the context of the problem situation under study, thus may be to render certain storage areas of the nervous system inaccessible to scanning.[13]

Golovin's hypothesis is that creativity is blocked when too many channels are used for input and too few are free for scanning. Simi-larly, too many stressful stimuli tend to shut down the organism, producing only low arousal, which is the nervous system's way to safeguard itself.

Of course, sometimes low arousal is very appropriate. For example, if your car is stalled on the San Diego Freeway, and you are required to direct traffic around you in the midst of the rush hour, it would be highly convenient to have this experience at a low level of arousal. At other times, however, it may not be useful. You could be so overwhelmed before a big interview as to fall asleep, or be paralyzed into inaction during an important exam.

In addition, whether the stimulation is either pleasant or unpleasant, it will still produce the same arousal results. Researcher D. E. Berlyne reports:

> In states of daze or ecstasy brought on by an overabundance of intense and varied stimulation, the body may show extreme excitement and a good deal of motor activity while blunting of consciousness and suppression of intellectual activity suggest a relatively inactive cortex.[14]

This blocking of functioning to safeguard the organism has a more extended role in the specific patterning known as "habituation." According to neuroscientist Alaric Arenander, "Habituation is one of the physiological components of the 'orientation reaction' to new stimuli. . . . The physiological indicators of such reaction often include a blocking of the alpha rhythm of the EEG, an increase in heart rate, and a drop in skin resistance." Based on how our individual nervous systems react, each of us orients automatically to any event that happens around us without seeming to think about it. Someone coughs and we are alerted. A dog runs past us and we check it out. We are actively processing the environment. The orienting reflex guides our perceptions and actions by setting up an evaluation of every event and comparing it with something in our past. If there is no new knowledge, we lose interest. After the person has coughed ten times, we habituate to the sound and no longer need to deal with it. Or we hurl some cough drops in his direction or move away.

We can look at the blocking of the creative process from this vantage point of habituated physiological functioning. Maslow called the creative impulses "weak impulses" that have been "drowned by habit." This hindrance to creativity caused by habitual response is described as the fixated response of set perceptual patterns to the environment. Gerard, among others, points to too early closure as a cutting off of creative activity caused in part by the detrimental effects of a good memory: "One pays for it by having a nervous system that somehow fixes so easily that it loses pliability . . ."[15]

Harvard psychologist Ellen Langer calls the mental results of such overhabituation "mindlessness," which she defines as "a state of reduced cognitive activity in which a person responds to the environment without considering its potentially novel elements and instead relies on old distinctions rather than creating new categories."[16] Thus, once you become skilled at something, your mind is no longer creating. When people are mindless, they no longer *can* think about what they know very well. In this way, one's thinking has become *too* patterned.

Designer Paul MacCready who invented the first man-powered aircraft believes it was his complete lack of experience in aircraft-wing structural design that gave him the creative edge over his more technically educated competitors. Patterned thinking, says MacCready, allows us to assimilate complex inputs, but it may prevent new ideas from being received without bias.[17]

Obviously, we need to habituate or we would be overwhelmed by stimuli. We need the stability along with the flexibility. But once your nervous system is functioning smoothly, you must also be able to unstructure useless, rigid patterns in order to incorporate more integrative, useful ones. We need to break up habits with subsequent reintegration, to create what psychologist Clark Hull called "assembly of habit segments never previously associated with each other." To achieve this, the first step is to rid ourselves of the old habits.

Losing the Stray Dogs:
Breaking Up Is Hard to Do

It has been said that habits are like stray dogs that hang around because we feed them every day. The reason it's so hard to break them is that they are literally "grooved" in our nervous systems. An extroverted, controlling person has difficulty sitting still and letting others do the job; out of habit, he jumps up and interferes, knowing he's making a mistake, but he can't stop himself. A shy executive, despite what he knows intellectually, continues to be unable to assert himself at the conference where *he* is the leading authority. Many self-help experts, with all good intentions, offer all kinds of psychological advice to help get rid of bad habits and weaknesses. Often we read the advice, say "Yes" or "Aha!," but a day later we may not remember or follow any of it. Or we may think, "But I *know* all that already."

Habits continue to elude the experts because most of us need a *physiological* change in order to break useless habitual behavior--something more basic than thinking about change, something more basic than thinking itself, something that actually creates change in us, *despite* ourselves!

Because habitual patterns are fixed at the level of the nervous system, they must be dissolved at that level. N. E. Golovin suggests that we look for a neural procedure that emphasizes the increased use of novel patterns as a way to repattern the flexible nervous system: "It is this inherent variability, characteristic for each individual, which allows any particular neural network pattern in his cortex to be randomly varied during successive, individual states of the overall system."[18]

Forty years ago, writer Aldous Huxley proposed that one's individual consciousness is connected to a universal consciousness by the human nervous system. He also thought the human nervous system must of necessity act as a "reducing valve"--reducing the input of universal consciousness, so as not to be overwhelmed. Today we find that since it is only through the nervous system that we can experience anything, rather than reducing the connection, we are really seeking to expand it. We are ready for technologies that strengthen human physiology in order to be able to "load" experience not only without damage but essentially to help us become physiologically ready for greatness, for an individual connection to such universal consciousness without being overshadowed.

A nervous system that functions at a fuller capacity would certainly be indispensable for increasing one's full mental and creative capacity and sustaining it. This growth is not only possible, it is natural. The latest developments in brain research show us why.

Great Brains

The human brain is a mirror to infinity. There is no limit to its range, scope or creative growth. No one knows what great leaps of achievement may be within reach of the species once the full potentialities of the mind are developed. As we create an ever higher sense of our cosmic consciousness, we become aware of our ever higher possibilities.

NORMAN COUSINS

At the beginning of the century, psychologist William James estimated that on the average we use perhaps 5 to 10 percent of our full mental potential. However, recent research indicates that the brain contains a much higher number of brain cells than previously realized, and now it is believed that we may only use up an average of less than 1 percent of the brain cells available to us in a lifetime.[19] So even though we may lose an estimated one thousand brain cells a day after age twenty-five, there are clearly a huge number left to us.

When we take a test, we might worry whether our brain can be trusted to hold all the information we want. In actuality, it's more a question of whether we've learned the material correctly. Because for all intents and purposes the capacity of the human brain is infinite, it can hold whatever we want it to, and in a given lifetime, we could never "run out of brain." Researcher Peter Russell gives us an interesting picture of this startling capacity of the brain:

> A transistorized computer capable of all the human brain can do would not fit inside Carnegie Hall. . . . Conversely, the whole of the world's telephone system is equivalent to only about one gram of your brain--a piece the size of a pea.[20]

The questions physiologists and neuroscientists ask most often are: How does that little piece of matter, which each of us has been given, provide the experience of the infinity of human life? And what answers can it give us in response to the Big Questions? Not surprisingly, the brain most fascinates those who are most familiar with its magnitude. Commented Dr. Candace Pert, a neuroscientist at the National Institute of Mental Health (NIMH):

> I don't feel awe for the brain. I feel an awe for God. I see in the brain all the beauty of the universe and its order--constant signs of God's presence. I'm learning that the brain obeys all the physical laws of the universe. It's nothing special. And yet it's the most special thing in the universe.[21]

Yet, despite our deep appreciation of the brain, we still know very little about it. It is a very complex business. For starters, it contains somewhere between ten billion and one hundred billion neurons. The possible interactions between these cells has been estimated at well over the number of atoms in the universe. Of these neurons, it has been estimated that only 2 to 5 percent are constantly in use. It is the loss of these neurons that is said to account for "brain death." Actually, however, brain death occurs primarily not because neurons are lost but because the arteries bringing oxygen to the brain constrict as a result of high blood pressure or arteriosclerosis. So really, as far as neurons are concerned, comparatively few can ever be lost in a lifetime. This is because the brain is constantly growing.

How the Brain Grows on Learning

The growth of the brain doesn't just happen automatically, simply because we've been born. Indeed, if the brain were set at birth, we wouldn't really be able to learn *anything* new. What *is* programmed in the brain, via DNA, is the most fundamental expression of biological intelligence, the ability to grow and change in a consistently orderly way. And because the brain is tremendously flexible, the most flexible piece of work we know of in the universe, its potential for growth is virtually unlimited. But the way we *use* it, to enable it to grow, is highly significant.

At age seventy-six writer I. F. Stone learned Greek as part of a study of Greek civilization. But his accomplishment was not unusual. It has been demonstrated that seventy-five- to eighty-five-year-olds learn languages as rapidly and as well as high-school-age students (though neither group learns as quickly as young children). Neuro-scientist Donald Hebb has concluded that with age, you learn to use your brain more efficiently. As you learn more and more, the neural connections become streamlined. In old age you've basically learned how to learn better. We do lose some functioning, but as a way of paring down excess synapses so as to create orderliness, a situation we may deplore until we learn that by the time we reach age seventy, our memories hold at least one hundred trillion bits of information. . . . A little streamlining might not hurt!

The brain not only changes and grows with amazing flexibility, but it seems to be a kind of focal point for evolution. Commented researcher Robert DeSimone of NIMH, "When we see something, the brain changes, apparently permanently." The brain is thus shaped and reshaped by experience, and ultimately just by the act of thinking itself. It should not be surprising then that a big thinker like Einstein would have grown a more developed brain than the vast majority of us. Recently, Dr. Marian Diamond and her colleagues at the University of California at Berkeley demonstrated just that. They dissected the cerebral-cortex section of Einstein's brain and found it contained a much higher percentage (73 percent) of support or glial cells per neuron area than the average number found in a control group. The glial cells are known to nourish and support neurons, and to increase in number with enriched learning experiences, of which Einstein himself was well aware. Noted Dr. Diamond, "Activities of this area fit many of the comments Einstein made about his conceptual processes."[22]

In another important study conducted by Dr. Diamond's team of researchers, elderly rats--equivalent in age to about seventy-five human years--were placed in an enriched environment full of mazes, wheels, toys, and fellow rats. A control group consisting of rats of the same age lived alone in an "impoverished" environment. The rats in the enriched environment were found to have increased the actual dimensions of their brains and the activity of their brain cells. The percentage of glial cells also multiplied, as did the nerve-ending surfaces that allow for more intercell communication.

Overall, the studies showed that brain cells can become more active and more connected to each other with proper stimulation at any time of life. According to Dr. Roger Walsh of the University of California at Irvine, they demonstrate that "there is much more neural flexibility in old age than we had imagined."

On the other hand, if there is environmental deprivation, cell growth may actually be restricted. In Dr. Diamond's study the brains of the "impoverished" rats decreased in size. In another study, conducted by Nobel researcher David Hubel, the brain cells in the visual cortex of kittens deprived of sight at an early age grew abnormally.[23]

Similarly, brain cell growth associated with language is also dependent on environmental stimulation. The major spurts in brain cell growth in the language center of an infant's brain occur first when the baby starts responding to voices (at six to twelve months) and when it starts to recognize word meanings (at twelve to eighteen months). The parts of the cell that grow are called the "dendritic projections," and they send and receive information to and from other cells. If they remain unstimulated, no growth occurs. Researcher Dr. Arnold Scheibel at UCLA says that the dendritic projections' growth is "like muscle tissue. They grow more the more they're used." So, when you learn a new language as an adult, he adds, "it's dendritic fireworks."[24]

Perhaps the best news we have about brain growth is that even when the brain becomes grossly impaired as a result of illness or accident, it can continue to function and, in many instances, it regains its abilities in remarkable ways. It is well known, for example, that Louis Pasteur made many of his great discoveries after a stroke had paralyzed half his brain. Most stroke victims eventually recover certain functions, not simply because the old neural pathways heal, but because new pathways are developed--since the brain can respond anew to new needs. On a recent TV show, brain scans of several people who had had large portions of diseased tissue removed to save their lives demonstrated how brain function had spontaneously been restored in other parts of the brain because of its capacity to form new connections.

It is almost as if the cells themselves have an innate intelligence and can make new choices. Yale University neuroanatomist Patricia Goldman-Rakic concludes: "The new connections that occur after an injury to the brain show that the brain's anatomy is not rigidly

fixed. . . . The uninjured cells reroute how they grow and intercon-
nect."[25] This indicates that every cell in the brain is endowed with
intelligence and can not only react but also *learn*.

The Development of Creative Intelligence: How the Brain Learns

Over the past decades, we've come to understand the value of a
regular program of physical exercise. But what are we doing to exercise our brains? After all, the human brain is the best gift that nature
has given us. What are we doing to grow our virtually infinite brain
capacity?

During the first three years of life, the human brain develops most
quickly, spurred by biological guidance. But when does complete brain
growth occur? It used to be believed that brain growth was "finished"
just after adolescence, at about ages twenty-one to twenty-five years.
But we know now that the brain keeps growing with use. In commenting on the significance of her recent findings, Dr. Diamond noted:

> We've been too negative in how we view the human brain.
> Nerve cells can grow at any age in response to intellectual
> enrichment of all sorts: travel, crossword puzzles, anything that
> stimulates the brain with novelty and challenge.[26]

Even in our dotage, we all have an enormous amount of learning
ability left, in the form of brain power we've only just begun to
access.

We tend to forget that our bodies are always changing because the
changes are so slow and unobtrusive. Bone tissue, for example, is
gradually destroyed and replaced via specialized cells so that every
seven years you get the equivalent of a whole new skeleton. Brains
change too, but much more quickly and significantly. That biological
changes in neural pathways take place whenever learning occurs implies that the intelligence measured by I.Q. scores, as well as creative
functioning and all higher mental processes, are in no way fixed; all
will vary with learning.

The part of the brain most involved with intelligence and creativity, with what psychologists call "abstract thought," is the part of the cortex known as the "frontal lobes." This brain area is much larger in human beings than in apes, for example, and takes so long to develop biologically that it isn't even ready for use until ages four through seven. According to brain researcher Karl Pribram, it is this part of the brain that allows us to envision a future, to maintain an "image of achievement"; it promotes a neural motor response that computes forward to the next action, such as that which occurs in sight reading music, where the next notes are mentally registered even while the current notes are played. Pribram believes that the frontal lobes of the brain are also responsible for retaining longer-term plans and allowing for the extended elaboration needed for great achievement. Thus, the "lifetime achievement" of every individual has a neurological basis within the frontal cortex. Here is where we can biologically form long-term goals and plans for the future.[27]

However, the growth of consciousness, of creative intelligence, doesn't start only with the frontal lobes in the cerebral cortex. Consciousness is actually found throughout the entire body and brain. So, when we say we want to develop consciousness, we are considering the whole brain.

Because of the brain's incredible capacity to make neural connections, it is not unlikely that each of its major functions--learning, creativity, and memory--is virtually infinite, since each depends on the brain's infinite interconnections for development. As Darwin concluded more than one hundred years ago, "Human evolution has no end point . . . with man we can see no definite limit to the continued development of the brain and mental faculties . . ."

New Models of the Brain

Based on the split-brain research of neurosurgeon Roger Sperry and others, the most widely held theory of brain function has been the dual-hemispheric-function model. The findings indicated that the left hemisphere generally governs language and the logical, analytical processes, and the right hemisphere governs integrative, intuitive, holistic, and spatial functioning. In behavioral terms the left hemisphere was thought to preside over language and reasoning, whereas the right hemisphere was in charge of bodily and perceptual functions along with imagery and patterns. It was believed that hemispheric specialization has both advantages and disadvantages, but it was also generally agreed that Western cultures have overemphasized training in left-hemisphere function to the detriment of spatial, emotional, and intuitive functioning in the right hemisphere.

Recent research, however, indicates that the functions of the hemispheres of the brain are a lot less biologically set than previously thought. True, each hemisphere reflects different processing styles, but how these styles develop, and in which hemisphere, is more complicated than a simple left-right split.

For example, studies conducted by the late Dr. Norman Geschwind and his colleagues at Harvard Medical School concluded that the infant's brain is shaped by certain experiences of the mother before birth which regulate the levels of the sex hormone testosterone present in the womb. Maternal stress and diet are among the factors that cause testosterone levels to vary. Speech, spatial abilities, and right- or left-handedness, rather than being predetermined hemispherically, are affected by testosterone, which also determines which side of the brain will control these effects. Dyslexia and mathematical genius, although entirely different in function, are apparently caused by the same phenomenon--unusual levels of testosterone that create abnormal cell development, particularly in males.[28]

In addition, the function of the two hemispheres of the brain can be modified through interaction with the environment. Culture therefore has a definite biological effect on the way skills are organized in the brain. Cultures that rely on spoken and written language for communication fulfill the brain's biological potential to learn language, and may create a dominance of left-hemisphere functioning. Conversely, cultures that rely more on visual and imagery processing will have created a right-hemisphere-dominant mode of learning.

For many years, research psychologist Judy Kearns has tested visual and spatial skills in aborigines and white Australians, using natural and manmade materials. The aborigine children have no difficulty distinguishing among and recalling the positions of about twenty stones of the same approximate size, a task the white children find almost impossible, but the white children have much less trouble recalling positions of different manmade objects. Dr. Kearns's findings indicate that each group of children uses a different part of the brain to solve the puzzles: The aborigines use spatial (right hemisphere) skills while the whites use verbal (left hemisphere) skills. She has concluded that the biological basis for the system of learning among each group therefore differs.[29]

An interesting study conducted in Japan by researcher Tadanobu Tsunoda demonstrates to some extent that the language one learns as a child may in fact influence the way the left and right hemispheres develop specialized functioning, and that this too is culturally determined. He found that Japanese who are raised in Japan have different language patterns from Westerners and consequently, according to Tsunoda, different divisions in right- and left-brain function. The most obvious distinctions are that the Japanese process all the vowels, as well as all Japanese music, animal sounds, and nonverbal human sounds, in the left hemisphere, whereas Westerners process isolated (nonlanguage) vowels and other nonlanguage sounds in the right hemisphere. The only two right-hemisphere processes common to East and West are mechanical sounds and Western instrumental music.

According to Tsunoda's research, Japanese and Americans brought up in Japan developed "Japanese" brain function, whereas Japanese raised in America had "American" brain lateralization. And because both illiterate and literate members of each group had the same results, Tsunoda concluded that spoken rather than written language produces the particular style of hemispheric brain functioning. Perhaps the most fascinating finding is that Japanese cognitive and emotional functioning are found together in the dominant hemisphere (the left side in right-handed people), not separated as in the West. Tsunoda speculates that this is because the intuitive and analytic modes function in a much more harmonious way in Japanese culture. The environment, the traditions of the tea ceremony, flower arranging, indoor-outdoor architecture serve to blend the intellect and the heart.[30]

It may well be then that the different functions of each hemisphere of the brain are not so predetermined and rigidly separated at birth as previously believed. Indeed, the latest direction in brain re-search is toward a more integrative view of brain function. "A lot of old theories about right brain and left brain are nonsense," observed Daniel Weinberger of the NIMH. "Things are not as localized as we thought."[31]

Researcher Justine Sergent at the University of Montreal offers another interpretation of how the right-left functions become dis-tinct. She found that the left hemisphere is better at "detail" work, whereas the right hemisphere is a "good guesser" and interprets gen-eralities more quickly. Sergent says these differences occur because the cortical cells in each hemisphere fire at different rates according to whether information is "detailed and complex" (left) or "scanty and diffuse" (right). She concludes that brain processing may not be a matter of analytical versus holistic, but may be based rather on a sensory model of exposure time and acuity of image. Therefore, lan-guage, because it is more detailed, ends up in the left hemisphere, and imagery, because it is more diffuse, ends up in the right.[32]

What do these latest research findings tell us about greatness? For one thing, they help us realize that the way we look at the brain very much influences the way we understand and educate for creativ-ity. For years the theory of bimodal consciousness based on the hem-ispheres of the brain dominated physiological research on creativity. The main creativity model used in this century, Wallas's four-step schema, reflects this binary functioning. "Preparation" and "evalua-tion" reflect the analytic mode, and "incubation" and "illumination" reflect the intuitive mode. Because we know that the whole brain must function in an harmonious manner to be consistently creative, it had been thought necessary to balance the two sides of the brain by alternating between the functions of each hemisphere.

But a model of the brain that relies on the separation of left-right-hemisphere function implies a "crystalized intelligence," a fixed picture. As we've seen, brain researchers are now offering a more hol-istic picture of "mass distribution" of potential, which allows for some specialization but also for less dependency on either hemisphere. Each hemisphere may indeed be capable of functioning simultaneously in the analytical and intuitive modes; what is needed perhaps is a more integrated view of how the brain functions as a whole, in a unified way, during the physiological state of "restful alertness," which gives rise to heightened creative experience. After surveying all the latest research, a recent *Newsweek* article concluded:

> The brain, then, is less a collection of isolated little players, each responsible for a different melody in the mental symphony, than a unified orchestra, with small numbers of neurons conducting an ensemble of millions.[33]

Perhaps the more useful model then, in keeping with our quantum vision of the universe, would be a quantum view of brain function. This view now has substantial support from a great number of studies on . . . um . . . memory.

❖

"Memories . . ."

Memory function ranges from genetic recall (the infant remembers to suck; the adult, to breathe and sleep, etc.) to memory of life events, factual memory, memory of words, perceptual memory (the smell of flowers, the sounds of music, and so forth). Other memory functions include visual imagery, learned activities, and collective cultural "archetypal" memories.

After lengthy research, we now believe that memory function is stored and distributed *throughout* the brain, wherever processing has occurred. In this way, memories seem to be "wired" into nerve cells and can travel across synapses. We also better remember things that occurred during times of heightened emotion and perception, such as where we were when we acknowledged our first true love.

Some scientists have proposed that memory is "imaged" holographically, and that is why, when we use images to think, we can envision the Big Picture. Basically, information can be retained in memory in two ways: episodically and "in wholes." The ability to retain episodic information means that each image can be isolated. Children remember in this fashion, but the process starts to decay around age nine or ten as "patterned learning" and full development of memory function begin. (This is why we may have difficulty remembering early childhood experiences because the way in which we remember has changed.)

Because memory has been the most researched aspect of brain function, we have learned how to improve its use better than almost any other function. For example, we know that good memory seems to require rest between operations. Research has shown that if we add rest periods between learning tasks, the better we learn. And along with rest, the key to good memory is based on association. Without meaning and association, we forget easily.

After age eight, when we start to recall in wholes, in patterns, the patterns get stronger and stronger as they are reinforced through learned experience. And memory is most strongly reinforced when you purposely link what you want to remember with an already existing pattern. Psychologists call this "association" or "subjective organization." Thus, we learn to learn through patterns and rhythms. Since these patterns are grooved in the brain from prior experiences, we are able to retain information in our physiology; linking patterns have established the associations. A "tree" of associations becomes our entire life experience. The greater the number of associations, of linking patterns, the more brain connections there are, and this is how the brain grows.

As we've seen, association processes really begin at the level of cell and neural connections; the knowledge of how to make connections is structured in the DNA code. This is most likely why connectedness or association is the basic principle of memory function. Says mystery writer Dorothy Sayers's central character Lord Peter Wimsey, "Most people don't associate anything--their ideas just roll about like so many dry peas on a tray." But he concludes, "Once you let them string their peas into a necklace," they'll find out everything.

Over a hundred years ago, Sir Frances Galton walked down a familiar street in London mentally free-associating each object he saw with specific memories, many from childhood. He was amazed at how lively his mind became as he noticed, by his own count, three hundred "objects of association." As a result, he remembered numerous incidents in his life. Up until that day, without his consciously thinking of them, all the objects along the street had become too familiar, too routine, providing no memory triggers.

Galton's experience was based on what is called "context association." It enables us to tie anything in with anything else once we place it in context. This is how we create a heightened experience to capture memory through association. Some memory experts believe that the act of memorization occurs entirely by association. More memories give more potential associations; the memory function keeps growing and thus the brain "grows" in knowledge in a holistic, "start from anywhere" quantum way.

The Quantum Brain

In the past we've tended to think of the brain as a computer, but in fact such functioning is just a tiny part of its capabilities. According to one eminent researcher, biologist Gerald Edelman of the Rockefeller Institute, "The brain is *not* a computer. It's more like a garden. Every time the brain does something, it's different."[34]

The basic difference may be that brains behave "quantumly," whereas computers think "straight." However rapidly they can give answers, computers must function in a linear, one-step-at-time fashion. Unlike the brain, they can't take an intuitive quantum leap. Explains Scott Fahlman of Carnegie-Mellon University: "They don't do the kind of thinking where there is an almost instantaneous flash of recognition--the kind you or I get when figuring out a problem."[35]

The more we learn about how the brain works, the more it reminds us of the workings of the quantum universe. Even its physical setup has been identified as "nonlinear." Writes Anthony Campbell: "The human brain--and therefore the human mind--seems to be built in such a way that it always tends to organize all the information it contains into a comprehensive whole."

Since we now know that memory function is distributed throughout the entire brain, we are beginning to apply this knowledge to other brain functions, which perhaps only *seem* to be specialized because full development has not yet taken place. Says researcher Robert Livingstone, "The nervous system appears to be made up less of 'independent' linear pathways than of mutually interdependent loop circuits." Similarly, the most recent research "suggests a whole new kind of organization in the brain," according to Dr. Robert Robinson of Johns Hopkins University, which indicates that "behaviors are distributed throughout the brain,"[36] not pinpointed to one spot. And N. A. Lassen, a Swedish researcher, reports that "it appears that for the brain to 'understand' the surrounding world, to perceive its meaning, and to take action, the cerebral cortex must be activated not only locally but also totally." Lassen's observations support his hypothesis that the total activation of the brain, (i.e., activation of all its parts) through performance of tasks, "increases general brain activity as well as cerebral blood flow and oxygen uptake, and that this reaction is related to an increased level of awareness."[37]

This picture of the brain is analogous to our picture of the unified field--the brain also is more like a field where everything interconnects than a collection of parts. And when a quantum brain functions in a quantum universe, every thing, event or particle--though each lives in its own dimension--is interconnected with everything else to such an extent that the study of one specific element could theoretically give detailed information about every other element in the universe, just like in a hologram where every point reveals information about every other point. According to Campbell:

> If you illuminate the hologram suitably with a laser beam, the object becomes visible . . . and perspective and depth are preserved. . . . If you snip off one corner of the hologram and illuminate that, the *whole* of the original scene is reconstituted, even if not quite as sharply. This is because information about any single point on the original object is distributed evenly throughout the hologram.[38]

It is thus conceivable that if we were truly to know ourselves, if we were to use our brains perfectly, we could know anything we wanted about any other part of the universe. Not only could the whole give us information about any single point, but any focal point could tell us about the whole.

And how does this picture of the brain help us to understand greatness? It shows us that greatness, like every other aspect of human development, is built from the ground up, from the most basic levels of physiology, from every single cell. Behaviorally, it tells us that we ought to be able to recognize greatness in even the subtlest gesture of a great person, as in our initial vision of a great teenage basketball player. Just as in a great poem where every word is right, so, in a great person every move would be perfectly in tune with natural laws. Like a hologram, the whole picture of greatness would be contained in each instance of behavior, even in each cell, each strain of genetic material, each neurological response to the environment.

In this brief look at the brain and its development, we've seen that the growth to greatness requires a parallel growth and maintenance in physiology. Later on, in Chapter Seven, we'll learn how to ensure that this development takes place.

Now let's turn to another aspect of the physiology of greatness, to perception. How do we exercise the capacity, as William Blake did:

> To see a World in a Grain of Sand,
> And a Heaven in a Wild Flower,
> Hold Infinity in the palm of your hand,
> And Eternity in an hour.

Sensation Seeking

Researcher Marvin Zuckerman studied a trait he called "sensation seeking." He found that although the majority of people "shut down" after a certain amount of sensory arousal, others, the sensation seekers, require much higher levels of sensory stimulation.

Today, more and more of us are becoming sensation seekers. We seem to need increasingly intense perceptual stimulation in order to enjoy life. Our music is played as loud as we can comfortably stand it, and this loudness threshold has been increasing for decades. We also require increasingly intense visual stimulation at the movies and on TV. At the same time our attention span is becoming shorter and shorter. This results in a lessening of perceptual activity. In addition, we have the noise--the continual noise of modern living--not just in our ears, but in our eyes and all the other senses, noise that tires us out perceptually so we become immune to anything except the most demanding sensory input. However, what we define as noise can mean different things to different people.

According to K. C. Cole, great scientists "have a special talent for . . . separating the signal from the noise and also knowing when what sounds like noise might contain the quiet whisper of important information." People with high levels of creativity in general are found to be acutely sensitive and tend to require very *little* input. In order to create and to avoid having the creative impulses "drowned out," many great people choose to remove excess stimuli, just to have a chance to hear *inside* as well as out.

French writer Marcel Proust, for example, wanted only his own memories and imagination to enter his vivid writings, and to eliminate outside stimuli, he always wrote in a cork-lined, soundproof room. The contemporary American sculptor Louise Nevelson noticed that she needed very little outer information to stir up her inner imagery experience: "A white lace curtain on the window was for me as important as a great work of art. This gossamer quality, the reflection, the form, the movement, I learned more about art from that than I did in school."

❖

Perceptual Motion

It is only recently that we have understood that perception is a changeable component of human development. We used to think of the act of perception as passive and nonparticipatory--something that just happens to us--but today we know that it is a far more creative process. Even in the womb, babies have been found to distinguish between all sorts of perceptual inputs, including musical selections. Audiologist Michele Clements, for example, has demonstrated that a majority of babies generally like Vivaldi and Mozart (their heart rates are steady and kicking declines) and dislike Beethoven and Brahms and rock music (violent kicking ensues).[39] Thus, we can say that the brain, from its earliest development, is capable of selecting what it wants and what it doesn't want to sense. In most cases, it acts as an editorial filter, screening our experiences.

Because of this interactive process, anthropologist Edward Hall suggests that perception is "a transaction between man and his environment in which both participate." And, as easily as we can change and rearrange the outside environment, we can develop the inside one, too, by developing our senses.

Yet we have often neglected to train our sensory apparatus and we've thus become somewhat lazy. We're most used to receiving information through sight because this is our most dominant sense; 75 percent of the information to the brain comes through the eyes. However, researchers believe that other senses could be far more highly developed if they were as reinforced as sight. For example, it's been discovered that a sensitive human nose can detect over ten thousand different smells in combinations of only seven odors and is capable of detecting the presence of a single molecule of gas. If we learn to use more of our brain's potential, we would indeed smell better! This is partly because smelling is actually closer to thinking than the other senses. According to biologist Lewis Thomas, "The cells that do the smelling are themselves proper brain cells, the only neurons whose axons carry information picked up first-hand in the outside world." That is why smell is such a good memory evoker. And we can become better smellers, says Thomas: "There are after all some among our species with special gifts for smelling--perfume makers, tea tasters, whiskey blenders--and it is said that these people can train themselves to higher and higher skills by practicing."[40]

Like all brain functions, the senses can actually unfold more and more as we grow to maturity. According to art researcher Rudolph Arnheim, the growth of perception takes place as the perceiver expands his or her awareness of each experience, as the brain chooses what is important for its current use and development. In this way perception is very much altered by experience, by the changing environment. Yet, says psychologist Ulric Neisser:

> Perception involves more than the pickup of currently available information. There is always an element of anticipation, of readiness for what will appear next. Infants' skills of perceiving develop smoothly into skills of expecting and imagining. Imagining, thinking, and remembering free us from the immediate environment.[41]

You might have misread the subheading at the start of this section as "perpetual motion." Because of our expectations, we often do not perceive what is there at all, but rather what we *expect* to perceive. Not only "seeing is believing" but often believing is seeing. Yet this subjective interpretation of the environment is what enables us to transcend the senses, to go beyond our typical sensory locked-in patterns and allows us to *imagine unseen phenomena* such as the quantum world.

Perception and the "Q View"

Although we like to assume that we all see the world alike, in fact we don't. As we discussed earlier, our individual perceptions of the "out there" world are *not* all there is. We are left with the basic conclusion that knowledge is different in different states of awareness. And this applies equally to our perceptions. It is fascinating to consider that our perceptual framework of reality is based solely on our individual human abilities. The outside world changes according to our individual awareness, according to our capacity to use our own physiology. When tired, we see grayness and dullness; when rested and alert, we experience a more vivid reality. When we say, "It's beautiful outside today," we also really mean, "It's beautiful *inside* today."

Our human perceptual abilities are what actually make the environment human. Human ear bones, for example, amplify sound twenty times. Without them, our world would be silent. (But if they were just a fraction more sensitive, we would constantly hear the collisions of molecules in the air as background noise. Nature is kind.) Similarly, because of depth perception, we perceive three dimensions where there ought to be two, and emblazon the universe with our human ability to distinguish thousands of color shades. But, as we sometimes forget, it is *we* who do the seeing.

We do not "see" only with our eyes. More properly, the eyes participate in the whole process of visual experience. As the poet Allen Tate wrote, "The idiot greens the meadow with his eyes." So do we all, according to brain researcher Sir John Eccles:

> I want you to realize that there is no color in the natural world or no sounds--nothing of this kind; no textures, no patterns, no beauty, no scent. These are all in fact perceptions which come to us because of our senses and in some way we don't understand, they are transmitted into thought, perception, experiences . . .[42]

How then do we create the conditions that favor the experience of "seeing anew"; how do we cleanse the windows of perception?

Renewing Perception

It has been demonstrated that perceptual experiences become more clear and vivid at more refined levels of human awareness. These refined experiences occur when old patterns are broken and new experiences are "permitted." "Genius," wrote William James, "in truth means little more than the faculty of perceiving in an unhabitual way."

But we generally forget to do this. As we saw earlier in this chapter, once we've constructed systems and categories to explain our experiences, they often prevent us from experiencing them firsthand. We become committed to old patterns, particularly to the meanings of things through language that interfere with fresh new experiences and understandings. Our verbal commitments, says creativity researcher Frank Barron, dominate our experience to the exclusion of new vision. He notes that we are "so habituated to language" that we cannot hold nonverbal material in our consciousness. And because nonverbal thinking is exactly the way most creative people create, we need some kind of training to think in new ways, to see an object in a new context, away from habitual associations.

Nonverbal experience is known to be one way of reopening the perceptual doors. Former President Dwight D. Eisenhower loved to paint because, he said, "When I paint, I have the feeling my eyes are reborn. I now see things that I never saw before." Many artists feel the responsibility of restoring this immediacy of experience, not just for themselves but for all of us. They help us change our ordinary ways of perceiving, help us see anew. When a skeptical critic remarked to the English painter Joseph Turner, "But I have never seen a sunset like that," Turner replied, "But don't you wish you could, sir?"

Sometimes the artist himself unexpectedly learns to see in new ways that tranform his vision. When we think of Van Gogh's paintings, we may recall the vivid yellows of his landscapes. But we know now that Van Gogh took foxglove, an organic form of digitalis, a drug that can cause a "yellow vision" in which one sees yellow even where yellow doesn't belong. Van Gogh's vision--extraordinary as it was--was not really extraordinary to him. He painted what he saw, what his unique perceptual situation allowed him to see.

In *Drawing on the Right Side of the Brain*, art instructor Betty Edwards uses a standard psychological boundary breaker, drawing upside down. This releases the mind from content orientation and allows it to experience an entirely different spatial orientation. Looking at things upside down gives one a whole new perspective; an inverted painting may offer a different sense of tint or shading, a new view of balance. Try looking at that big moon near the horizon upside down and it looks "normal" again. (This is because the horizon seems farther away than the high sky, so we believe the moon is farther away when it's on the horizon.) Or turn your head upside down and observe someone talking; notice the usually hidden liveliness of the activity of his lower lip! Or look at your room in the mirror and see things reversed: You'll feel as if it's a different room--especially when you look at colors and shapes.

Another way we break the boundaries of perceptual habituation is to go away from our usual routine and return again. You'll always notice how intense the city seems after a vacation in the country. And when you return from vacation, it is always a pleasant surprise to see how that same old house can look so good when you were previously bored with every stick of furniture and champing at the bit to leave it.

What these experiences allow us to do is to break old perceptual patterns and to release us from narrow vision, from "one-way looking." And we can learn to favor new ways of looking by awakening our inner perceptions.

❖

Inner Perceptions: Image-ination

Heard melodies are sweet, but those unheard are sweeter.
JOHN KEATS

From our inside perceptions, we create our universe. In fact, none of us really needs to depend on the outer senses. As biochemist-biologist Roman Vishniac said, "All the events of nature are inside you. When you close your eyes you can still see, and if you close your ears you can still hear. You are dominant, you are the master; but you must be the master of yourself . . ."[43] What we consider to be "real" are actually inner perceptions and symbols, which the human mind imbues with meaning. Other species give different meanings to the world. Birds find a Ferrari useful only as an occasional toilet, and horses are not exactly thrilled by VCRs. Most human inventions are meaningless to other species because they are based on human thought patterns, constructed solely out of human experience.

The ability to rely on inner perception has always been a significant condition for greatness. Great people look inside to find more comprehensive patterns and special keys to unlocking the universe. And in this way, inner perception becomes the most valuable sense of all--enabling us to create a real world on the inside through our imagination.

Everyone has the ability to "image" or to imagine even if he lacks the ability to think in words. Imaging and thinking are very close, but "imagery thought" doesn't rely on language. Thus, the use of mental imagery is universal. However, even though it is universal, great creators are often better imagers. Charles Dickens, for example, was said to have had highly developed imagery skills and vividly pictured his stories as he wrote them. Charlotte Brontë also saw her novels enacted before her (inner) eyes and wrote what she pictured.

Dr. Ann Roe, in her research on scientific creativity, found that the more creative scientists used more visual imagery than others who relied on verbal thinking.[44] Abstract thinkers like mathematicians and artists have to think in images because there is no verbal language to express their thoughts. But imagery thought is also the most vivid kind of thinking and has been described as the most pleasurable--most compelling, dreamy, and sweet.

Einstein described his own imaging experience:

The words of the language, as they are written or spoken, do not seem to play any role in my mechanism of thought. The physical entities which seem to serve as elements in thought are certain signs and more or less clear images which can be "voluntarily" reproduced and combined. . . . The above-mentioned elements are, in any case, of visual and some of muscular type.

Conventional words or other signs have to be sought for laboriously only in a secondary stage, when the mentioned associative play is sufficiently established and can be reproduced at will.[45]

Images often stay alive longer than words, even for a lifetime. As a young man, Milton visualized his *Paradise Lost,* and the vision stayed with him and developed throughout his life until, when he was old and blind, he completed it.

The image the artist uses might be an entire inner movie or a single "frame." When he began *The French Lieutenant's Woman,* John Fowles remembers:

It started . . . as *a visual image.* A woman stands at the end of a deserted quay and stares out to sea. That was all. This image rose in my mind one morning when I was still in bed half-asleep. It corresponded to no actual incident in my life (or in art) that I can recall . . .[46]

The image can also be an "audial" experience. The reported experiences of great poets indicate that many of them hear sounds and rhythms before the meanings of words come to them. Yeats heard a buzzing sound; Wordsworth identified his precognitive experience as a kind of "booing." Similarly, many of the great composers have inner musical perception. It may at first seem incomprehensible that Beethoven, who at twenty-six had lost his hearing, could compose music. But evidence shows that musicians hear in their minds the way painters visualize in their minds.

New York Times critic Harold Schönberg described his mental musical "hearing" in *Facing the Music.* He always had music playing in his head. His wife says that if she asked him while he was sleeping what he was listening to, he'd mumble the name of the piece without waking up. He "read" chamber music and symphony literature the way other people read books, hearing it inside and memorizing as he went along.

When such inner perceptual abilities are developed in very specific channels and associated with memory, we call it "eidetic ability" or "photographic" memory.

Eidetic Ability

Some of us are able to remember a map in perfect detail or a book or a dance--depending on one or more highly developed sensory abilities. This process is generally experienced in childhood. Retaining this ability to absorb sensory information in a very complete way and recall events in rich detail in adulthood is said to be one of the typical, although not always universal, characteristics of genius.

Conductor Arturo Toscanini could conduct a vast repertoire of symphonies from memory. Many great musicians, like Mozart, Tchaikovsky, Scriabin, and Weber, had auditory eidetic ability--they could recall musical passages in perfect detail--music they had heard only once, or, in the case of Mozart, music he had heard only in his head and was able to reproduce on the concert stage weeks later, having never played it.

If a person with visual eidetic ability--a photographic memory--is asked for information out of an encyclopedia she has read, she just turns the pages in her mind until the appropriate page is reached. An artist endowed with eidetic ability may be able mentally to project a vision of his painting onto a canvas and "trace" the projection.

Because it's much easier to remember images than actual words, the ability to "feel" in images is in fact a very common technique that people who want to develop good memories use. They associate numbers or words in a list with specific images and then recall the images instead of the words, to which they then can associate back.

When all the senses contribute to the "feeling" of images, another kind of integrated perception is experienced. Anthropologist Margaret Mead was not only a brilliant researcher, she also enjoyed a form of highly developed perception called "synesthesia," which integrates the five senses to act in accord with one another. When perception channels become more subtle, they become less bounded and may actually cross. "Cross-sensing," or synesthesia, enables you to hear color or smell sounds. The poet John Keats experienced this perceptual unity, and his poetry is filled with synesthetic imagery, such as "O turn thee to the very tale/and taste the music of that vision pale."

Perhaps the most dramatic and vivid description of synesthetic experience comes from one of the greatest mnemonists or memory experts of all times--a Russian man whom psychologist A. R. Luria studied for thirty years and called "S." S had a "virtually unlimited" memory. He could recall thousands of lengthy lists of words or numbers even after twenty years had passed. For him each number or word was characterized by a specific image. But he also had an ability to see sounds or even taste them. For example, he heard film maker Sergei Eisenstein's voice as "a flame with fibers protruding from it . . ." He experienced a musical tone as "a brown strip against a dark background [accompanied by] the taste of borsht"; a much higher tone was "something like fireworks with a pink-red hue. The strip of color feels rough and unpleasant and has an unpleasant taste--rather like that of briny pickle . . . you could hurt your hand on that."

He described the "feeling-value" of perception as something more subtle than perception itself:

> I recognize a word not only by the images it evokes but by a
> whole complex of feelings that image arouses. It's hard to express
> . . . it's not a matter of vision or hearing but some over-all
> sense I get. Usually I experience a word's taste and weight, and I
> don't have to make an effort to remember it--the word seems to
> recall itself. But it's difficult to describe. What I sense is
> something oily slipping through my hand . . . or I'm aware of a
> slight tickling in my left hand caused by a mass of tiny,
> lightweight points. When that happens I simply remember,
> without having to make the attempt.[47]

Of course, fascinating as it is, most of us are fortunate *not* to be blessed with S's ability; the effort required to forget the useless information when not needed was a strain for him and detracted from other aspects of his life, leaving him quite limited in creativity. However, in its less intense, and no doubt more enjoyable form, synesthesia is found more often in more creative people. "It's like a special gift most of the time," reported one woman. "Almost any music to me is like the opening scenes of *Fantasia* or a laser-light show. The minus side is that sound is very distracting when I'm trying to work because I can't 'turn off.' " About 10 percent of us can experience a primary sense accompanied by a secondary sense;

most commonly, sound produces both an auditory experience and an accompanying visual image. And according to Dr. Lawrence Marks of Yale University, a leading expert in this field, even though synesthesia is inherited to a certain degree, "most people have the capacity for at least some form of synesthesia if we paid attention to it." Thus, like all forms of perception, even this unique ability can be far more developed in any of us.

So, although our senses are to some extent physical response mechanisms, as we've seen, there is a vast range of usage and capacity associated with them. And we find that when our senses are further developed, refined *and* integrated with other processes like thought and feeling, we experience a profound benefit: We discover a "sixth sense"--our intuition--which enables us to rely on and use all our senses on a much more abstract level. In the following chapter, we'll see how perceptual and thought processes develop into intuitive capabilities, which the majority of great people seem to have in abundance.

6

— ❖ —

GREAT THINKING:
ONE GOOD THOUGHT DESERVES
A MOTHER

The Importance of Thought

My contemplation of life and human nature . . . had taught me that he who cannot change the very fabric of his thought will never be able to change reality, and will never, therefore, make any progress. . . . The fact that change should take place first at a deeper and perhaps subtler level than the conscious level was one I had established as a basis of action ever since I discovered my real self in Cell 54.

ANWAR SADAT

It has often seemed to me that something great has only to be *thought* in order to exist indestructibly.

RAINER MARIA RILKE

We in America have everything we need except the most important thing of all--time to think and the habit of thought.

Norman Cousins

Few people think more than two or three times a year. I have made an international reputation by thinking once or twice a week.

G. B. Shaw

Any thought can change the entire course of society. Society may think it's passing right by you, said Buckminster Fuller, but if you're doing dynamic things mentally, you can stick out your foot and turn the whole society around with one well-placed thought. And those whose thoughts are most powerful will in fact influence us all.

Great people are generally powerful thinkers; they think with their valves open; they admit new ideas, and so they live in a big world, a big reality: "One thought fills immensity," wrote William Blake. And in this way, great thinkers provide deep continuity for all societies, no matter what cultural differences may be present on the surface.

Not surprisingly, great people tend to be aware of the importance of their thoughts and thinking processes. The sixteen-year-old Ralph Waldo Emerson, during his junior year at Harvard, began keeping a journal of ideas and thoughts which he called "The Wide World No. 1." He kept it for over fifty years; it grew to two hundred notebooks and was eventually published as a sixteen-volume work. His respect for the value of thought itself in influencing society was considerable. In *On Education,* he wrote:

> Consent yourself to be an organ of your highest thought, and lo; suddenly you put all men in your debt, and are the fountain of an energy that goes pulsing on with waves of benefit to the borders of society, to the circumference of things.

Great thinking, however, doesn't have to be based on laborious study or on rational intellect. In his day Edison was considered a kind of wizard--the "Merlin of the Nineteenth Century." But most of his knowledge came through experimentation, not books; his solutions were arrived at by "thinking in a way I could never explain." Not knowing where the boundaries of invention stopped, he quickly went beyond them and kept going until he had solved the various technological problems he encountered.

Children tend to think in this innocent and abundantly unrestricted way: The average four-year-old asks an estimated 437 questions a day. Children also enjoy very *flexible* thinking, which clearly influences the adults around them. As a result, people who spend the most time around children, such as parents, pediatricians, and schoolteachers, have been found to be more creative and flexible in their thinking than the adult population as a whole. Kindergarten teachers, in particular, score exceptionally high on tests of imagination, compared with other occupational groups.

However, although children may have great imaginations, they generally don't *connect* their thoughts very well and therefore lack certain ingredients for great thinking, like pattern recognition, sequential thinking, and uninterrupted focus. Mere abundance of thought is not enough, either in a child or in an adult.

It is estimated that each of us thinks about 57,000 thoughts a day.[1] But how many of those thoughts are more than ruminations; how many do we act on or use constructively? In fact, greatness is more likely to come about because of *one* wonderful thought that we act on with utmost attention and perseverance until, we could say, the thought is "done." Einstein was a prime example of a "one-thought" thinker, and no one, wrote C. P. Snow, "has ever been able to think more obsessively, and for longer on a single issue." That's because the thought--"How does the universe work?"--was a huge one and completely compelling for him.

Thinking for Pleasure

The whole of science is nothing more than a refinement of everyday thinking. . . . When I have no special problem to occupy my mind, I love to reconstruct proofs of mathematical and physical theorems that have long been known to me. There is no goal in this, merely an opportunity to indulge in the pleasant occupation of thinking.

ALBERT EINSTEIN

It will be found that a quiet life is characteristic of great men, and that their pleasures have not been of the sort that would look exciting to the outward eye.

BERTRAND RUSSELL

The sole purpose of any activity is to make living more enjoyable, and the activity of thinking itself is in fact the most profoundly "human" form of pleasure. In this regard, "you go to my head" may be a more accurate way of describing love than "I've got you under my skin." Or even "deep in the heart of me."

And often what we experience in our thoughts or "hear" in our heads is more pleasing than what we are able to translate and express. It is always something of a shock to sing what we feel to be quite a beautiful song, well rehearsed in the shower, and realize that our friends are barely keeping it together behind those indulgent smiles. What we have enjoyed is the pleasure of the inward experience. In this way Einstein experienced the thrill of discovery completely on the mental level without any direct confirmation from the sensory world he was exploring. His theoretical or "thinking" discoveries were not verified in the physical universe until many years later.

Researcher H. J. Campbell has described three stages of pleasure seeking in humans:

(1) Feeling-doing--an early stage of mainly sensory input and with little higher-level activity like thinking;

(2) Thinking-doing--a stage that includes most of life's activities, where thought is put into action and makes an impact on the environment. At its most developed levels, we enjoy creative thought in action, such as art, music, and inventions;

(3) Thinking only--this highest stage of human pleasure is found in mathematical and philosophical thinking, where thought itself, without any expressed activity, provides pleasure.[2]

Campbell's progression is a physiological approach to the way we learn and experience pleasure, based on the sequential and evolutionary growth from pure sensory experience to pure thought experience. Gradually, as the brain matures, the importance of sensory input declines. Of course, it never becomes irrelevant, but eventually the higher regions are sufficiently developed anatomically to receive and give out information so that interchange between the thinking regions and the pleasure areas can be largely self-sustaining.

This pleasure in mental activity is not exclusively human. Animals, too, enjoy solving problems merely for the sake of solving them. When rats are trained to go through a simple maze as well as a more complicated one to get to food, they will choose the more complicated, lengthier maze even though the reward is the same. And researchers at Dr. Harry Harlow's laboratories at the University of Wisconsin have found that monkeys enjoy solving puzzles with no reward at all.

But the pleasure humans derive from thinking comes from the development of the process itself, from the desire of the mind to seek finer and finer patterns and connections leading to an experience of a unified whole. As images combine into associative patterns, new ideas are born and the sensation of even further integration is a joyful "Aha!" "The essence of all new ideas is the formation of unexpected patterns," writes Anthony Campbell. And this brings a sense of relief and pleasure to the thinker. As critic I. A. Richards reminds us: "We should not forget that *finer organization* [my italics] is the most successful way of relieving strain, a fact of relevance in the theory of evolution. The new response will be more advantageous than the old, more successful in satisfying varied appetencies."[3]

Emerson also identified "finer organization" as the way to seek and hear "nature's laws" as poetry:

> For poetry was written before time was, and whenever we are so *finely organized* [my italics] that we can penetrate into that region where the air is music, we hear those primal warblings, and attempt to write them down, but we lose ever and anon a word, or a verse, and substitute something of our own, and so miswrite the poem. The men of more delicate ear write down those cadences more faithfully, and these transcripts, though imperfect, become the songs of the nations.[4]

So how does each of us discover and create the songs of the nations?

Desire: The Inception of Thought

> We all have this creative desire to do something. . . . We all
> want to do something, to reach something, everyone in his way.
> When I find a person who lost this desire, such a person is
> almost dead.
>
> ISAAC B. SINGER

If we wish to be blessed with good ideas, first we must actively want
them: Jacques Hadamard and others who have studied the attain-
ment of creative insight have concluded that desire is of utmost importance in the creative process.

Generally speaking, desire is the energy component of all human
motivation. Without desire, nothing moves toward accomplishment.
Desire is the fire, the energy of thought--the spark that enlivens. It
propels us, often with amazing force, into creation. Indeed, desire is
the natural way in which we recognize and accede to the personal
growth to greatness.

The specific desire for knowledge enables us to learn--to enter
continually into new worlds. It can start as a tiny seed of feeling, of
wanting to know, and can lead to a lifetime of greatness. Or it can
wither and die. But when it stays alive, it can turn from simple desire
into creative thought and from thought into constructive activity.

Writer Isaac B. Singer describes this phenomenon as follows:

> I get up every morning with a desire to work and to write a
> story, or to work on a novel, to do some creative work. This
> desire is made of the same stuff as . . . the businessman's desire
> to go out and do business, the desire to get patients, or to write a
> book. This desire, even though it has millions of forms is the
> same desire: to do something, to create something. I don't think
> that only writers and painters and musicians are creative. All
> human beings are creative.[5]

And desire is never contrived. It just arrives, says composer Aaron
Copland, like hunger:

> How does it come about that you feel hungry? You don't know,
> you just feel hungry. The juices are working, and suddenly you

are aware of the fact that you want a piece of bread and butter. It's about the same in art. If you pass your life in creating works of art in one field or another, you recognize the "hunger" signs and you are quick to take advantage of them, if they're accompanied by ideas. Sometimes, you have the hunger and you don't have any ideas; there's no bread in the house. It's as simple as that.[6]

From desire comes thought--an idea, hopefully a good idea. But it isn't just *any* desire or *any* thought that will prove most useful for becoming great. That kind of thinking comes in three packages: positive and deep and intuitive.

We've all probably heard of the "power of positive thinking," but it's also important to remember that any thought is only as powerful as the depth of consciousness from where it is drawn. The most powerful thought seems to come from a more settled, "intuitive" level of the mind. And because great thoughts arrive from a more highly organized and energetic inner source, they tend to be more effective, more dynamic, and seem to attract more cooperation from the environment. Let's look at each aspect of great thoughts to see how this happens.

Positive Thoughts

If we think of defeat, that's what we get; if we're undecided, then nothing will happen for us. We must just pick something great to do, and do it. Never think of failure at all, for as we think now, that's what we get.

MAHARISHI MAHESH YOGI

It's a psychological law that we tend to get what we expect. If you live expecting bad things, you will get them. This will be true, at least to a degree because you will actually, by your expectations, be bringing bad things into being. On the other hand, if you put in your mind a picture of bright and happy expectations, you put yourself into a condition conducive to your goal . . .

NORMAN VINCENT PEALE

If you want to fly, you must think lovely thoughts.

JAMES M. BARRIE, (*Peter Pan*)

If we say we want to be great, but inside we believe this isn't possible, our own greatness will elude us because we are not self-believers. What we deeply believe, not what we say we want to believe, seems to be what happens. Theologian Paul Tillich calls it the "hidden content" of prayer. And all great thinkers understand this. "As one thinketh in his heart," said the Prophet David, "so he is."

Over a hundred years ago, Harvard psychologist William James became the first modern researcher to identify the value of positive thinking--ahead of Dr. Norman Vincent Peale, Dale Carnegie, and Napoleon Hill. Wrote James, "One of the greatest discoveries of my generation was that human beings can alter their attitudes of mind."

Rather than deny reality, positive thinkers create a *different* reality based on the kind of focused attention that belief engenders. James explored his findings in *The Will to Believe* and concluded, "These, then, are my last words to you: Be not afraid of life. Believe that life is worth living, and your belief will help create the fact."

If our thoughts do indeed have influence, then how we think of others will affect them either positively or adversely, depending on what we have in mind for them. And how intensely we desire it. In the 1970s, for example, we kept reminding each other of President Jimmy Carter's failures, and pretty soon we were believing collectively that he was failing, as indeed he was. However, in the sense that President Carter represented all of our collective wishes, he (or we) actually succeeded: We wanted him to fail and he did just that.

In times of war leaders of nations tend to have the good wishes of the country focused on them, and, as a result, are generally more popular than peacetime presidents. Says researcher John Naisbitt, "In a crisis we choose Lincoln and F.D.R. In between we choose What's-his-name. . . . We have not attracted strong leaders except in times of crisis."[7]

In general, collective negative thoughts about a leader may weaken him further and also create a chaotic national consciousness. This can be a powerful tool if we desire to oust the leader (as in President

Nixon's case) or it can create a weakened leadership (such as Carter's). But if we accept that leaders are created by the needs and wishes of the times, then it is *we* who succeed in creating a Lincoln or an FDR.

Our wishes only *seem* to be unimportant and isolated. In fact, they are profoundly necessary in all fields of life. The contemporary artist Agnes Martin has observed: "Life does not move ahead due to the work of a few geniuses as is generally believed but due to the positive wishes of all those who have faith in life." The highly successful publisher of *Ebony* magazine, John Johnson, averted all negativity toward his success by hiring only those employees who believed the magazine would succeed.

However, positive wishes are not, of themselves, always effective unless they are projected from the most powerful level of consciousness available.

❖

Deep Thinking

A man's life is what his thoughts make of it.

MARCUS AURELIUS

We say, "It's the thought that counts." And that's very true. But we must also evaluate the *quality* of the thought: Is it a vital, powerful one, or not? This is what Alfred North Whitehead meant when he said, "The vitality of thought is an adventure. Ideas won't keep. Something must be done about them." Film director Sidney Lumet described this process:

> The idea will hit and then without my knowing it, another idea will wipe it out; then depending on its persistence, depending on its importance, depending on what role it's playing, it will keep intruding in little bursts, literally, and then depending on circumstances, either crash through or be wiped out.[8]

A strong, clear thought will create a corresponding reality in the physical world. And thus it grows. A weak thought dies in seed form.

For example, you might say to yourself, "I think I'll give a party." If it isn't a very strong thought; that is, if it really isn't what you want to do deep down, your next thought may be "Maybe not . . . too much trouble." On the other hand, if it is a strong thought, it will bring its own energy with it, and food, music, and guests will combine perfectly at the very time you had decided upon. With a lively thought, you'll start to feel good about it and a series of "action" thoughts will follow.

Powerful thinking comes from a deep level of the mind. And it happens most easily when the mind is not agitated, but free of stress and fatigue.

In the process of acquiring knowledge, information passes through the senses and settles in the depths of the mind, at the level of the delicate impulses of thought. But the information will not settle in the depths of the mind if, because of certain blocks, it cannot reach that level. This is why we seem to remember the pleasant, happy moments of our lives more easily than the uncomfortable ones, simply because we experienced them under conditions more free of stress. As a result, they could "sink in" more.

The same is true of the process in reverse--knowledge given out. For example, a college student is asked to write a paper. If she is able to settle down to quiet, comprehensive thinking, undisturbed by accumulated stress, the process of expressing what she knows is effortless; thoughts flow freely, as she has access to a full range of knowledge stored within her mind.

Education that "works" is aimed at developing a process of learning which enlivens the silent, deep levels of thinking. Learning to think on the quiet levels of the mind leads to enjoying the maximum value of knowledge. Often in school we are taught about *things*, but not about our own mental capacities; how to read with maximum efficiency, how to "rest" the brain or how to "attend" so that the brain can fully function. To be fully awake and aware allows for complete mental functioning and gives us an opportunity for all our great ideas to flow in and out. In this way learning to think freely *and* deeply is the real basis for a great life.

When we can think deeply, we begin to perceive thought early on in the process; we experience it in its infancy, and this leads us to what we call *intuitive* thinking.

Intuition: The Power of Refined Thinking

All greats are gifted with intuition. They know without reasoning or analysis what they need to know.

ALEXIS CARREL

Intuition, or what's called the "sixth sense," occurs when perception, thinking, and feeling operate together at very subtle levels of awareness, when we associate very refined levels of feeling with a subtle aspect of the mind or senses. When we use intuition, a pattern of events can be perceived from very little data. We could call intuition "inside knowledge" or "insight knowledge," but it can be most simply described as the "feeling of knowing."

We've all had intuitive experiences, like knowing a certain friend is going to call seconds before the phone rings. When we trust this "feeling of knowing," we can then pick up the phone and say, "Hi, Allan!" even before he speaks.

Although we use intuition in everyday life, it has not been really "proven" in psychology because no really good procedure has been developed to test it. However, this situation is changing. Psychologists like Amos Tversky and Daniel Kahneman, among others, have been studying the various ways in which we like to think, called "cognitive biases." According to their research with scientifically trained subjects, "the bias for the intuitive" manifests consistently.

When we say we're intuitive, we mean we're able to sense reality on a very fine level and "know" accurately what's happening or about to happen. It's not that we're able to know something that's impossible to know, but rather that we're aware of it at a more subtle level than we are used to experiencing.

For example, by using intuition, we could know the answer to a problem without going through all the mental steps. Seven-year-old Emilie can intuitively calculate four-digit by four-digit multiplication problems in her head because the solutions just "appear," she says, "in color," and because of this she knows she's got the answer. At any given intuitive moment, we are aware of the dawn before the sunrise, while ordinarily we are aware only of the sunrise. To those who have never been awake before the sunrise, this awareness could seem very odd. To people with lively intuition, these experiences are quite normal; they are merely another way to know things, apart from analysis. But even intuitive thinkers must learn to trust their intuition. And this is a lesson for the greats, too.

Beethoven was well known for his indecision in committing his musical ideas to a final version. Unlike Mozart who knew his ideas were perfect from their inception on, Beethoven rewrote constantly. Once when a curious publisher had peeled away eight layers of paper, each pasted on top of the other as alternative versions, he found that the ninth and final form that had finally satisfied Beethoven was identical with the original!

If you are successful in trusting your feelings, you can learn to rely on your intuition. You're probably using it anyway because it's so extraordinarily useful in every field. This sixth sense enables you to know what's coming. Because great thinkers have the ability to perceive subtle thoughts, they often seem "ahead of the times," but they are really just picking up on what is about to be experienced by all of us.

Scientist Michael Polyani describes a creative scientist's intuitive vision as comparable to using a long stick to feel one's way in the dark: The attention is on the far end of the stick, not on the end in hand. This is almost exactly film maker Ingmar Bergman's experience of how his intuition works: "I throw a spear into the darkness. That is intuition. Then I must send an army into the darkness to find the spear. That is intellect."[9]

Intuition in Business: Inner Market Research

Although intuition is not yet taught in business schools, even the most hard-headed successful business people rely on it to make decisions. Companies pay enormous amounts of money to hire executives who possess unerring business judgment, who have a "gut feeling" for the marketplace. For example, when television was first becoming widespread, George Long, president of Ampex Corporation, foresaw a day when recording TV programs for future use would develop into a huge market. Based on this feeling, he led his company to the top of the industry in videotape development and manufacturing.

Most top-level executives have been found to think "multidimen-sionally"; that is, they can synthesize a great deal of apparently un-related information, see patterns emerging in periods of change, and consider consequences several steps ahead. In other words, they are intuitive.

A research group headed by John Milhalasky and his associates tested hundreds of business managers for their pure intuitive ability. Effective decision making was found to be highly correlated with intuition. In one experiment with twenty-five managers, each had held a top decision-making position for five years. Of the twenty-five, twelve had doubled their companies' profits in five years, and eleven of those twelve scored very high on the intuitive test. The man who scored the highest had increased his company's profits al-most twentyfold.[10]

According to Dr. Rashi Glazer, associate professor of marketing at Columbia University, "Intuition is a kind of information-gathering designed to reduce uncertainty. It enables a business person to gather information most efficiently, with less effort." And this is how the intuitive scientist operates as well.

❖

Intuition in Science:
The "Cave of the Hot Winds"

The "cave of the hot winds" was the name given to the office of theoretical physicist Victor Weisskopf by his colleagues at Los Ala-mos. They so named it because of his ability to solve problems out loud by intuition. Says Weisskopf, "I just guessed but I was usually right. . . . It was important then because we were dealing largely with the unknown."

Scientists are usually dealing with the unknown, and so require the abstract "feeling" skills of intuition. And most scientists recog-nize their own use of intuition. Researchers Platt and Baker, ques-tioning a group of scientists about their experience of the creative process, found that many based their research on intuitive "hunches"; 33 percent used frequent intuition, 50 percent did so occasionally, and only 17 percent used no intuition.

The truly great scientists, of course, use their intuition almost unerringly. According to Buckminster Fuller, "If you don't know that something exists, there's no way you can look for it, yet mind has the unique capacity of finding things out through intuition. And this gives man his marvelous capacity to discover generalized principles and employ them." Einstein arrived at his results, writes his biographer Jeremy Bernstein, "by a phenomenal intuition of what they should be, by a deep inner contact with nature." For example, he intuited that the path of starlight would bend in passing through the curved space near the sun. (This prediction was verified much later by other scientists.)

Two Nobel Prize-winning physicists, Richard Feynman and Brian Josephson, have each recently explained how they use intuition. Josephson describes intuition as "the ability to observe on a sort of universal scale." He says: "It's probably the same sort of channel that's used in remote viewing--the ability that some people seem to have to describe physical settings that they have never directly observed. It's as if you can see inwardly things that you cannot see directly." Similarly, Feynman knows he uses intuition because, he says, "I need a qualitative idea of how the phenomenon works before I can get a quantitative look."

If you only think analytically, you are forced to consider choices in a hierarchy of possibilities. You are looking at things in a piece-by-piece way, not as part of a natural flow of ideas, but broken down into incomplete parts. Intuition reduces the available information to the "feeling" level; patterns, not individual parts, become more significant. Virginia Woolf described good writing as "the unusual power of following *feeling*" until it manifests as thought. Intuition allows the picturing of the whole by feeling it, feeling it mentally.

❖

Sight and Insight:
Indirect and Direct Cognition

You cannot go on seeing through things forever. The whole point of seeing through something is to see something through it. It is good that the window should be transparent because the street or garden beyond it is opaque. How, if you saw through the garden, too? . . . If you see through everything, then everything is an invisible world. To see through all things is the same as not to see.

C. S. Lewis, *The Abolition of Man*

Philosopher Susanne Langer refers to two kinds of knowing: "discursive," which includes language and the scientific method, and "nondiscursive," which is nonverbal, intuitive, "felt." We could also call these two processes "indirect" and "direct" cognition.

Usually, we tend to see and then think about what we have seen. We call this "observation." It implies two steps--seeing and then categorizing. This is indirect cognition. In direct intuitive cognition, knowledge comes immediately. It does not require categorization. This was how Dante initially awoke to his vision of the Paradiso. It came to him as a direct experience: He saw the entire Creation as a book--God's book: "I saw within Its depth how It conceives all things in a single volume bound by love, of which the universe is the scattered leaves." Then he tried to analyze, to categorize, and when he started to interfere with the clarity of his own experience, his beloved Beatrice had to remind him: "You dull your own perceptions with false imaginings and do not grasp what would be clear but for your preconceptions."

To a great extent, language itself is a conceptual barrier to direct cognition. By the time we are able to form hypotheses (by age eleven, according to psychologist Jean Piaget), we begin to operate as problem solvers, conceptualizing verbally, cognizing only indirectly through cultural reference, inexorably linked to established mental patterns. Because of the kind of education we typically receive, by the time we're adolescents, thoughts have become constricted and routinized; we long for the unpatterned openness of our childhood creativity. More than language is needed to go beyond these learned patterns. We need ways to see *behind* thought, to go beyond the critical and analytical. This is the value of direct cognition, which is the perceptual result of intuition.

Many intuitive experiences seem to contain the *visual* quality that Dante described, a clear inner perception that various cultures have called "the eye of the soul" or "the eye of the mind." The American Indians call this faculty "in-seeing," "in-hearing" or "in-knowing." It could also be termed "in-tuition." And because, like all senses, seeing has subtler and subtler dimensions, it moves from the most outward experience of visual stimuli to the most inward "visionary" qualities, to direct cognition. For example, the sixteenth-century seer Nostradamus "saw," with great accuracy, the French Revolution, the death of Richard II, and the eventual rise of Napoleon and Hitler. For the seer, therefore, seeing means seeing the deeper and wider reality and it requires a different kind of sight. American Indian culture in particular is replete with reports of this kind of visionary experience. Blind seers, like the ancient Greek prophet Tiresias, have often been considered the greatest visionaries--intuitive knowers of the future whose vision is not clouded by the illusions of the visual world. Only after he was blinded was Samson said to have developed this inner vision of direct cognition.

The sensory mode of intuitive knowing also has very practical benefits. When that great "see-er" Nikola Tesla developed a machine powered by his discovery of alternating current, he tested his ability to visualize constructs prior to production. Tesla could project before his eyes a completely detailed picture of every part of each machine. These inner pictures were more vivid to him than any blueprint, and he could remember exact dimensions, which he mentally calculated for each item. He did not have to test each part prior to the total assembly. He knew they would fit because there was no difference between the motor he built and the one which he visualized. All his inventions were "tested mentally," because Tesla could run them for weeks in his mind, after which time he would examine them *mentally* for signs of wear. "If he at any time built a 'mental machine,' " writes his biographer, "his memory ever afterward retained all of the details, even to the finest dimensions."

Intuition from the Q

If we refer back to our quantum or Q model, we can understand intuition more clearly as a refinement of ordinary thinking and perception, operating at another level of the mind. We could say that intuition is logical analysis occurring at a finer time and distance scale where the cognitive processes are speeded up to the point of not being perceivable--and we get the information without experiencing the process of information-gathering or selection itself. In this way the intuitive thinker is operating from the Q level, from the holographic perspective, where a tiny bit of knowledge gives the whole vision. And even for the most exacting scientist, this is a tremendous advantage. Here is how biologist Konrad Lorenz describes it:

> Intuition . . . is able to draw into simultaneous consideration a far greater number of premises than are of our conscious conclusions. The most important advantage of intuition is that it is "seeing" in the deepest sense of the word. . . . Even the most exact and inartistic of research workers is invariably guided by intuition in the choice of his object, in the choice of the direction in which to look.[11]

Intuition is the mind working within itself, awakening to its own knowledge by direct cognition, unencumbered by conceptual constructs, in which perception becomes a simple matter of self-awareness. In short, intuition is simply a way to perceive greater and greater connections. It's the ability to have feeling and thinking knowledge occur at the same time. We could call it the "Q advantage." Operating from a deeper, more unified level of inner awareness, the creator is "clairvoyant," clear seeing, able to perceive phenomena at a more unified level of integration.

Tesla thought there were "finer fibers" in the brain that enabled us to perceive truths which could not be attained though logical deduction. His intuition was once again correct. Greatness may very well be inextricably linked with a physical quality of intuition. Physiologically, like most aspects of higher development, intuition has been found to be correlated with frontal brain-wave functions. Because of the pliable nature of the brain, it may be that experiences of "great moments"--of clear intuition and a perception of wholeness--actually serve to restructure the nervous system to accommodate and develop the intuitive mode.

Another way to look at this is to consider that powerful intuitive thought could enliven greatness because thought itself is a subtle *physical* manifestation of creativity. Because it has energy and purpose, a given thought can actually create physical reality. We know, for example, that thinking about the sun produces a physiological condition different from that produced by the thought of cold. And thus the thought affects not just our mind but our physiology, too. Researchers have called this phenomenon "ideomotor action." Author Joseph Pearce cites studies by Price and Carington, and reports:

> An idea or response tends to fulfill itself or execute itself automatically through the muscular apparatus of the body, and will do so unless other ideas are present to inhibit it. Price suggests that this is indicative of a wider operation in life, namely that all ideas have a tendency to realize themselves in the material world in any way they can, unless inhibited by other ideas.[12]

Pearce further describes this "self-fulfilling prophecy" activity as "filling the empty categories."

Filling the Empty Categories

> Anything is possible. You must only educate people to know that.
>
> WHOOPI GOLDBERG

As a child, I spent what seemed like a lot of time traveling by car with my family. And like many children, I counted things out the window--red convertibles, license plates from a single state, Cadillacs, etc.--usually up to a hundred per category. And it would appear to my child's way of thinking that I had created these items--actually made them appear--for, all of a sudden, once I'd decided on the category, they would pop up in large numbers everywhere I looked, even when I wasn't really thinking about them. Psychologists say that this is because my mind was attuned to these objects and so it was "set" to see them, a way of mentally picking out certain like items from all others with great efficiency.

But the child's-eye view was really more in keeping with the Q view, in which one would be *creating* these objects just by desiring their reality. According to Pearce, by setting up empty categories we structure a possibility and then proceed to make it happen, make it come true. And empty categories can simply be filled by a strong belief, both individually and collectively.

For example, tennis pro Stephen Briggs has observed that the great tennis champions are able to sustain the thought that, no matter what, no matter how far behind they are, they *will win*. Just projecting the thought that they'll win may give their opponents the sinking feeling of inevitably losing! And in a broader sense, our changing images of ourselves are also empty categories or self-fulfilling prophecies. In the words of Dr. Willis Harman of the Stanford Research Institute, "We can think of personality change as depending upon change in self-image . . . fundamentally involving a change in the person's perception of himself and hence of the possibilities open to him."

Authors Peters and Waterman describe the work of Peter Vaill, who studies "high performing systems" like businesses, orchestras, and football teams. According to Vaill, such systems behave as self-fulfilling prophecies. Vaill cites the emergence of a "private language and set of symbols": Members feel "up" because something has worked, and, if allowed, they start to act in a new way. As they act in a new way, more good things happen. "Peak experiences . . . lead members to enthuse, bubble, and communicate joy and exultation. . . . People eat, sleep, and breathe the activity. . . . A Hall of Fame phenomenon arises . . . members acquire an aesthetic motivation and finally an air of invincibility leads to the same reality."[13]

Category filling not only occurs individually and in groups, it also appears as a basis for societal and global change. Once somebody has come up with a new category, it's available for us all. In other words, according to physiologist Rupert Sheldrake, a "morphogenetic" field is created with each new invention, each new idea. That "shape" is now in the universe, and other inventors and thinkers will pick it up and play with it.

By structuring all possibilities, thought that becomes manifest as reality, even a previously unheard-of reality, is a kind of code for physical life--the DNA, we could say, of matter. It contains the essence, the basic content of the object. But how does thought actually unfold into concrete reality?

Attention: One Good Thought Deserves a Mother

Thinking can be either directed and engaged or undirected and random. Similarly, all conscious activities can be engaged in with full attention, partial attention, or no attention at all. Whether one is reading, watching TV, talking on the phone or watering the garden, one can be fully engaged in the activity or fully disengaged. People who tend to be actively engaged in what interests them and disengaged in what doesn't are on the road to greatness. Because if you can fully attend to what you want to do or accomplish, you are nine tenths of the way there. So, what does it mean to "fully attend"?

Great people generally use their ability to observe the birth of thought--they know how to collect their thoughts at the abstract beginnings before the thoughts become concrete and specific. They have learned how to focus attention on the initial stages of the thinking process automatically; in other words, they have learned to get in early.

And this initial attention is vital: *The habit of "early" thinking is the key to great thoughts.* For in that way one can "raise" them from birth.

Because if thought is a seed, it needs to be properly cared for as it grows into full existence. As every parent knows, giving birth to the child is just the beginning. One must nurture it, attend to it, support it, and love it until grown. So it is with an idea. Socrates preferred to think of himself as an intellectual midwife helping to "deliver" an idea at birth rather than as a teacher. And Norman Cousins writes: "What is most valuable in the Socratic method is the painstaking and systematic development of a thought from its earliest beginnings to its full-bodied state."

Great ideas are in some sense born, but they also die if not attended to with the right kind of care, focus, and love. The way we think and feel about our thoughts very much influences their development. Obviously, we need to believe in our thoughts, just as we do our children, to love them and nurture them until they flourish. So, we can say that "one good thought deserves a mother," and if we could identify one single factor which contributes most to the *structuring* of a great achievement from the initial thought to its fulfillment, it would have to be "mothering" attention.

Let's look more closely at this requirement. Attention has two components: (1) what we attend *to*, and (2) what we attend *with*-- the two together make up what we usually call the "power" of attention.

❖

What Are We Attending To?

My experience is what I agree to attend to.

WILLIAM JAMES

What we mean by something to attend to is simple. It's where you put your attention at any given time. It can be any thought, perception or feeling, anything that activates your brain. Where you put your attention literally creates your experience, your reality. A solo rock climber was asked if he had ever been frightened when the margin of safety on the sheer surfaces became almost nil. He said that at those times, he pretended he was "only two feet off the ground . . . and that usually did the trick." With this thinking, he had climbed the north face of the Eiger, alone.

Great people know they create their own reality, and for this reason, they like to put their attention on finding out about what structures the universe, on love, on things that might contribute to the health and happiness of society. Great experiences come from attending to great things. Otherwise, there might be a tendency to think only of little things that just fill up time. Little petty thoughts make little petty products--like gossip. (Not to mention what Big Petty Thoughts make . . .) Put simply, when it comes to creating reality through attention of thought: (1) You get what you ordered from the catalog; or (2) you get the floor for which you pushed the button.

Thus, if we want to be great, we have to take conscious care about where we put our attention. We also call it goal-setting. Goal-setting works because it enables your attention to flow in the direction you want instead of being diverted by anything else that comes along. You construct the process in advance and focus on what you *really* want. For years realtor Donald Trump, creator of the Trump Tower in Manhattan, would drive up Fifth Avenue near Fifty-seventh Street and think, "This is the most valuable piece of property in the world. I want to buy it." And eventually he did. He set a goal--a big one but not an unrealistic one, given his circumstances--and put his attention on it continually. The historian Thomas Macaulay began his career at age six by writing what he titled A *Compendium of Universal History*. He never stopped. From age twelve, John McEnroe never doubted he would become a tennis champion. He sustained the vision, treading the narrow, deep path of a one-pointed commitment.

Once you have put your attention on something, whether a business goal or a relationship or anything else, you may notice things picking up in the direction you have chosen. The means to accomplish it seem to gather about you in the environment; it's almost as if nature likes to have a goal to support.

But it's your belief that creates this support--and the belief must be real and exclusive. There can be no wavering. As William James advised: "If you can only care enough for a result, you will most certainly attain it. If you wish to be rich, you will be rich. If you wish to be learned, you will be learned. If you wish to be good, you will be good. Only you must then *really* wish these things and wish them exclusively and not wish at the same time 100 incompatible things just as strongly."[14]

Belief is thus a kind of continual form of powerful attention. "One person with a belief," wrote John Stuart Mill, "is equal to ninety-nine who have only interests."

Instead of being afraid of the unknown, great people structure what they want to happen--not by coercion but by simple attention. The success expert Napoleon Hill had one famous secret of success: "To put all your eggs in one basket--and then watch the basket." Essentially, your belief will make whatever you want succeed. Christopher Jencks and his associates at Harvard University have reported that "the sense of internal control or how much one believes success is determined by one's own personal initiative rather than by external events, does affect success."

But it isn't the amount of time you attend to something that makes it happen; it's the *quality of the attention. It's what we attend with* that counts.

❖

What We Attend with: The Power of Attention

Thought is a man in his wholeness, wholly attending.

D. H. LAWRENCE

The power of attention is really a function of your consciousness. It lights up whatever you're attending to. No matter how much you may want something, if you have no attention to put on it, nothing will happen. Conversely, the more powerful your consciousness, the more light you shine--the more likely you will get what you desire.

The real key to powerful attention is to develop an ability that lets us attend easily to anything without effort or strain. It means that the thinking process must be stress-free. Attention is always most powerful when it is *free of tension;* one could really call it "a-tension."

In his study of self-made millionaries, Blotnick found that most of them had developed an ability to attend to their inner thoughts even while carrying on some surface transactions. "People who have spent years absorbed in their work finally develop the phenomenal ability to talk without rupturing the connection to their thoughts. . . . They have learned how to go through the motions of being sociable and cooperative, but through it all maintain a high state of involvement with their work."[15] This outward-inward attention is developed when the process of being aware of one's thoughts is well-established, drawing on a dynamic connection to the silent, unbounded source of thought. Attention is always more concentrated and powerful when connected to this subtler field of thinking. Not only are you paying attention to your environment, you are quietly aware of your own thinking process. As you pay attention to the more abstract "earlier" thoughts and to subtle feelings, you are accessing your intuition more fully.

Moreover, when you put your attention on something, you affect it and it affects you--there is some exchange of characteristics. You are not necessarily aware of it, but just the information you receive from it produces changes in your brain. At one level, it's a kind of learning, but at another level, it's actually a *physical* exchange, that can either enhance or sap your energy.

When a speaker says, "Let me have your attention," the request has several implied outcomes. First of all, the speaker wants something from the listeners; that their individual thoughts have one focus--the speech. Then if what she says is of sufficient interest and liveliness to keep you focused on the content of her speech, rather than on the lint on your jacket, she has succeeded in keeping your attention. But what she really wants, although she may not be entirely conscious of it, is your flow of mental energy toward her, to capture your powerful awareness. Because it's *your* attention and that of the rest of the audience that enlivens her speech.

The exchange of energy through attention can be both positive or negative, creative or destructive, depending upon the desired result. One of the most amazing events attesting to power of attention took place during the sixteenth century. A group of several hundred conquistadors left Spain and set off for the New World. When they arrived at what is now the Texas Gulf area, they were shipwrecked. Only a few survived and one, Cabeza de Vaca, years later recounted his adventures among the native Indians in a letter to the king of Spain. At the outset of an eight-year period before returning home, he and several fellow survivors were approached by the Indians and warned that if they were not able to heal the sick, they would be killed. So they became doctors. With the power of group attention and an unrelenting desire to remain alive, these soldiers did indeed restore the health of a large population of ill Indians. Cabeza wrote to the king:

We had to heal them or die. So we prayed for strength. . . . To our amazement, the ailing said they were well. Being Europeans, we thought we had given away to doctors and priests our ability to heal but here it was, still in our possession. . . . After all, we were more than we thought we were.

It was a drunkenness, this feeling I began to have of power to render life and happiness to others. Yet I was concerned about it. . . . What occupied me was whether I myself knew how to use it, whether I could master it, whether indeed it was for me to master--perhaps being a self-directing power that came through me. But after one accustoms oneself to the idea, it is good to be able to give out health and joy whether one man have it, or whether we all have it. Had this thought occurred to your Majesty? Never before had it occurred to me.[16]

It is apparent that both individual and group belief systems can serve to transform patterns of behavior into new realities. Once we know this, we can help our friends and families considerably by putting our attention on wanting the best for them. Parents have tremendous influence on the development of their children in this way; by their positive attention, they can help fill the category of personal greatness.

The only sociological factor that has ever been significantly correlated with greatness is that greatness "favors" the first child in the family. Approximately 70 percent of the top scientists were first children. And of the first sixteen astronauts, fourteen were either only or eldest children. Why the eldest or first-child bias occurs may actually be a function of one-pointed attention by parents on their child's greatness. Alma Wright, Frank Lloyd Wright's mother, envisioned him as an architect *prior* to his birth. She hung pictures of the great cathedrals and architectural monuments of the world in the baby's room-to-be. When he was a youngster, she supplied him with beautiful building blocks and colored pieces of cardboard, which she herself designed. Whether we agree with her approach or not, there's no doubt that her son did grow up to become a great architect.

In a more general way, many parents who have raised great children often spontaneously elicit the best qualities in them through their own belief in their potential. They create the mental set for confidence and success. A mother who wants the best for her child may not in fact be overly possessive. She may just be setting up conditions for positivity. W. Clement Stone credits his success with the positive attention of his mother's "generosity and determination." Designer Diane von Furstenberg recalls how she internalized a lifetime goal of "freedom to come and go as I please" from her mother.

But greatness, although easy to create, is also easy to destroy. As parents, we can make children into nothing, we can shrink their hearts, their ambitions with a cruel statement or two, especially if they are uncertain of their strengths. A teacher can have this effect, too, but not as profoundly as a parent. A parent who sees only the best happening for the child stirs that value in the atmosphere, so that the child benefits from it and internalizes the vision of himself as good, worthy, brilliant, loved, and "able to do anything." It can set the proper inner environment and category for all future goals-- and it is the future which is the magic territory of greatness.

Thinking Ahead:
From Intuition to Fruition

All the real part of your life has a real dream in it; some of the real dream part of you coming true. You know in advance when you are really following your life. These things are familiar because reality is here. Coming events cast light.

DOROTHY RICHARDSON

Great individuals often envision the future with almost the same clarity as the past and present. The German philosopher Ernst Bloch described the feeling of intuitive thinking as anticipation--a quality of human consciousness he defined as "dreaming ahead" or "dreaming forward." But this quality is more than just dreaming. It is either a vision of a not-yet-arrived future, or the creation of a possible and ultimately real future in the mind. This future vision is what leaders are required to create. Writes Henry Kissinger:

The dilemma of any statesman is that he can never be certain about the probable course of events. In reaching a decision, he must inevitably act on the basis of an intuition that is inherently unprovable. If he insists on certainty, he runs the danger of becoming a prisoner of events. His resolution must reside not in "facts" as commonly conceived but in his vision of the future.[17]

Seeing the future means seeing deeply into the laws of nature and tuning in at a subtle level to what is about to surface, seeing the full panorama, not just a section of it. The power one gains from this method of creation is enormous, but it is sometimes frightening to others who can't yet see it.

During the thirteenth century, Roger Bacon, a Franciscan friar, made discoveries far beyond what was currently known, using intuitive thinking and experimentation. His vision of what would come was crystal clear. He predicted the coming of automobiles, planes, suspension bridges, and power machinery. To his contemporaries, Bacon's knowledge appeared to be black magic; he was ordered to stop writing and teaching, and for years was confined to his monastery. We are quite a bit less superstitious today and will occasionally listen to our modern seers. We paid heed to the late Buckminster Fuller, who was perhaps our greatest Western futurist. He explained his ability to predict and create the future as follows:

> By means of becoming a deliberate comprehensivist, I have come in view of an enormous amount of information that has allowed me to make accurate projections of most of the big changes that have occurred in the past 50 years or so. . . . Because I'd deliberately got to living and thinking 50 years ahead on a comprehensive basis, I inadvertently got myself into a strange position. I began to live on that frontier and it was like any wave phenomenon: I was living where it was cresting and things happened to me long before they happened to the rest of society.[18]

But we all have Fuller's ability to think ahead. The ability to look into the future with any certainty is less mysterious when we recognize that the future itself is created in the present.

People can either live in the past, the present or the future. When we are unhappy in the present, we tend to live in the past. As we learn to trust ourselves, the present becomes more livable and we are freed from the bonds of the past. This is what has been said to be real freedom--to live fully in the present. Great people tend to live easily in the present, but are rarely afraid of, or unaware of, the future. They can live mentally in the future, not just in preparation for it, but really to see it and structure it. This is how they differ from most of us, because most people have very little understanding of how they create the future. No one plans to be ill or to have a war; it just happens. Without knowing why, we notice "bad things happening to good people." However, this may be because "good people" are sometimes unaware that they are using their thoughts to their own disadvantage. They are creating just what they *don't* want to happen.

"The world we create--the world of slums and telegrams and newspapers--is a kind of language of our inner wishes and thoughts," wrote poet Stephen Spender in *The Making of a Poem*. He suggested that "if the phenomena created by humanity are really like words in a language," we can choose whatever language we want to project and structure the future.

What is your language--what thoughts, words, and images do you want to use to create the world? To make such a choice, you must first be aware of what values you hold near and dear and what you wish to have happen in the future.

A study conducted at the Center for Social Policy at Stanford Research Institute (SRI) offers a description of this process by Fred Polak:

> Awareness of ideal values is the first step in the conscious
> creation of images of the future and therefore the creation of
> culture, for a value is by definition that which guides toward a
> "valued" future. . . . The rise and fall of images of the future
> precedes or accompanies the rise and fall of cultures. . . . In the
> end, the future may well be decided by the image which carries
> the greatest spiritual power.

Polak contends that intuition and inspiration are prerequisites for future thinking, providing not just the ability to visualize but actually to "envision" and thereby create the future.

The SRI study concludes: "It is your vision of your own future which will likely determine your life. An awareness of ideal values may be the first step in the conscious creation of the future."[19] Parents who want to protect their children from negative and unrewarding TV shows are instinctively aware that children are the most susceptible recipients of society's images. In fact, Harvard psychologist David McClelland reports that the stories adults tell children are the most significant source for the values a society upholds. Children grow up following what they believe are the desired values of their community and nation. If a child believes in a happy, uplifting future, she automatically starts to move in that direction in her thinking and behavior.

Images of the future are extremely powerful thoughts, and therefore become powerful determinants of cultural behavior. To create the best world possible, the SRI report stated that all future images of human life must include:

- a holistic understanding of life;
- an ecological ethic emphasizing life-in-nature and the oneness of humanity; and
- a self-realization ethic that places the highest value of all social institutions on self-development.[20]

According to Dr. Jonas Salk, "Wisdom is becoming the new criterion of fitness. . . . We are engaged in the process of selection by the decisions that we make to support certain ideas. It is important that we help people with those qualities of mind that are of universal value."[21] Salk's vision, which he calls "survival of the wisest," is that we join those great universal thinkers in imaging a perfect future, creating an age of happiness, fullness, and enlightenment. Doing anything else may only lead to a lesser life and possibly even to disaster.

We've seen how unfortunate futures are easily created. Once a student is labeled a loser within the school system, for example, he starts to behave like one. Conversely, research has demonstrated that when teachers hold high expectations of their students, this alone can cause an increase of twenty-five points in the students' I.Q. scores.

University of Georgia researcher Paul Torrance, who has studied classroom "miracles," has found that teachers who expect the most wonderful things from all their students, get them. His research indicates that because of this, children who are considered "hopeless, unteachable non-readers" become average or superior readers; those who have well-established vandalism patterns turn into productive altruists; the emotionally disturbed become outstanding achievers; the apathetic become enthusiastic; and those who have been labeled mentally retarded can move on to superior intellectual functioning and school achievement. And all because their teachers put attention on these happier possibilities.[22]

Similarly, with proper attention one can create "invincible health" in a sick body. Years ago, Dr. Morris Abrams, a well-known scholar and former president of Brandeis University, was told he had leukemia and six weeks to live. Despite a background in logic and scientific thinking, he refused to believe he would die. He structured his thinking in terms of healing and medical care, and overcame his disease. Norman Cousins writes of a similar experience in his compelling book *Anatomy of an Illness*. Nowadays, very ill patients everywhere frequently use this overall healing technique.

And while the value of proper attention in our individual lives is obvious, we have to reexamine our collective thinking along these lines, too. For example, images and predictions of the effects of nuclear war are meant to bring corrective action, but it is possible that in reality they may produce even more fear and negative thinking, which could contribute to further stress and tension within us all and inadvertently help create a future that none of us wants.

Today, most societal prophecy is "doomsday"-oriented, and we become so prepared for this belief that we feel odd if we *don't* believe it. Whereas we may be great optimists when it comes to our individual lives and those of our family and friends, the majority of us still accept a negative global future as a reality. The results of a recent survey conducted by *Newsweek* magazine showed that 51 percent of U.S. citizens "believe that it is likely or somewhat likely that U.S. hostilities will escalate into a third world war."[23] We have to ask ourselves if we are not reinforcing with our collective attention the possibility of such an undesirable future.

Perhaps because the news is generally "bad," we accustom ourselves to bad news being real and good news being of the sort they tell us at the end of the program, as a light joke to make us feel better. On a typical newscast, it has been estimated that for every five "bad" news items, we're allowed only one piece of "good" news. Now, what does that do to us? It means that our psychophysiology is exposed to five times more negativity than positivity. And how does it affect our thinking, our feelings, our activities? It simply creates a world outlook that *expects* unhappiness--negative becomes normal; the positive is only expected one fifth of the time. And if the books we read, the movies we see, the art we absorb are not fully in keeping with such expectations, they're not considered true, but merely fantasy--not in touch with the times. (Perhaps as a result of an overload of negativity, because it isn't really natural to feel constant negativity, many people fall into a habit of disengagement, so as to not be overshadowed by the harshness of what they are asked to take in. But the cut-off experience may continue into realms where they don't want to be "cut off," such as in relationships and in the growth of their creativity.)

Not only does disaster consciousness seem very unfavorable for collective mental health, the ultimate danger is that if enough people believe in disaster, that's what they'll get. Fortunately, however, we can learn to replace these images with those of a future we *do* want.

Futurist Alvin Toffler presents such a view. He writes:

> Man will become incomparably stronger, wiser and more perceptive. His body will become more harmonious, his movements more rhythmical, his voice more melodious. His ways of life will acquire a powerfully dramatic quality. The average man will attain the level of an Aristotle, of a Goethe, of a Marx.[24]

The individual images we want to create and live with will have to be the result of group agreement about the future. Our leaders will have to reflect this group image and help unfold our own vision of the future. Henry Kissinger observes that the task of the leader "is to get his people from where they are to where they have not been.

225

. . . Leaders must invoke an alchemy of great vision. Those leaders who do not are ultimately judged failures, even though they may be popular at the moment." Finding and expressing the most life-supporting and life-enhancing images will be the ultimate manifestation of greatness in our era.

Imaging a Great Future

If there were in the world today any large number of people who desired their own happiness more than they desired the unhappiness of others, we could have a paradise in a few years.

BERTRAND RUSSELL

Here is a four-step "thinking program" we can undertake in order to successfully image any future we want:

1. Clarity of Image: Our thinking process seems to depend on, and perhaps in the end is identical with, the ability to have a mental "image" of the world. It is a skill we can develop--the ability to keep something in mind when it is out of sight.

2. Continual Forward Thinking: "All progress," wrote Samuel Butler, "is based upon a universal, innate desire on the part of every organism to live beyond its income." Each of us thinking beyond our present accomplishments and circumstances to achieve something even greater could take us all where we want to go.

3. Flexibility: We need the ability to change our minds, or plans, and move quickly toward a more favorable and evolutionary activity. We can only grow by letting go of everything that holds us back in any way.

4. Desire for Immortality: Wrote Arthur Koestler, "Every writer's ambition should be to swap one hundred readers now for ten readers in ten years' time and one reader in one hundred years' time. . ." If what you are focusing on starts to be more satisfying to you, more loving toward and more responsible for others, then you will start to tap into your own immortality--to see yourself as the true creator not only of your own life, but of the world--both present and future.

With the above in mind, you will be able to think and image yourself into greatness. And in so doing, you will be participating in a collective societal imaging leading to greatness for us all.

In the following chapter, we'll see what more we might be able to do individually to guarantee the growth of this move to personal greatness.

7

❖

TECHNOLOGIES FOR DEVELOPING GREATNESS: FROM SILENCE TO ACTIVITY

Educating for Greatness: The Adult Prodigy

If it is possible to teach genius instead of merely hoping it will come along, the future will belong to the society that first discovers how.

EUGENE AYERS

Contrary to popular myth, talent does not automatically rise to the top, like cream in milk.

FRED M. HECHINGER

For he who knows the country gives the direction to him who asks the way.

NINTH MANDALA, *Rig Veda*

Greatness obviously doesn't occur all by itself. We can't just sit around and wait for it to hit us. We've seen that even though we have long understood that human development is virtually limitless, we have done very little to unfold greatness in ourselves and others. Until the nineteenth century, the dominant belief about greatness was based on the concept of the "born genius," that highly developed capabilities were for the most part genetically determined. Then we began to understand how significantly the learning environment stimulates brain function. As educator John Dewey wrote, "The purpose of education is to enable a person to come into possession of all his powers." By now it is clear that while the *origin* of some of our behavior can be traced to genetic (i.e., inherited) factors, the actual course of our development is primarily structured by the demands and opportunities of the inner and outer environments in order to unfold genetic possibilities. Still, the issue has remained--with all we understand about the importance of education, why haven't we been educated for greatness?

Because greatness enjoys higher-level physiological and psychological growth. Education would be most valuable if it provided *"better conditions"* for bringing about this growth. Therefore, we could ask: What do we really need to set the right conditions for greatness to occur?

Today, even though it's the first time in history that formal education is available throughout our entire life span, there is a considerable emphasis on being "realistic"; setting lesser, more easily achievable goals so as not to be up the creek later on. At colleges and universities, students are now said to prefer the practical courses, ones that were virtually ignored a decade ago. There's nothing inherently wrong with these choices; society seems to be supporting them at present, but what does realism really mean? Does it mean we adopt a smaller, less worthy personal outlook because the world is a static reality to which we respond, or do we expand because reality can be shaped to our desires?

If we believe psychologists like Jerome Bruner, the world is in no way static; rather, our ideas of the world transform it. We know that great people are more than passive observers. They seem to create their own realities. Others may live in an already created, prescribed world, but great individuals recognize that change is their own creation. They live, as we've learned, in a quantum world where what you want to happen, happens. And we now have ways to educate ourselves for this self-referral, lifelong creation.

However, before we explore the dynamics of such transformations, in order fully to accept our possibilities for personal greatness, we have one more greatness myth to dispel, and it's a big one: It presents greatness in the light of human suffering. Sad to say, the history of greatness has been unduly burdened with a negative portrait of great people. And this misunderstanding has promoted a psychological attitude that may diminish the entire evolutionary value of greatness for both the individual and society.

❖

"Creative Suffering": The Mistaken Mystique

As long as we insist on associating pain and achievement . . . every major accomplishment will be stuffed into a mold made of a mixture of Michelangelo's Sistine suffering, Beethoven's turmoil, and Van Gogh's distress. Needless to say, the farcically inflated depictions will subsequently be rehearsed everywhere by aspiring artists, writers, composers, musicians--and millionaires.

SRULLY BLOTNICK

We noted previously that until not so long ago, psychology had only studied greatness as an aberration--by looking at the unusual, trying to deduce what greatness is from isolated behaviors. In this way the psychology of greatness implied separateness. Great people were different from the rest of us. And the main difference seemed to be that they were crazy and we were not.

Somehow it seemed appropriate that Leonardo da Vinci was unhappy, that Beethoven was paranoid, that artist Paul Klee was schizophrenic, or that composer Robert Schumann was manic-depressive. Never mind that this information did nothing to help us gain a similar mastery of science, music or art, but actually distanced us further from the attributes of greatness. Years ago Dr. Havelock Ellis cited this psychological "diagnosis" as the *repeal* of genius:

It is a consolation to many . . . that Nietzsche went mad. No doubt also it was once a consolation to many that Socrates was poisoned, that Jesus was crucified, that Bruno was burnt. But hemlock and the cross and the stake proved sorry weapons against the might of ideas even in those days, and there is no reason to suppose that a doctor's certificate will be more effectual in our own.[1]

In addition to madness, it was also proposed that greatness actually required great suffering: In order truly to know the full range of the human condition and express this experience to others, one had to live the most miserable life. It was a romantic idea perhaps, but not a useful one. And yet even today, in a *New York Times* article, the unhappy, suicidal photographer Diane Arbus is honored less for her work than for her depression, and researchers reportedly continue to look for the association between genius and emotional illness.[2]

It's surprising that personal suffering has become associated at all with personal greatness. We know that many artists like Rembrandt had to work in severely impoverished circumstances (while other artists like Velasquez and Cezanne lived in comfort). But no one would affirm that great creativity arises because we have *physically* suffered; why then do we think we require *mental* anguish?

Peak creative experiences are certainly better understood as an *antidote* to suffering. As the German poet Heine wrote, "By creating I could recover; by creating I became healthy." Ballet dancer Suzanne Daley describes the "relief" from suffering in performance: "People who perform notice that even when everything is going wrong, it's a different world because you're performing . . . it's almost a relief to get to the theater. I think that's probably why people perform when they're sick or injured."[3]

We create *despite* anxiety and torment, not *because* of it. It is in their works that the greats seem to resolve their torments. Beethoven, wrote Selden Rodman, was a most extreme example of an artist completely unable to solve any of the problems of ordinary life. He was the ultimate "dropout" by the standards of his day. And yet although he had enormous personal problems:

All of them are solved in his music. . . . His music is the resolution of all these conflicts, and the projection of this encompassing, majestic acceptance and nobility. With the result, that Beethoven's music uniquely appeals, not only to the other musicians . . . but to the common man, who responds to the symphonies as no other composer has ever been able to reach them and touch them.[4]

According to a number of researchers, there may be more troubled life in creative people because of their more intense sensibilities associated with seeking larger dimensions of knowledge and experience. But it is also true that even though you may be depressed, if you can express yourself through your work, your sad as well as your happy feelings, that is a positive not a negative process. Says composer Aaron Copland:

> Too much depression will not result in a work of art because a work of art is an affirmative gesture. To compose, you have to feel that you are accomplishing something. If you feel you are accomplishing something, you won't feel so depressed. You may feel depressed, but it can't be so depressing that you can't move. No, I would say that people create in moments when they are elated about expressing their depression![5]

Similarly, writer Isaac B. Singer maintains:

> I would say that being very much depressed, being, let's say, in a real crisis of depression, is not conducive to one's writing, quite the opposite. I had, myself, a number of years in which I could not write. This was when I came to this country from Poland. . . . I wrote and rewrote, and nothing came out of it . . . a real depression can make a writer impotent.[6]

In his pioneering book entitled *The Neurotic Distortion of the Creative Process*, psychoanalyst Laurence Kubie challenged the conviction that psychological illness is necessary for creativity. He documented how automatic, repetitive response patterns serve only to inhibit the free, direct discovery and expression of the artist, rendering him like other neurotics, rigid and constricted. Playwright Jean Cocteau described this kind of experience: "In the midst of my work these symptoms grip me, forcing me to resist that which is pushing me along, involving me in some strange crippled style of writing, hindering me from saying what I would."[7]

Various research findings support the conclusion that if anxiety or stress is present, new associations and deeper integration of material are restricted and that "any increase in stress interferes with problem solving." Both children and adults are unable to be creative in frustrating, psychologically stressful situations: ". . . Anxiety-induced drive does not lead to . . . creative productiveness."[8]
Mathematician Morris Kline concludes:

> I would say the mind has to be very much alive and very free in its ability to make associations at the time that one is trying to solve a problem. If he is tired, for example, ideas do not present themselves. I would think a happy state of mind is far better than a depressed one. A depressed state affects one's willingness to think, let alone the ability to think. One can force oneself to work only on something that's more routine or that really was worked out before and needs revision.[9]

What, then, is the complete psychological portrait of greatness? We can't claim it forever crazy. We have to acknowledge that greatness is a more integrated reality because to do otherwise would certainly diminish its real value.

❖

Becoming Great: Another look at the Creative Personality

Creativity researcher Sidney Parnes tells the following story:

> A first grader had not yet learned to read or write except for a few numbers and letters. She found it difficult to remember the days when certain events were to take place in school. One day she came home to her parents and exclaimed, "We're going to have a party at school, and this time I won't forget the day--I have written it down." Her parents looked at her inquisitively, knowing that she couldn't write. When she eagerly opened her note, they saw merely the figures "22." They looked curiously at the little girl and asked, "You mean the 22nd?" The little girl answered, "What does '22nd' mean? My note means the party's on Tuesday."[10]

We know that children invent all the time, using what little symbolic knowledge they have to maximum advantage. And if we continue to be creative as adults, it's because, like children, we avoid getting locked into repetitive patterns of seeing the world. In other words, we continue to grow. And the growth is *integrated*, not one-sided. Dr. Frank X. Barron and his colleagues at the Institute for Personality Assessment and Research at the University of California have studied creative people for decades and found them to be energetic, independent, self-sufficient, mentally healthy and emotionally stable, intuitive, aware, open to experience, and able to integrate effectively.[11] Barron concludes that they are "individuals of unusual personal force" who create change in the world. Similarly, according to creativity researchers Paul Torrance and Laura K. Hall:

> These people seem to have a power that goes well beyond the usual criteria of expertness in their fields. . . . They seem able to give energy and inspiration to those with whom they come in contact. . . . This ability seems to be associated with compassion, intuition, friendliness, and happiness.[12]

Other major personality assessment studies of creative individuals have borne out these psychological descriptions. They have essentially concluded that creativity is a result of the full expression of psychological health and an integrated life. Like Terman's gifted children, who were physically as well as mentally healthier than their classmates, great creative persons function from a more supportive, more integrative basis in all aspects of their lives. Wrote psychologist Carl Rogers:

> When man's unique capacity of awareness is thus functioning freely and fully, we find . . . an organism able to achieve, through the remarkable integrative capacity of its central nervous system, a balanced, realistic, self-enhancing behavior as a result of all these elements of awareness.[13]

How can we then prepare ourselves for *this* kind of "realism," the kind that recognizes that the world is indeed our oyster and that we can be great? In other words, how do we overcome personal or societal limiting conditions?

As we've seen, the *experience* of greatness seems to be synonymous with psychophysiological "health," even if only momentary. Marghanita Laski reports that greatness is accompanied by feelings of "physical and mental well-being," wherein "harmony and satisfaction have replaced stress and dis-ease." The experience of creation occurs if and when the psychophysical energy that was previously used to maintain old patterns is freed to be applied in a fuller, more integrated way as a result of the natural tendency to progress towards higher levels of growth. This is what Maslow calls the innate drive toward self-actualization: "Capacities clamor to be used and cease their clamor only when they are used sufficiently." But he says, "We are generally afraid to become that which we can glimpse in our most perfect moments . . ." In *The Farther Reaches of Human Nature*, Maslow calls this fear of "something greater than yourself," "the Jonah Complex." Running away from "your fate" or what could be more positively regarded as one's own greatness is not uncommon. People who have the desire and the capabilities to lead bigger lives but won't take the chance are more unhappy than anyone. They worry about failure even before they engage in any action at all.

The first thing we have to do as adults is accept our own birthright to be great. And once this is acknowledged, we also need great self-images. We must feel "larger than life" if we are to behave in large ways. We need heroes, just as children do, whether we admit it or not. And even if it's a best friend or a spouse who believes in you, everyone has something to teach you about your own greatness. But we also need teachers, even in adulthood, who can put us directly on the track of greatness.

As teacher-author Bel Kaufman has pointed out, "The road less travelled is not necessarily the better road." Beethoven had his Czerny, Plato had his Socrates. Indeed, almost all greats, as we said, had some mentor or mentors in whom they could observe greatness at work. A teacher can teach through personal contact, through writings, through a painting, through a kind action. Any way we can, we learn to absorb the best lessons of the masters. Great teachers teach by enabling us to unfold what is already within us. Said the eminent piano teacher Nadia Boulanger, "Loving a child . . . is to bring out the best in him. . . . My role is above all to try and understand what he is, not what I am."[14] Teachers also provide us with models and kinds of outlooks that we can use to enhance our own growth and clarify our own values. We look for basic things, ways to grow and develop. And through this kind of education, we learn to call upon and enjoy the full orchestra within us.

Becoming Great: Learning to Learn

When I look at a row of little boys, I often wonder which of them it is who is hiddenly in touch with the enduring powers of the world, and how they will look forty years later. There seems to exist no key to these enigmas. The dunces of genius and the real dunces look very much alike; and the boys of brilliant promise cannot be prophetically classified.

JOHN JAY CHAPMAN, (JOHNNY APPLESEED)

On his way home from receiving the Nobel Prize in Stockholm, physicist Richard Feynman stopped by his old high school in suburban New York and looked up his I.Q. scores. To his delight, he found his I.Q. had been measured at around 125, above average but nothing spectacular. According to his wife, winning the Prize was "no big deal" for him, but winning it with a pretty ordinary I.Q. was something!

Greatness doesn't really have an "I.Q." Rather, it has a gift for learning. As we've seen, the human mind is infinitely flexible, becoming smaller or larger according to what we do with it. So how and what we learn is physiologically as well as mentally important for our growth to greatness. One of the best examples of a participant on this path to greatness was Abraham Lincoln. Even as a youth, he adored learning. Observed Lincoln's cousin Dennis Hanks:

Seems to me now I never seen Abe after he was 12 'at he didn't have a book some' ers 'round. He'd put a book inside his shirt an' fill his pants pockets with corn dodgers, an' go off to plow or hoe. When noon came he'd set down under a tree, an' read an' eat. An' when he come to the house at night, he'd tilt a cheer back by the chimbly, put his feet on the rung, an' set an' read. Like as not Abe'd eat his supper thar, takin' anything he could gnaw at an' read at the same time . . .

Aunt Sairy'd always said Abe was goin' to be a great man some day.

Lincoln's stepmother, Sarah Lincoln, recalled how her stepson clung to knowledge from every source:

> When old folks were at our house, he was a silent and attentive observer, never speaking or asking till they were gone, and then he must understand everything, even to the smallest thing, minutely and exactly. He would repeat it to himself again and again, sometimes in one form and another, and when it was fixed in his mind to suit him, never lost that fact or his understanding for it. He would hear sermons, come home, take the children out, get on a stump or log and almost repeat it word for word. His father made him quit sometimes.[15]

A recent study of 120 world-class artists, athletes, and scholars, conducted by Professor Benjamin Bloom and his colleagues at the University of Chicago, found that for talent to emerge, it has to be nurtured in the home and in school, and it demands intensive and continuous technical and emotional support. Bloom concluded that no matter what the initial characteristics (or gifts) of the individuals, unless there is proper encouragement and training, gifted youngsters don't generally achieve high accomplishments. "No one," he said, "reached the limits of learning in a talent field on his or her own."[16]

But when should encouragement begin? Just watch a baby try to figure out his environment, and you see how extremely fluid the intellect is. In the first few months following birth, the brain undergoes its most rapid growth. The senses of the newborn are already quite developed and can be easily stimulated to continue to grow and develop quickly. Consequently, babies who hear lively conversation around them and are engaged in family talk learn to speak sooner. We know that a baby learns even in the womb. She is already distinguishing her parents' voices. Also certain sounds and rhythms, such as the mother's heartbeat, produce beneficial effects. Learning may begin in the womb, but when does it end? As we saw in an earlier chapter, there is a great deal of emphasis on child development in our culture but not as much as may be desirable on adult development. Can what we learn after twenty-one ever produce as much growth as what we learned before. We need ways to promote such development, to foster creativity and learning throughout our lifetime. We need a technology of greatness.

For a start, we may want to know what procedures the greats

themselves use, if any, to shed their little selves and become larger. Did Wordsworth eat apples, did Florence Nightingale jog, did Napoleon accomplish his goals by sleeping only a few hours a night? And if we have any concerns about becoming great, could these be alleviated by experiencing for ourselves the naturalness, the ease, the effortlessness of greatness?

Becoming "Fit for Greatness": Successful Divers

. . . Each admirable genius is but a successful diver in that sea whose floor of pearls is all your own.

RALPH WALDO EMERSON

Suppose you live above an underground symphony hall but you don't know it. One day, a neighbor comes by and tells you to put your ear to the floor. All at once you hear beautiful music--the music has always been there, you may have been faintly aware of it, but you hadn't been listening to it. Getting in contact with that "floor of pearls," the unbounded field of life, is similar--you actually have to move toward it or you may never really know what it is. To contact our own floor of pearls, we all need to learn to become "successful divers."

As we've seen, this is a resource all great people seem to enjoy--a place where they can "go mentally" for ideas. Obviously, we all want to know how to experience perfect, flowing, unrestricted creativity, and how the great creators captured *their* moments of insight. But unfortunately, most people, including the greats, don't always know how their experiences of greatness arise.

We concluded earlier that most great individuals have had to rely on isolated moments of creative insight rather than on sustained access to a field of creativity. And these moments seem to come at the most unlikely times. There is, for example, the story of the chemist Kekulé who discovered the chemical bonding of the benzene ring by dreaming of a snake with its tail in its mouth. Mathematician Henri

Poincaré's "moment" occurred while he was getting on the bus; Archimedes experienced his in his bath; Aquinas was eating dinner when he had one of his great insights. Einstein reported that "ideas came to him so suddenly while he was shaving that he had to shave carefully to avoid cutting himself with surprise."

Great people usually describe these revelatory experiences with great clarity and precision: They are often able to recall the exact circumstances under which the idea or vision came because they experienced a heightened awareness during those moments. But unfortunately, much research into human greatness has focused on the *circumstances*, on the form--whether dream or daydream or "sudden idea"--in which a particular discovery was made, not on the kind of awareness that accompanied them. One physicist described the settings for these famous insights as the three "Bs": the bus, the bath, and the bed, "where the great discoveries are made in our science."

But these descriptive circumstances obviously tell us nothing about how we can have such experiences, or even how those who have had them can repeat them. Forever climbing aboard buses may not do it. We need to understand the actual process.

The Creativity Components of Greatness

> It often happens that you have no success at all with a problem; you work very hard, yet without finding anything. But when you come back to the problem after a night's rest, or a few days' interruption, a bright idea appears and you solve the problem easily.
>
> GEORGE POLYA

In 1926 when J.R.R. Tolkien was a professor at Oxford, he was reading a student's thesis. One page, for some reason, had been left blank, so he picked up his pen and wrote: "In a hole in the ground there lived a hobbit." According to Tolkien, his literary life was launched by the line that "just popped into my head."

"Popping into one's head" is the way the birth of ideas has traditionally been described. The "creative process" has long been viewed as mysterious and unpredictable. Although there are hundreds of definitions available, the mechanics of the process have eluded scientific theory.

Still, some valuable overall descriptions have emerged. In the same year that Tolkien wrote the first line of *The Hobbit*, a four-step model of the creative process was developed by G. Wallas in the the following sequence: preparation (a period of acquiring knowledge and cognitive skills); incubation ("off-consciousness," "mind resting," inattention); illumination ("Aha!," insight, the "flash" of past knowledge meeting present awareness); and evaluation (verification and application). Wallas's model has proven to be an enduring description of the various aspects of the creative process, and it is worth looking at more closely.

Preparation is one's accumulated knowledge and experience up to the instant of new creative insight. Obviously, moments of creation are derived from prior knowledge and experience. To have a "physics" insight, you need a "physics" preparation. To use language effectively, you need a large data base of words. Shakespeare, for example, had a vocabulary of fifteen thousand words, five times the vocabulary of his day. Dr. Herbert Simon, a Nobel Prize recipient in the field of artificial intelligence, believes that the masters of chess have much more highly developed long-term chess memories, and that these memories turn into subconsciously remembered patterns, or what Simon calls chess "vocabularies." While the class A player may have a vocabulary of around two thousand patterns, the chess master has a vocabulary of around fifty thousand patterns. Similarly, all of us have some kind of pattern vocabularies--Simon calls them "old friends"--that channel our creativity and prepare us for our great moments. Preparation is thus an intellectual condition that influences the kind rather than the quality of the creative experience.

The last step of the creative process--evaluation--is more or less a procedure of analysis and verification that gives direction to activity, according value and directing thoughts and ideas into the proper channels of behavior toward accomplishment. These two "rational" steps--preparation and evaluation--are generally taught through traditional school education.

The two "intuitive" middle steps of Wallas's model--incubation and illumination--have become the principal focus of exploration in developing technologies to enhance the creative process. The need for a period of incubation is almost universally recognized. This process was understood by the ancient playwright Aristophanes, who said, "If you strike upon a thought that baffles you, break off from that entanglement and try another, so shall your wits be fresh to start again." Researcher Marghanita Laski writes that all powerful creative experiences "begin by being, to no matter how slight a degree, withdrawal ones."

Thus, incubation is also called "the rest hypothesis": As we saw, research on perception demonstrates that resting the mind breaks lazy, fixed patterns of thinking, eliminates "functional fixedness," creates new solutions, and allows the brain the opportunity for new neural connections. The mind is described as being at rest but also awake and alert, seeming to operate from a different level of consciousness than the usual focused attention of ordinary thought processes. It is a state, said the painter Cézanne, in which we are "seeing innocently." Kubie's "preconscious," Ghiselin's "preconfigurative consciousness," Rugg's "transliminal mind," and Thurstone's "prefocal activity" are among the psychological descriptions offered for this "aware" silence. Rugg speaks of it in the Eastern sense of a mood of "letting things happen," taking things as they come. It can be a state "wherein perception and understanding themselves are absent," where "the intuitive mood of inside identification is established."

It is from this stage of incubation that the creative "flash"--the illumination--is said to be born. Bertrand Russell gives this description of it: "[The problem] would germinate underground until, suddenly, the solution emerged with blinding clarity, so that it only remained to write down what had appeared as if in a revelation." We become aware of its inevitability when, according to Wallas, "our fringe-consciousness of an associated train is in the state of rising consciousness which indicates that the fully conscious flash of success is coming."[17] In other words, we know we're about to get it. And it results in the "'Aha!" experience.

Sometimes the incubation and illumination phases are so deeply intertwined that they are not felt as distinct but rather as a functioning creative unit. Singer-composer Lionel Richie experiences it as "a radio that is constantly playing in my head. I get the music and the melody at the same time. The station just turns on and I'm listening. . . . The words are a little muffled, that's the only problem."

Inventor Nikola Tesla described his experiences in detail in an effort to teach others his technique:

> After experiencing a desire to invent a particular thing, I may go on for months or years with the idea in the back of my head. When I feel like it, I roam around in my imagination and think about the problem without any deliberate concentration.
>
> Then follows a period of direct effort. I choose carefully the possible solutions of the problem I am considering, and gradually center my mind on a narrowed field of investigation. Now, when I am deliberately thinking of the problem in its specific features, I may begin to feel that I am going to get the solution. And the wonderful thing is, that if I do feel this way, then I know I have really solved the problem and shall get what I am after.
>
> The feeling is as convincing to me as though I already had solved it. I have come to the conclusion that at this stage the actual solution is in my mind subconsciously, though it may be a long time before I am aware of it consciously.
>
> Before I put a sketch on paper, the whole idea is worked out mentally. In my mind I change the construction, make improvements, and even operate the device. Without ever having drawn a sketch I can give the measurements of all parts to workmen, and when completed all these parts will fit, just as certainly as though I had made the actual drawings. It is immaterial to me whether I run my machine in my mind or test it in my shop.
>
> The inventions I have conceived in this way have always worked. In thirty years there has not been a single exception. My first electric motor, the vacuum wireless light, my turbine engine and many other devices have all been developed in exactly this way.[18]

We have to conclude that Tesla was in easy rapport with a tremendous resource of inner creativity. He depended on his prodigious memory to bring his inventions from his mind into his laboratory. He had a remarkable ability to keep track of even the smallest detail of each phase of every project. In an effort to teach this capability to his staff, he would not permit them to take their finished drawings to the shop; he made them destroy the drawings and work from memory. He believed that this ability was achievable in everyone if they would just make the effort. Unfortunately, he was not as good a teacher as he was an inventor, and he didn't offer a way to improve the memory capacities of his staff members so that they, too, could actualize such abilities in themselves. According to the "rest hypothesis," the mind's ability to attend to itself must be improved. If we are not a Tesla, this requires some deeper kind of learning or some specific technique.

Having acknowledged the need for incubation leading to illumination, researchers have concluded that of all the inner supports needed for greatness, the keeping of an open mind, a mind "free and relaxed," is primary. As creativity researcher Brewster Ghiselin concluded, "To clear the mind for creative action, something more positive than relaxation and less restricted than voluntary diversion is required."

It is very encouraging to look at all the good things available today for self-improvement. But it is also confusing. What techniques can really prepare us for greatness?

Mental Technologies for Greatness

About thirty or forty years ago, specific mental techniques for becoming more intellectually productive and more creative were advanced in education and business. These methods--notably "brainstorming," developed by Alex Osborn, and "synectics," developed by William J. J. Gordon--were actually problem-solving techniques. Brainstorming required a small group of people (ideally, seven) to share as many ideas as possible without self- or group-editing or criticism. The technique was partly based on J. P. Guilford's divergent-thinking research, which indicated that the more ideas one brought out, the more likely that one or two would be good ones. By coming up with fifty solutions to a problem instead of just a few, we would be considered more creative. However, this view is somewhat limited because people with developed intuition tend not to brainstorm. They don't need to; they filter out all irrelevant material prior to the decision-making process. The ability to use the intuitive sense is thus the fulfillment of the need for brainstorming: The solution presents itself automatically and so negates the necessity for the decision! Still, until the intuitive skills are developed, brainstorming has proven to be a helpful technique that continues to be in widespread use.

As Aristotle observed, "Metaphor is the special mark of genius, for the power of making a good metaphor is the power of recognizing likeness." Synectics also called for generating new ideas, but used the tool of metaphor to structure the idea-making session with exercises to make "the familiar strange" and "the strange familiar." The purpose was to break mental sets or boundaries, to induce the kind of thinking by analogy often used by great thinkers as a primary means of developing new insights through familiar ideas. William James had found that creativity is generally accompanied by an "ability for 'similarity association' to an extreme degree"--that is, the ability to think in analogies, a skill that synectics develops well.

Currently, ways to unfold greatness have been promoted through the use of attitudinal techniques, which rest on the proposition that greatness can be nurtured with the right attitude--by maintaining a *desire* to be great. Today's popular success-oriented courses were started fifty years ago when they were originally developed by Dale Carnegie, Napoleon Hill, and Dr. Norman Vincent Peale. They help people establish a framework for success based on goal-setting, optimistic attitudes, positive thinking, and positive group dynamics. They attempt to re-orient our mental gears, and there is little doubt that these techniques help in some ways, at least to give good direction.

Another available mental technology is visualization, which seems to work if you're good at it. Author Robert Louis Stevenson, for example, used a visualization technique for his writing; he had a cast of characters whom he called "Brownies" who would act out his stories for him mentally. There are also affirmation techniques, verbal visualizations, saying things to yourself like "I will win the award," "I am a prosperous, successful person" as ways to focus on a "mindset" that moves you toward your goals. Such techniques aim to develop a clear mental construct in order to create a reality of one's own choosing.

These thought-changing techniques do work to some extent. But, as we concluded in Chapter Five, what they can't seem to do is change your *physiology* to any significant degree. Telling yourself you want to change is a good first attitudinal step, but ultimately it requires a more basic physiological approach. To use a modern analogy, you may have the correct software but not the proper hardware. And no amount of software instruction can change it. Stevenson's Brownies came from somewhere. You have to use more brain to get more ideas and more energy. To break old habits, you have to tap the *neural* level of development.

❖

The Need for a Mind-Body Technique

As we've seen, being great requires a physiology that allows us to support greatness fully in our thoughts, ideas, and activities. If we can use more than 1 percent of our full physiological potential, we can solve more than 1 percent of our problems!

It is clear that creativity is most fluid at certain times, when the integration between the workings of the mind and body is most complete. Therefore, a technique for perfecting our physiology, and on that basis our thoughts and activities, must also be a physical tool that can change the functioning of the body to support powerful shifts in awareness, great moments of creation, permanently.

It has been known for centuries that greatness depends on the cooperative, interdependent growth of mind, body, and spirit. Plato, for example, attempted to establish one of the first Western educational mind-body programs for greatness. He outlined a systematic course to gain direct knowledge of that which underlies all mental energy and awareness--what he called the "Good." In order to experience the Good, he said, mind and body would have to be developed in an integrated manner. He suggested that the first two or three years of school be devoted to gymnastics and music in order to tune the body and senses. The next ten years would be spent in the study of mathematics to develop the mind. Then, five years of study of philosophy, which would be followed by fifteen years of giving oneself to society through public service before returning to the philosophical quest. In this way he hoped the student would have achieved a balanced integration of body, mind, and heart.

When we speak of a technology for structuring all aspects of great-ness--physical, mental, emotional--there are two equally important directions in which to move: "in" and "out." We need to culture the ability to go within, to sink into silence through deep rest, and we need to set out goals for dynamic action. In doing so, we learn how to activate the full resources of the brain, by letting it rest and by improving its ability to direct activity.

Locating Silence

> Objects around are perceived, and from them the individual
> proceeds to the contemplation of his own inner being . . . then
> inactive meditation is quitted for activity; by the close of the
> day, man has erected a building from his own inner sun.

G. W. F. HEGEL

> Purity and stillness are the correct principles for mankind.

LAO-TZU

Our ability to experience life at its deepest comes from being able to access a silent basis for living. Silence is indeed golden in that it exists as a profound source of creativity verifiable by all of us. Ac-cording to research undertaken by psychologist Barry Ruback and his associates, you can get more ideas by being quiet than by talking. It's the silence *before and after* talking that counts. So all good brain-storming sessions really begin and end in silence.

By listening to what one writer calls "the voice of the silence," one starts to hear one's own true voice beyond all the language, chatter, noise, and musical offerings of the day. This attunement to silence is said to be an attunement to nature's voice--to an eternal means of communication, a unifying language so true, so direct, as to be understood easily by all humanity. Wrote T. S. Eliot:

> Words, after speech, reach
> Into the silence. Only by the form, the pattern

Can words or music reach
The stillness, as a Chinese jar still
Moves perpetually in its stillness.[19]

Take away a musician's orchestra, he will still play a single instrument. Take away the instrument, he sings or whistles. Take away his ability to sing or whistle, he still hears music. And take away his ability to hear, he can still hear music in his head. It's apparent that silence is lively. Without pen, paper or speech, we can still think. And without even a thought, we still experience lively silence itself. This is because silence is also active. Indeed, it is the source of all activity. Into this silence come a poet's images. As Wordsworth understood it: "They flash upon the inward eye which is the bliss of solitude."

The great religious seekers have long recognized the need to contact silence. Because this silence is blissful, suggested Thomas à Kempis, "the great holy men where they might, fled men's fellowship and chose to live with God in secret places." But according to Dr. Albert Schweitzer, "It is not necessary to go off on a tour of great cathedrals in order to find the Diety. Look within. You have to sit still to do it." And as Thomas Merton reminds us:

> The contemplative has nothing to tell you except to reassure you
> that if you dare to penetrate into your own silence . . . then you
> will truly recover the capacity to understand what is beyond
> words and beyond explanations.

In Psalm 23 the technique of becoming quiet is taught: "The Lord is my shepherd; I shall not want. He maketh me to lie down in green pastures: he leadeth me beside the still waters." Then, as a result, "He restoreth my soul."

We all know the expressions "The earth stood still" or "My heart stood still." The stillness describes what lovers feel when they reach each other on that silent level of love. What happens when one has either brief or sustained contact with this silent field? It becomes very evident that this is the secret place where greatness is structured.

But because silence is also apparent in a finely functioning physiology, people who are aware of it can hear it and see it even in the midst of dynamic activity. They use it as the basis for their work. Contact with it, observed composer Johannes Brahms, is "a wonderful and awe-inspiring experience." He continued, "Very few human beings ever come into that realization, and that is why there are so few great composers or creative geniuses in any line of endeavor. . . . The term subconscious is a very inadequate appellation for such an extraordinarily powerful state of mind. . . . Superconscious would be a better term."

This crystal-clear silence is traditionally the setting in which the artist experiences her own process of creation. The deeper the inner quietness, the more perfectly and precisely the vision is realized. As novelist Franz Kafka wrote:

> There is no need to leave the house. Stay at your desk and listen. Don't even listen, just wait. Don't even wait, be perfectly still and alone. The world will unmask itself to you, it can't do otherwise. It will rise before you in raptures.

Adds Brewster Ghiselin, in *The Creative Process*, "Silence is . . . sustaining, not an emptiness. It is a substantial profundity of being." The resource of creativity therefore lies in this settled, silent state. Without it, there is no natural experience of one's inner life to call upon--no ground state of discovery.

Just how real is this silence? Can we locate it and actually measure it? According to recent findings by geneticists, this is almost possible. They have discovered the "silent regions of the gene"; "the [silence] between those pieces of information is needed to manufacture a protein." This discovery is important because it informs us that *silence is structured into the very basis of life*--into the genetic material itself.

The laws of nature enable every seed to have precise knowledge of when to sprout and under what circumstances. DNA is the human blueprint for "sprouting." It's fascinating to know that not only is silence in genetic material interlaced with information, but, according to anthropologist Paul Bohannan, "it seems that the silent regions of the gene sometimes speed up, and sometimes complicate the protein formation." It appears, then, that the silent regions must also be active. It is not fully known what these genetic silences do. "It may turn out," observes Bohannan, "that the silent spaces of the gene hold the key to some of the intricacies of genetic structure, or even a new science. [So] the silent spaces of the culture are the cradle of our future."[20]

How We Use Silence

There is only one necessary plan--the plan of nature. We must live according to natural laws, and by virtue of the power which comes from concentrating upon their manifestation in the individual mind . . . by attending to what is within.

HERBERT READ

Imagine you are an automotive engineer designing a new car. To do so, you have to evaluate the needs of the individual driver and of society in general, environmental needs, governmental regulations, the latest technological possibilities pertaining to fuel, structural materials, etc. You must estimate the costs, know how other cars--the competition--have been built and the aesthetic taste of the car-buying public. Then you must put all that information together. The success of the car you ultimately design will depend on how many pieces of information you can take in, how clearly you have stored them, and how well you use them. Since it is the depth and integrity of your vision that will project that car onto the road, how do you go about designing it?

All these pieces of information will have to interact with each other and sort themselves out in the silence of your mind. In this quietness each new possibility opens a new door, is tested against other possibilities, and eventually all the useful thoughts are included and organized most efficiently and effectively. Then you say, "Eureka!" The whole process may take a single moment or it may take months of continually storing, sifting, and exploring. But it is a spontaneous process . . . it can't be forced; it has to be effortless. All you can do is be as alert as possible. If you start to interfere with this "in" and "out" flow in some way, you might miss a vital connection. You have to keep in mind the whole project at all times even while looking at the parts.

Each of us operates more or less in this way in everything we do. We take a thought (or an inspiration, a vision, an idea for something, a feeling) and make it happen "on the outside." For maximum success what is needed is: (1) a large, comprehensive vision of where the thought is going; (2) the ability to focus on it every step of the way until it is realized to our satisfaction; and (3) continued contact with the field of silence.

When silence and activity meet, this is a most powerful combination for greatness. Activity based in silence is a principle of all good business negotiations. According to the most successful sales people, it is the silence that sells, not the pushing, the forcing of "the close." The "yes" comes from silence--the "yes" is the fullest, most unrestricted aspect of the buyer.

If you observe great people, you see they have a great deal of inner silence. *Tonight Show* host Johnny Carson, for example, after a quarter of a century of doing the same show, is still successful primarily because he is alert yet quietly understated, and that quality seems to have more long-lasting power than surface flash. The audience laughter comes from their experience of this field of silence. First, there's the story, then the pause, the silence, then the punch line. This is what's called "timing." Carson has it; Jack Benny certainly had it: the deeper the silence, the greater the contrast when the punch line comes--or when the music stops at the end of the performance and we experience the audible silence. In this way music makes us aware of our own silence--and what may be the very essence of our own nature. Music reminds us, says violinist Yehudi Menuhin, that "there is something constant in ourselves . . ."

Silence is also a basic component of true education. With a great teacher, silence prompts you to ask questions. It allows a student to attune his or her thinking to the teacher's greatness. A teacher uses silence, knowing that it is within its flow that knowledge is most powerful. Indeed, in every field we can become aware that deep silence dominates no matter what is going on "on the surface." If one is able to be in silence, then the local environment telescopes backward and more universal values dominate.

Anthropologist Edward Hall studied all the behaviors that occur silently in various cultures: the distance we maintain with others as we relate to them, how we move physically forward and backward, according to our traditions--the ways we meet in silence. Silence can mean avoidance, it can mean fullness, it can mean fear, and of course it can be the greatest expression of love, the universal language of deep, direct communication. In any case the quiet levels of experience seem generally to be the most powerful. If someone yells, "I love you!" how does that feel, compared to hearing it whispered?

In *The Language of Silence*, Alan Boone describes how a native of the African jungle taught him about silence as the ultimate field of communication:

> My newly acquired friend had lived in the jungle for over forty years. During this time he had mastered, to a superlative degree, the science and art of right relations. As a result, he could instantly establish silent good correspondence with every living thing he met . . .
>
> I managed to discover his "magic secret." When he and a wild animal, for instance, came into visual contact with each other for the first time, they would both instantly stop and become as motionless as statues. Then they looked across at each other with almost expressionless faces. For the conventional observer it would be a dramatic and shivery experience--one in which he would wonder which of them would do the most deadly damage to the other.
>
> But neither bodily damage nor any killing would result from that unexpected meeting between those two supposedly implacable enemies. Instead, it would be the beginning of a swift balance in inner as well as outer relations.[21]

As we learn to listen to silence and as we learn to listen to life underneath it, we learn to appreciate our own greatness. We stop listening only to the stereo and start to hear our own internal music. Or words. Or see our own pictures. Or experience our own most loving, most full selves. Dag Hammarskjöld called this contact with silence the *point of rest* "at the center of our being." There, he wrote:

> We encounter a world where all things are at rest in the same way. Then a tree becomes a mystery, a cloud a revelation, each man a cosmos of whose riches we can only catch glimpses. . . .

It opens to us a book in which we never get beyond the first syllable.[22]

Since the most powerful aspect of life is not outside us but inside, the ability to "listen in," to be perfectly subjective yet not complicated and "noisy" in our thinking is a helpful way to get to our true nature. In his *Star Wars* trilogy, film maker George Lukas called it "The Force"--the most pervasive, powerful, yet hidden aspect of each of us. Only, we as individuals must be in touch with it. And once we are in touch with it, we have no choice *but* to become great-- we've opened ourselves to the source of greatness.

A Technology for Structuring Greatness Through Meditation

Teach us to sit still.

T. S. ELIOT

"I require quiet and myself to myself more than any man when I write," observed Tennyson. The need for silence is apparent to most great men and women and yet, although learning to "sit still" is a matter of necessity for greatness, how to experience it is a different matter. Writer Flannery O'Connor would go into her writing room for four hours every morning and not be bothered at all if she came out without getting a syllable onto the page. "I go in every day," she explained, "because if any idea comes between eight and noon, I'm there all set for it."

This is actually a technique taught by success experts, and it is known as "sitting for ideas." Every day one sits quietly for a certain time period without being pressured. However, this purposeful sitting must be useful and efficient; without settling down physically *and* mentally, it's often more a waste of time to keep waiting for a good idea.

Great moments, as we've seen, come when awareness seems to

expand--this has been described as both a heightening and a unification of experience--when we experience an entirely different state of consciousness or awareness. What a different state of awareness means is that we are functioning in a physiologically different manner. If we are to experience the subtlest values of our own inner nature, our own silence, we need to change our physiology easily and effectively in a long-term way. Mental silence accompanies deep physical rest.

Contemporary mythologist Joseph Campbell says that when we regain touch with the permanent silence within us, we lose our fear of death: "That's why there's such a movement now towards meditation," he observes. Norman Cousins reminds us how "it took a serious illness to get me to put meditation ahead of mobility." Often people who have gone through a severe physical trauma learn this. Of course, we do not have to be seriously ill to become aware of the need to go within. In fact, it seems more a matter of regaining what we once had rather than creating a new structure.

There are a number of technologies, methodologies, and programs that have been developed to restructure the physiological and psychological components of development. From biofeedback to Rolfing to visualization to a healthy diet, so many good ways to enhance our mind-body integration and unfold our greatness are available now. But as we've seen, a procedure that allows us to experience silence is also necessary, something even more settling than sitting in quiet contemplation. And nothing I have found comes closer to a genuinely effective technology for becoming great than the Transcendental Meditation (TM) program, which has been available now for nearly thirty years.

The TM technique is both very old and very new. Its origins are very old, but it is very new in its availability and in its potential contribution to the history of greatness. For the first time, repeatable, regular experiences of "great moments" are possible for everyone, not just for the precious few. And, as corroborated by extensive research, TM offers the nearest thing to a failproof method by which an individual can cultivate a more refined physiology, expand his or her thinking awareness, and experience a taste of a reality known in the past only to the greats. Yet because greatness ought to be available to everyone, perhaps the most noteworthy aspect of the TM technique is that it works for everyone: Anyone who can think can meditate.

We've seen that in order to experience the depth of inner silence, one would need an impediment-free nervous system so all thoughts and activities would be as free to be as "awake" as possible. A technique like TM would be necessary for changing our physiology and maximizing our creativity, brain function, and stress reduction so as to set up ideal conditions for greatness. Because the TM program has been available worldwide for decades, a very large collection of experimental research on higher states of consciousness has accumulated on evaluating its short- and long-term effects, both during the practice itself and in daily activity. The research results suggest that TM does indeed create beneficial physical, mental, and even social conditions for greatness.[23]

The data include a very important finding: a biological definition of silence, a psychophysiological description of the process of allowing one's awareness to settle down into complete, thought-free silence, to "awareness of itself." Such a correspondence between mind and body is demonstrated during the practice of TM by respiratory rates that are lower than those normally achieved in deep sleep. During these periods of spontaneously quiet respiration, meditating subjects report such experiences as "Everything feels synchronous and complete in that state--the mind stops thinking, the breath is very light, the body seems to stop, yet awareness is full."[24]

Overall, the research conclusions indicate that the integrated complex of psychophysiological changes taking place automatically during the practice of TM is generally consistent with a major change in the nervous system toward a permanent state of higher development, of maintaining silence along with activity. Neuroscientist Alaric Arenander describes the mechanics of TM as the process of the mind orienting itself to new physiological states. The nervous system starts to synthesize the rest and activity systems of the brain; the EEG picture of brain waves during the practice of TM is unlike any other state of consciousness in that it combines both deep rest *and* complete alertness.

As is well known, the Transcendental Meditation technique is the contribution of Maharishi Mahesh Yogi, who has long been considered a master in the Vedic tradition. What Maharishi originally discovered and what he has been able to teach others are the dynamics, or principles, of how to unfold the growth of consciousness. He outlines these principles as follows:

1. The natural tendency of the mind is to expand its boundaries.
2. The attention of the mind is spontaneously attracted toward a field of greater and greater enjoyment at the finer levels of thought.
3. The technique of Transcendental Meditation is natural and effortless, unlike rigid control techniques, thus enabling the mind easily to experience the field of pure, silent, unbounded consciousness.[25]

Reaching or attaining a state of pure consciousness is structured through a simple daily practice (twenty minutes, twice a day) that directs the attention inward and allows the mind and body to settle down. Research on the effects of TM indicates there is a significant reduction in oxygen consumption, in the breath and heart rate, and in lactate concentration, along with other metabolic and autonomic indicators of a settled physiology.

While these physical effects are occurring during TM, awareness becomes less and less directed and, as the energy used in directing thought is decreased, boundaries dissolve, the levels of physiological excitation are reduced, and awareness itself appears to expand. Then one arrives at that state of perfect rest, which Maharishi calls "pure consciousness," the state of least excitation of consciousness, or the unbounded level of reality. We could also say it is the personally experienced underlying field of silence.

This settling down to the experience of pure consciousness, pure silence, is the goal of all forms of meditation. What makes the TM technique unique is that it is easy to learn, effortless, and natural, giving immediate results that are repeatable, consistent, and long-lasting. This happens because TM uses the natural tendency of one's attention to go to more "charming" levels of thought; the mind is said to settle down spontaneously to its own nature, which is described as blissful. (And in my own experience, I find that the daily practice of TM is indeed blissful.)

Because this state of pure consciousness is believed to be the nature of consciousness itself--and all mental activity is understood to be excitations of that basic state--Maharishi describes pure consciousness as the "source of thought." As we've seen, because of the high noise level characteristic of most everyday perception and thinking, this source of thought, and its more subtle values or fine impulses, are ordinarily not experienced. With the TM technique, you are able to experience a thought in its more subtle states--states of lower noise, we could say--until the faintest thought impulse is left behind and you experience the silence that both underlies and lies between thoughts; you actually experience that state of consciousness that underlies all thinking. As one's awareness emerges from this state, the entire process of thinking has been renewed from its source, and more profound and creative thought inevitably follows, along with increased clarity of perception and intuition. So, rather than becoming reclusive and withdrawn from practicing TM, you actually end up participating more fully in the world around you. As Nobel physicist Brian Josephson explains:

> I think Transcendental Meditation has enabled me to use intuition effectively to a much higher degree than I used to be able to. . . . I had some good experiences with [it] from the very start. It was as if, instead of being immersed in a kind of mental fog--immersed in my own thoughts--I suddenly became aware of the outside world.[26]

What TM seems to do is enable us to access the deeper, more insightful levels of consciousness and ultimately integrate them with the more localized boundaries of everyday activity. Over time, the thinking processes gradually enjoy a greater ability to attend to both surface and depth with equal ease. Clear, logical thinking begins to join easily with more fluid idea-making.

Another way to understand these effects is in terms of reducing physical stress. As the automatic mental process that occurs during TM settles the mind to more comprehensive levels of thought, the underlying stress in the nervous system is removed without effort. And as a result of the reduction and removal of stress, as a large number of research studies on the effects of TM have documented, there is a wide range of physical, mental, and emotional benefits--

from normalized blood pressure to increased ego strength. Thus, the integrated psychophysiological state needed to support moments of greatness becomes stabilized.

These results occur because every state of mind produces a corresponding physical manifestation in the body. As stress is released from the nervous system, the mind is freed from such physiological restriction. Thus, to the degree that these more subtle mental processes are unencumbered by the effects of stress, what is known as incubation, or an effortless waiting period prior to having a great thought, becomes more a matter of choice; creative thought therefore becomes a virtually continuous experience, based on a stress-free nervous system, not merely a stage in an occasionally recurring process.

Not surprisingly, comparisons of the results of practicing TM and the reports of great creators suggest that the technique produces the relevant experience and is therefore most likely also to enliven the automatic mechanisms involved in spontaneous periods of peak creativity, happiness, and pleasure.

Thus, individuals who practice TM report experiences similar to those such researchers as William James, Marghanita Laski, and Brewster Ghiselin have described as "great moments." These moments are also experienced as unbounded, free of content, and effortless. For example, one meditator found that "the experience was very blissful, superclear--it was infinite correlation, because I found that I was infinite, unbounded . . ." Another reported: "The predominant experience in meditation was a deep, expansive silence, stable and immovable in its character, with thoughts proceeding on the surface. . . . It seemed as if there was no coming or going, only absolute pure consciousness moving within and for itself."[27]

Based on Vedic principles that originated five thousand years ago, Maharishi has recently synthesized a description of the behavior of consciousness with the latest discoveries in the physics of the unified field. As we discussed before, quantum physics demonstrates that there is a level of material existence that is truly unbounded, not concrete. Physicists recognize that the different objects we perceive are actually, at subtler levels of existence, undifferentiated energy. At their most basic level, they exist as part of a single unified field of nature out of which all space, time, and matter are structured. Similarly, according to Maharishi, although our perceptions and thoughts are characterized by specific boundaries, the more subtle levels of thought are more unbounded; so, as the mind experiences subtler levels, it becomes less bound, less localized until consciousness itself becomes infinite. This undifferentiated field is the silence we experience inside. And even though we may think that our minds and thoughts and images are nonmaterial, they, too, are just wave forms resonating at different frequencies, manifesting from that field.

Accordingly, the TM technique has been incorporated into what is called the "Maharishi Technology of the Unified Field." This is a subjective approach to experiencing and understanding the unified field of consciousness, which, in Maharishi's words, "identifies the conscious mind with the unified field, rendering all thought and action spontaneously in accord with natural law. . . . Since the unified field is basic to all other levels of natural law, experiencing this field brings the advantage of the infinite creativity and organizing power of all the laws of nature to any individual . . ."

The full contribution of the Maharishi Technology of the Unified Field will no doubt be seen from many other perspectives in the future. For now, however, it can be simply evaluated as proof of the ability of everyone to experience a more refined physiology, leading to higher states of consciousness, as well as highly effective overall technology to access the unified field--and thus our own personal resource of greatness--at will.

Squeezing Silence into Action: Unboundedness into the Boundaries

Now, let's look more closely at the "outward" phase of structuring greatness. We've seen how silence can be cultivated by using a technique that taps greatness within each of us, and that with daily practice, the powerful field of silence can spontaneously begin to flow into every activity. We could call the best and richest union of this silence and activity "moving silence," which becomes the ultimate vehicle for greatness to become manifest.

We are all born with the ability not only to know the unbounded unified field of silence, but also to coordinate it with the environment. Once we know both aspects of life, we can start to make sure that they coexist.

To bring about such dynamic coexistence, first the unbounded has to be experienced, then it has to be brought into given boundaries-- into a game, a dance, a relationship, a political speech. The meeting of the two is often felt as the "Aha!," the illumination following the deep rest of incubation, a subtle feeling of "rightness." We then take that feeling and concretize it further in thought and action, perhaps expressing it in such a way that others can know it, too. We "squeeze" unboundedness, something more undifferentiated, into specific boundaries. We gently squeeze the infinity of silence into sound or speech or color through the form of a symphony, a play, a painting. And this is how the more powerful aspects of life are brought directly and easily into any activity or structure.

We can understand our earlier discussion about the myth of "creative suffering" in this light. If you've had great moments of unboundedness, when everything flowed perfectly and effortlessly, you will inevitably feel a struggle later if you can't recapture or tap back into that flow. It's as if you're trapped in narrow boundaries; and without the ability to transcend or come in contact with the inner field of greatness, you feel diminished and frustrated. It is the *lack of flow* from boundaries to unboundedness that causes the despair. Suffering comes from being held back from our natural desire to create, perhaps as a result of some stress in the physiology, and joy comes from the creative flow.

From the opposite point of view, there may be a flow of creativity but we are trying too hard to control it, to hold on to a restrictive pattern: The "object" (the sculpture, for example) is perhaps being forced to conform to an unnatural boundary or form. Or we haven't found the right boundary. We may have the desire to re-create a past success, or to follow a modern but perhaps unfulfilling trend. The discomfort results from the onward force of evolution, because our boundaries, the frameworks within which we choose to express our creative selves, are continually growing and expanding, and we need to support their progress--which is really our own development--even if not entirely in keeping with current fashion.

Yet boundaries, the right ones, are essential. Great creators especially seem to benefit from using a given form into which the flow of creativity can pour and be molded. The symbolic framework serves as a picture of the whole into which each part can be placed. Philosopher Immanuel Kant focused on a particular tower from his study window to think out his categories. The playwright Henrik Ibsen composed his work using a group of visual cues he kept on his desk. Poet Robert Browning described how he planned *The Ring and the Book:* "I went for a walk, gathered 12 pebbles from the road, and put them at equal distances in the parapet that bordered it. These represented the twelve chapters into which the poem was divided."

One of our great modern mathematicians, Ronald Graham, director of the mathematical research division of AT&T Bell Laboratories, reports that he often relies on musical patterns to provide information about mathematical patterns: "I like to listen to [structured] music before I go to sleep and allow my thoughts to flow . . . Mozart, Bach, Beethoven, Brahms . . . the music plays and my mathematical thoughts flow, and they merge. . . . Music helps reinforce patterns that may be developing in the space between waking and sleeping."[28]

All forms of knowledge are really quite static until they are transformed into vibrancy by the contact with unboundedness. Arthur Koestler identified this process as the basis of Ernest Hemingway's greatness:

> Through his monotonously repetitive trivial dialogue, you get glimpses of eternity. . . . Eternity is a bore, you know, when you don't look at it through the window of time. So, to get those two together, I think that's really the essence of craftsmanship. That the trivial is transparent. It's transparent to the eternal. And the eternal is embodied in the trivial, in the here and now.[29]

With the help of a great artist, we can all directly experience unbounded awareness. As our expectations are challenged, we experience the joy of a sudden expansion of consciousness. Profound experiences of this boundary shift often occur during great performances. After watching magician Doug Henning's show, an economist at Stanford University remarked, "Seeing his magic makes me have to rethink my model of the world." What Henning himself has observed is that with the help of the unbounded field, he can create what he calls "wonder" in the audience. He says:

> When you're watching a magician perform and the fountains come up and they put the girl on the fountain, your intellect says, "There must be something hard in those fountains that lifts her up." Then the fountains are turned off and you become very alert and start thinking about wires from the ceiling. Then the magician passes a hoop of fire over the suspended girl and you can't believe it. . . . Your mind *stops* and your intellect disappears and you're left still seeing what you're seeing but you feel an upsurge of another kind of awareness. You've transcended your intellect, the boundaries disappear, and what you now feel is a joyful wonder. It makes your heart open up.[30]

When you are able to experience the unbounded silence and the boundaries simultaneously, you are operating in a greatness mode that is really the basis for all creative dynamism, even the most material. In fact, some of the best applications of this kind of "squeezing in" process can be found in the highly practical field of invention.

We could say that invention is a kind of marriage between the unbounded awareness of the inventor and the environment. Each has to surrender some of its own territory to the other. (Even the selling of an idea or product is a series of "surrenders" or "boundary breakers" between the inventor and the business environment.) To understand the requirements for successful invention, let's return to Wallas's four-step model: There needs to be preparation and evaluation--to know the language or technology of the field in particular, not only intellectually but through experience. (When researcher Eric von Hippel studied the source of innovation in the scientific instruments business, he found that of eleven major inventions, all came from users; of sixty-six "major improvements," 85 percent came from users; of eighty-three "minor improvements," about two thirds came from users.)[31]

But besides knowing the language, we also need to be able to produce ideas from silence to fit a technological boundary, to be able to deliver unboundedness to a technology. Obviously, the more familiar we are with both unboundedness and the technological field and its language, the better able we will be to invent something great. It may seem at first that these diverse requirements are in reality very different--that is, what we need to know to make electric skis is quite different from knowledge of the unbounded field. Even if we agree that electric skis could be made up of elements from that infinite field, how would they interface, if at all?

The answer is surely that nothing new or significant can be invented unless the mind of the inventor can tap into a field of creativity and channel it into the boundaries, regardless of what *kind* of boundaries he or she is dealing with, whether extremely narrow or extremely broad. So even if the size and scope of the boundaries differ, the reality of creating remains the same. Being an inventor means being able to determine the exact shape of the boundaries and allow unboundedness to infuse them.

Another way to look at it is that boundaries are what we consider needs or problems, and the "infusing" of them is what we call "solutions." A solution can appear easily as a simple direct response to an immediate need. For example, the ice cream cone was invented by the girl friend of a salesman at the Louisiana Purchase Exposition in 1904 who rolled up one of the flat wafers from her ice cream sandwich to contain the ice cream and used the other wafer to hold some flowers the salesman had given her. The Aqua-Lung was invented by Jacques Cousteau, who needed such a device for his research, and consulted a control-valve system specialist to complete the design. Similarly, Bissell invented the carpet sweeper because he was allergic to the straw on the floor of his china shop. (His invention would later be somewhat overshadowed by another: With no other testing materials at his disposal, Hubert Booth, the inventor of the vacuum cleaner, experimented with his filtering system by lying on the floor with a handkerchief in his mouth to see how the dirt would actually move when he drew in his breath.)

Breakfast cereals originated with the Kellogg brothers, who were vegetarians. They had started a health sanitarium in Battle Creek, Michigan, and found that a light breakfast helped them and their clients to think more clearly. The cornflakes served at the sanitarium were demanded by the patients at home, so the Kelloggs began to market them.

King Gillette's need was simple: Money. So he set out to invent something that was useful yet disposable, correctly figuring out the economics of an item that would have to be continually replaced, and the disposable razor blade was born.

Other inventions were created in response to physical needs. Alexander Bell taught language to deaf children, including his own son, and began the study of sound. The telephone was invented because Bell was trying to develop a hearing aid for the children using amplified sound. Similarly, the typewriter was conceived of as a way to emboss print for the blind.

In all cases, it is a clear boundary that seems to be the challenge that awakens the silence of pure consciousness. And as a result, the most dramatic "Why didn't I think of that?" inventions are created. For example, a draftsman to whom Walter Hunt owed money offered to pay four hundred dollars for all the rights to the various shapes into which Hunt could twist an old wire in three hours. Hunt invented the paper clip on the spot. It was easy for him, because like all greats, his awareness was established in the field of all possibilities; it was almost as if he was playing with unboundedness, shaping it to fit into the world. And when one's mind is operating from that field--the thought, the idea, the invention are always right; it's just a simple matter of thinking and doing to produce something great.

In our concluding chapter, we'll look at how all of us can enliven silence together in the world to produce an incredible resource--collective greatness. But first, let's summarize a few of the signs we've seen that indicate the growth to greatness has begun:

1. You recognize greatness in others; to that extent, you yourself are great.
2. You value life and think of it as precious, as a gift--and have a feeling of urgency about it. One indication is that you don't like to waste time on useless activities.
3. You feel happy in your activity. And despite objections or obstacles you may encounter, you feel that what you're doing is very right for you and very natural. You feel deeply *yourself* in what you are and do.
4. You set what you feel are big goals and carry them out. Your actions seem to develop ahead of time based on your intuition,

your ability to think clearly, and your ability to focus. You become very absorbed in what you think and do.

5. You also seem to have an ability to connect the beginning and end of your undertakings. You see the whole of what you are involved in; it emerges whole in your thinking, although you may proceed toward accomplishment step by step.

6. Your mind, body, and emotions all work together in an integrated manner, enabling you to have a lot of focused energy with moments of effortlessness. Often you don't feel it's *you* doing anything; it seems to happen through you.

7. You feel that although you are enjoying what you are doing, you are responsible for others, too; you want to structure a great future both for yourself and all humanity.

8. You sometimes feel you are connected to the universe in an intimate way, as part of a great flow of life, experiencing a deeper level of truth beyond local social and cultural values.

8

※

GROUP GREATNESS:
THE BEST OF EVERYONE

❖

"Nothing in the World Is Single . . ."

> The fountains mingle with the river,
>   And the rivers with the ocean;
> The winds of heaven mix for ever
>   With a sweet emotion;
> Nothing in the world is single;
>   All things, by a law divine,
> In one another's being mingle . . .
>
> PERCY BYSSHE SHELLEY

No one does it alone. "No matter what accomplishments you make," observed tennis champion Althea Gibson, "somebody helps you."

We watch while Academy Award-winners thank a group of family, friends, and mentors. Great people whose greatness is best reflected in their accomplishments almost invariably have strong social support, a sense of connectedness.

Sometimes support comes from within a family group, such as the Adamses, the Kennedys, the Mayos, or the McCormicks. Baseball player Dwight Gooden may have been born with great athletic potential, but he was also born into a baseball family--not a football or a political family. His grandmother swore he was his baseball-playing "granddaddy come back alive." Support for greatness could also come from an artisan tradition--in Eastern cultures in particular--whereby the artisan is connected to a centuries-old craft passed on through his family or his craft masters. Or it could come from a writers' association like Leonard and Virginia Woolf's Bloomsbury group, or a philosophical, religious, or spiritual group such as the nineteenth-century Transcendentalists.

Sometimes it is simply a working group. Good research groups often produce better results than individuals; a majority of scientists and other researchers find they benefit from collective working environments. The Edison Laboratory, Bell Laboratories, the Rand Corporation, and the Hoover Institution are some of the environments that generate this support. The support is not only psychological; these groups are necessary because most research is structured on what others have done before. In fact, this emphasis on group knowledge is said to have been the secret of Western science for centuries because it achieved a far more significant collective influence than the sum of all the individuals who contributed to it.

As each line of thinking is added to by thinker after thinker, chains of thought get built into our patterns of evolution. So-called brand-new ideas are often variations on old ones--cycles of ideas seem to come up again and again. (Consequently, a good technique for getting "new" ideas is to browse in an antique shop or read old magazines.) Even the innovations created by a solitary inventor, such as the Xerox machine, the FM radio, the Polaroid process, the zipper, ballpoint pens, and cellophane, were all built upon other inventions. Today especially, most scientific work is so specialized that it is really useful only in conjunction with the output of others.

On the surface it may seem, as Miranda Weston-Smith has written, that "civilization has been built on the discoveries and inventions of a handful of people. [Those] . . . who have made our heritage would not fill a double decker bus."[1] But those great individuals who form part of our heritage merely represent visibility; they are the "tip" of those groups and societies that have created and supported individual greatness.

Sociologists tell us that individuals, while remaining individuals, always act as part of a group. Sociology professor David Riesman called this phenomenon "the herd of independent minds." But very few of us feel like part of a herd; in fact, we generally feel quite the opposite. We have the distinct impression we are unique in our personhood. Biologist Lewis Thomas calls this "the paradox of individuality"--we all seem to be separate, but actually are deeply connected to and dependent on each other. Jung called this deep connection the "collective unconsciousness." "Under each of our individual 'consciousnesses,' " he wrote, "we are united as one " And our thought processes are united, too.

❖

Thinking Together: The World Mind

For masterpieces are not single and solitary births; they are the outcome of many years of thinking in common, of thinking by the body of the people, so that the experience of the mass is behind the single voice.

VIRGINIA WOOLF

To sit alone in the lamplight with a book spread out before you and hold intimate converse with men of unseen generations-- such is a pleasure beyond compare.

YOSHIDA KENDO

As the reality of a unified universe becomes more and more apparent in our scientific age--with input from physicists, biologists, ecologists, and communications specialists--we are coming to realize what poets like Francis Thompson have always known: "Thou canst not stir a flower, without troubling a star." Even science, according to such theorists as Gaston Bachelard, Thomas Kuhn, and Karl Popper, is not "pure," that is, entirely separate from the times; it, too, reflects the shifts in awareness, in consciousness, based on collective transitions in human thought.

We are also learning that the information we accumulate during our lifetime is not ours alone. It has arisen out of all human history. We can ask each other, "Are these my ideas or yours?" Emerson called this operating idea-experience storehouse "the mind of the world," and considered each genius to be expressing the world's mind. (The greats may express it better, but we are all capable of experiencing it, if only for moments at a time.) Emerson wrote:

> It is the mind of the world which is the good carpenter, the good scholar, sailor, or blacksmith, thousand-handed, versatile, all-applicable. . . . In you, this rich soul has peeped, despite your horny, muddy eyes, at books and poetry. Well, it took you up, and showed you something to the purpose; that there was something there. Look, look old mole! there, straight up before you, is the magnificent sun. If only for the instant, you see it.[2]

In the world's mind, ideas can travel long distances over time. One's ideas may be as much influenced by what Plato thought and taught as by what Joan Rivers talks about on late-night television. All our thoughts, ancient and modern, are connected, and so no thought I think is really new. My thoughts have been thought by others--even thousands of years apart. And this explains why human beings feel so connected to each other even across time and cultures.

Nowadays, anthropologists use the expression "cultural pool" to describe how all ideas in a culture are supported selectively in and by that culture. Each idea that survives is called a "meme": Memes are what Richard Dawkins named "units of imitation"--the way in which ideas and meanings are passed on through the medium of a culture. How quickly an idea, a phrase, or a joke travels through a culture is indicative of its appropriateness for a particular group at a particular time.

Since information is encoded and stored chemically in the brain, memes have a biological basis as well; they, too, are a kind of living

structure. And just as nature creates new species through the introduction of new patterns in the genes and chromosomes, the history
of thought travels the same evolutionary road through the biological
development of patterns of thinking. In every human transaction,
memes are acted upon and exchanged. When our memes are alike,
the exchanges are smooth; otherwise, we adjust. And in each adjust-
ment these "cultural genes" change the way our brain functions. (We
know, for example, that our attention spans have been changed
physiologically, shortened, by thirty years of watching television. In
addition, however, the ideas we absorb while watching TV have been
changing our physiology, too. . . .)

According to Dr. Jonas Salk, ideas are "as important as genes" for
the evolution of the species. And anthropology professor Paul Bohannan writes, "The better an idea, the greater its likelihood of survival." But the idea has to be communicated--and that requires a
group. He continues:

> Any individual's own personal structure is made up of a relatively
> small portion of the totally available memes, just as each
> individual carries only a relatively small portion of the totally
> available genes in the gene pool. . . . Every time one of us hears
> it, reads it, picks it up, and repeats it so that somebody else can
> hear it, then that meme is replicated. Thus, just as genes need
> plants and animals as survival vehicles, so memes need animals
> with highly developed brains and good capacity to communicate
> as their survival vehicles.[3]

Bohannan explains how good communication is the way in which
group ideas, or memes, last. (The idea that remains uncommuni-
cated dies with its author.) What is required for good communication is human consciousness. Strong cultural images are created this
way, often with lasting influences, which ensures their survival. For
example, American Indians, sociologist Robert Jay Lifton observed,
employ "a reservoir of shared cultural imagery--usually religious," which
is the basis for their powerfully unifying spiritual traditions.

By virtue of memes, we become in a sense a collective genius.
Each of us may have entertained occasional thoughts about being a
"Renaissance person," to have--as Arthur Koestler described it--the
ability to know "everything about everything." But it may not be

possible to become as informed as this in our era. Researchers at Bell Laboratories have estimated that there is more information in a weekday edition of *The New York Times* than a person in the sixteenth century would process in a lifetime. In fact, the last person on earth to "know everything" is said to have been the scientist-philosopher Leibniz, a contemporary of Newton's. So, in this sense there can never really be an individual Renaissance person who knows everything about every field. Therefore, for the sake of knowledge itself, we are obliged to join together to form a group mind, the knowledge we hold collectively being more complete than any of us could retain individually.

We may then wonder how collective thinking operates, in what medium, and whether it can bring about collective greatness.

❖

Cultural Support for Greatness

The reciprocal relationship between culture and creativity is such that a creative product is not really an invention unless it is socially accepted.

MORTON I. TEICHER

The best of human thought is developed, nurtured, and maintained by each successive societal environment. And the ideas that change least and survive best throughout history are in most cases the truest. Ptolemy's system of astronomy wasn't wrong in his day; he saw a particular unity in the diversity of nature, and his understanding was accepted and honored for a long time. His ideas were correct for his age, but were not unifying enough to plumb a deeper level of knowledge and create a more lasting belief. In this century Einstein's understanding of relativity has given us one view of the universe; if some other thought comes along that is more unifying and fundamental, it will be more powerful and we will all shift our thinking to it. This shift is already beginning to happen through an increasing acceptance of the latest theories in quantum physics.

But until the next thought shift fully occurs, Einstein's thought remains our reality--we have made it our own. And we have collectively agreed to create our universe based upon that thought. In the days when it was "known" that the world was as flat as a pancake, that's what the world was. Now that it's "known" that the universe is expanding, this is how we have come to rethink our concept of it after centuries of a Newtonian view. As these shifts in understanding occur, "the universe begins to look more like a great thought than like a great machine," concluded astronomer Sir James Jeans.

We also know that the way in which greatness becomes manifest will change according to the thoughts of the society and the coherence of the group mind. Indeed, greatness is such an abstract quality, so free of boundaries and thereby ultimately flexible, that the same people who became the great Christian philosophers in the twelfth century might have become today's Nobel Prize-winning theoretical physicists, and the individuals who became great medical doctors in the early 1900s might today be eminent mathematicians or research chemists. Leibniz might have been a great Wall Street economist or financier. As philosopher Elizabeth Haich observed:

> It does not matter whether such a man manifest his energies as a scholar, politician, statesman, ruler, philosopher, or as a performer, composer, painter, sculptor or author. The impact of his influence is the measure of his greatness. It is of no consequence where and when these men lived and worked--or are living and working at the present time.[4]

As we saw earlier, successful channels for greatness change with each society: Greatness tends to seek the most fully developed and supported channels. In all cases, for a society to be great, its channels for greatness must provide ways for the individual to express the highest level of societal integrity and wholeness. When a society supports this kind of integration, the creative activities of its constituents then become an intimate part of the traditions. Otherwise, they are scattered in a million personal channels. And when creativity is strictly idiosyncratic and not beneficial to society, it doesn't generally lead to greatness.

You see one youngster dancing in the street, moving fast, energy flying, but it's not a performance with a purpose--it's a kind of "letting off steam." It has a value for him, but not for anyone else. Whereas another youngster has a dance in mind, and is performing it using certain forms or patterns; historically, he might have been dancing as part of a complex tradition--as a member of a tribe in Africa or a community in Greece--where the dance may have had a very important artistic, religious, or social purpose. Without denying the pleasures of self-expression, it seems that greatness requires channels that are deeper and more integrative to serve not only individual expression, but to maintain the growth of society through communication of ideas and values.

Obviously, because of the variety of societal differences, any given tradition might be a natural path to greatness within one culture but not within another. For example, in European cultures greatness might be sought in long-established "European tradition" channels. If you are a French baker, for instance, you might pick up on the national desire for a perfect strawberry torte and set your sights on achieving it. Your goal is to bake the ideal strawberry torte as defined by French standards. If you succeed, you achieve a reputation as a great baker, and people come from all over to experience your tortes. You are great in the strawberry torte-baking tradition.

In America, where there have been very few long-established traditions through which greatness could accommodate a societal ideal, we might think, "What is 'now'?" In the field of tortes, we would try for the new . . . maybe a zucchini torte will catch on. In fact, the American tradition most in keeping with its national consciousness has been the tradition of novelty.

Composer-lyricist Betty Comden once said, "Good is always new." But we have tended to try to reverse that thinking, hoping for "new is always good." But "new" rarely produces greatness in and of itself, because often, as E. W. F. Tomlin writes, novelty for the sake of novelty is impoverishing: "Not novelty for its own sake but renewal within the traditional or inherited modes of expression, thereby extending that tradition and heritage, is what characterizes a work of art." He quotes poet T. S. Eliot, who understood the importance of this inheritance for the artist: "We shall often find that not only the best, but the most individual parts of [the poet's] work may be those in which the dead poets, his ancestors, assert their immortality most vigorously."[5]

True, in America the founding fathers threw off established tradition in favor of individual freedom, and we've come to cherish that freedom above all else. But it was a carefully thought-out freedom, a vision drawn from the most successful and powerful republics and democracies of the past. According to historian Henry Steele Commager, the goal of the founding fathers was not immediate gratification, but to design something valuable for all time--to establish a more unifying political framework. Greatness rose in their "collective political genius" by unlocking deeper truths, deeper laws and principles, and they created "every major political and constitutional institution which we now have . . . [and] . . . probably the greatest political treatise" to which "thousands of highly trained scholars at advanced institutes of government today have produced nothing comparable."[6]

But now, as citizens of a highly creative nation, comfortable in our changeability, accomplished in the understanding of the dynamics of individual freedom, we are starting to desire stable platforms for greatness, cultural roots from which to soar. We have often been on the brink of becoming a culture of almost total content, not much concerned with form. (Form is why a great poem can't be paraphrased or a Count Basie concert re-created on Muzak. Form gives the actual experience; content only the idea of the experience.)

When Aaron Copland took the responsibility for creating the first purely "American" classical music, he realized that:

> In the field of art, each country tends to produce a kind of art which somehow reflects national characteristics, and in the field of serious music, when I was a student, it was also clear that we hadn't achieved that yet in this country. From that came the desire to do something about it.[7]

And because we are seeking opportunities for greatness, we are eager for deeper channels of knowledge and experience in every field. For example, when Julia Child came along, we were ready for her. Her concern: "How can a society call itself great when its white bread tastes like Kleenex?" Her solution: to teach the traditions of good cooking to Americans, using her knowledge, her powerful intelligence and rich enthusiasm, qualities which, no doubt, would have distinguished her in any field. She helped make cooking into the art form it has always been in other countries, into a proper channel for greatness. Now our own American cooking traditions are being fully revived.

So, whether we create new traditions or connect to old ones, the bottom-line reason for tradition is simply the need for proper channels for greatness to flow easily. In connecting to the past *and* also to the future, greatness seeks these opportunities in every culture, as it seeks ways to bring out the best.

The Permeability of Ideas in Cultures: Upholding the Best of Us

And the music's not immortal; but the world has made it sweet.

ALFRED NOYES, *The Barrel Organ*

I just do the best I can do musically and in all parts of my life. And if I don't, there's something *inside* me that says, "Hey, you're not doing the best you can do." So there's a consistent [inner] check.

STEVIE WONDER

In art, you don't compete with anybody because, after all, if you do something good, nobody but you could have done that kind of good. You can only write your own kind of music. If you don't write it, nobody else will, so you're not competing in any real sense. It's just that master musicians set standards. If you can't do that well, then it's not going to be good enough to last and to sustain interest over the years.

AARON COPLAND

If we are touched by a poem or some music or a painting, it is a very personal experience. Not everyone is touched deeply by the same works. It takes receptivity, readiness, openness, prior knowledge, and experience.

So, what is the best? Most of us are dedicated comparers--we want to know what is better than what, who is better than whom. And, according to sociologist Leon Festinger's "social comparison" theory, people generally evaluate their own performances by comparing themselves with others. But when we start to compare scientific discoveries with artistic achievements, composers with each other, performances with performances, one's children with other children-- it's often with a sense of purposelessness.

Of course, we may like having critics help us decide what exhibits, concerts, and movies to spend our time and money on. But we can't forget that not only are we all different in the way we express greatness, but also in the way we evaluate it. And because individuals and cultures see and experience things differently, based on different states of awareness, different past experiences, and different traditions, arguments about the measure of greatness of particular works of art, for example, remain unresolvable. As pianist Arthur Rubinstein so wisely observed, "Nothing in art can be the best, only different."

What we can do, however, is look at the territory of influence as a measure of the global effect of greatness. A painting by your own child, for example, might touch you personally very deeply, but not necessarily because of its color, form, or quality of light. But if a lot of people are touched by the same work, if hundreds of thousands of people are drawn to it the way they are to Botticelli's "Venus" or Monet's "Water Lilies," it means that the work has captured something universally true and intimate. And if the vertical depth of your greatness extends through a wide horizontal territory of history, it means your influence has reached beyond the boundaries of your own culture.

We wonder how Shakespeare could have been so hugely appreciated by the uneducated working people of his time at the Globe Theatre. Perhaps it was because he gave them--and us--a way to experience something deeper within. His language, even if the meaning were missed, could be enjoyed for its sound, its poetry. His work has stayed universally charged throughout the centuries; his art has dissolved not only the class boundaries of his times, but boundaries throughout almost all cultures. Shakespeare is able, according to actor Walter Matthau, not only to make actors his collaborators, but to make audiences his collaborators, too, thereby permeating even the most rigid constraints of each age and culture with the brilliance of his insight into truth.

From this angle we could say that, on the "greatness" scale, how much influence and effect a particular idea or product has on all of us depends on its *permeability*--how closely it represents the all-time universal values, how well it travels across space and time, by virtue of its being upheld in society after society throughout history. The truer it is, the farther it will travel, and the greater its continuing historical influence. And in this way greatness demands to find itself-- its familiar universality--in the best representatives of each society through which it passes.

In *The Lives of a Cell,* Lewis Thomas speculates how we could express the best of our universe to an alien culture in outer space. What would represent us all and all we have been in our whole world history? He concludes: "I would vote for Bach, all of Bach, streamed out into space, over and over again. We would be bragging, of course, but it is surely excusable for us to put the best possible face at the beginning of such an acquaintance."[8]

As we contemplate Bach as "the best of us," we may ask what has kept Bach "alive." Is his music immortal, forever upheld by its own brilliance, or have successive societies of awake, perceptive individuals continued to enliven Bach? It seems that both are true. Nothing in life is totally static; as cultures change, no work of art or personal reputation of greatness remains eternally the same. As great and long-lived as Bach is, it's quite possible that a time could come when we outgrow him, when his music no longer satisfies us musically, or even when the arts and sciences we now know disappear and new expressions of human consciousness arise and are savored for centuries.

Our appreciation and expressions really change in relationship to evolutionary development. In an interview with Dick Cavett, Mikhail Baryshnikov compared today's ballet companies with those of the nineteenth century: "Dancers today," he said, "have better bodies--the men are jumping higher, are stronger, ladies have longer and higher extension--their balance is stronger." If today's dancers are stronger, then the dances they perform must be geared to modern capabilities. A dance choreographed for nineteenth-century abilities would not be as fully expressive of our progress. So, the group mind is intimately connected to the group body, to physiological evolution. And as we grow, greatness grows with us; greatness, to be great, must always express the best of us.

The Simultaneity of Thinking: The Group Mind at Work

The lightning spark of thought, generated in the solitary mind, awakens its likeness in another mind.

THOMAS CARLYLE

We may have heard the principle "What the mind of man can believe and conceive, it can achieve." But it's also true that what you can conceive, someone else can also achieve. In fact, what any one of us can conceive is probably being conceived of right now by hundreds of others. All of us come up with ideas all the time but don't necessarily raise and nurture them beyond the thinking stage. Yet we have all probably experienced thinking of something and, a short time later, reading or hearing that someone else has "discovered" what we had been thinking of. (Of course, then we may think-- not the usual "Why didn't I think of that?" but "Why didn't I do something with that thought?" The answer is, not every thought is ours to do something with--we are only going to "do something" about those we really become deeply involved with.)

As we saw in an earlier chapter, thought seems to have a life of its own. We all know what it feels like to think of something that all at once brings about a chain of interrelated events. This phenomenon was never well explained in the West until Jung described it as "synchronicity" or "meaningful coincidence," which he illustrated with the following true story:

A certain Monsieur Deschamps, when a boy in Orleans, was once given a piece of plum-pudding by a Monsieur de Fortgibu. Ten years later, he discovered another plum-pudding in a Paris restaurant and asked if he could have a piece. It turned out, however, that the plum-pudding was already ordered--by

Monsieur de Fortgibu. Many years afterwards, Monsieur Deschamps was invited to partake of a plum-pudding as a special rarity. While he was eating it he remarked that the only thing lacking was Monsieur de Fortgibu. At that moment, the door opened and an old, old man in the last stages of disintegration walked in: Monsieur de Fortgibu, who had got hold of the wrong address and burst in on the party by mistake.[9]

It's true that from a statistical point of view there will always be a certain number of coincidences. However, what Jung meant by synchronicity was that events that are significantly related, yet without any apparent causal connection, can and do occur in our lives based on something more meaningful than simple statistical coincidence, suggesting a hidden force that underlies all events and all natural laws.

From a scientific perspective, it now appears that Jung was right: Synchronicity is a real phenomenon of the quantum world, a world in which each of us creates reality, moment by moment, individually and collectively. The Q view explains coincidence. As science writer Rudy Rucker says, "Quantum mechanics not only allows for synchronous events, it even requires them. . . . Quantum mechanics predicts that once two particles have been near each other, they continue to instantaneously affect each other no matter how widely they may be separated."[10]

After decades of experiments attempting to identify other hidden causes that might account for this eternal bond, in 1982, University of Paris researcher Alain Aspect proved that quantum predictions are indeed true: Particles do seem to communicate telepathically and noncausally. Thus, simultaneity of thought, from the Q view, is not at all coincidental--even the tiniest particles of matter are capable of a kind of collective group consciousness. If this is true at the Q level, it should not surprise us if from time to time such a coherent group consciousness manifests in our everyday lives. And nowhere is there more vivid illustration of this than in the world of scientific discovery and invention.

History reveals that more often than should be the case from a classical view, nearly identical inventions are thought up simultaneously by different individuals working in isolation from each other.

As Joseph Needham points out: "Some ideas, some sciences, and some complicated inventions have a disagreeable habit of appearing (and even disappearing) almost at the same time . . ."[11]

A few examples of this simultaneity of events include: the discovery of oxygen by both Scheele and Priestley (1774) and, a century later (1877), the liquefaction of oxygen by Cailletet and also by Pietet; a kinetic theory of gases by Clausius and by Rankine (1850); the telegraph by three different individuals--Morse, Cooke-Wheatstone, and Steinheil (1837); electric motors by Dal Negro (1830) and by Henry (1831); the microphone by Hughes (1878), Edison (1877–1878), Berliner (1877), and Blake (1878); the telephone by Bell and also by Gray (1876); the flying machine by Wright (1895–1901), and by Langley (1893–1897) and others around the same time; reapers by Hussey (1833) and by McCormick (1843); and centrifugal pumps by Appold, Gwynne, and Bessemer (1850).[12]

Perhaps the most interesting synchronous event was the simultaneous formulation of the theory of the origin of species through natural selection, which was proposed by Charles Darwin as well as by another English naturalist, Alfred Russel Wallace, working entirely independently of Darwin. When Wallace sent Darwin his manuscript in 1858, Darwin immediately recognized his own theory. "I never saw a more striking coincidence," he wrote to geologist Sir Charles Lyell; even Wallace's terms "now stand as head of my chapters." *The Origin of Species* was published the following year, and Wallace's *The Malay Archipelago* was published ten years later.

Not only do inventions and scientific discoveries seem to occur synchronously, but the world mind creates other kinds of manifestations at the same time. We generally find that the more evolved the society, the more intelligence its creators express in their work, the more far-reaching the creations. The most profound expressions of human life so far have been developed both within highly developed societies, such as the ancient Vedic society, and those of classical Greece, the Renaissance, and early America, as well as globally from time to time throughout history. For example, a disproportionate number of the most influential Eastern religious teachers--Confucius, Buddha, Mahavira (the founder of Jainism) and Zoroaster--were all born within fifty years of each other. In this time period (550–600

B.C.) also, many of the Indian *Upanishads* were written. Obviously, the era was ripe for spiritual teachings.

Synchronous thoughts and connections that pop up in culture after culture are evidence that some kind of collective thinking is at work. And it is also apparent that collective support is required if an invention or a discovery is to be accepted and succeed. Simultaneous discoveries and inventions did not occur precisely when they did simply because the required technology suddenly became available. Most materials were available long before particular inventors used them. The hot-air balloon, for example, was simultaneously invented in the same year (1783), many centuries after the manufacturing of cloth, by Montgolfier and Rittenhouse-Hopkins. This implies that there is a need for cultural support--the group mind has to be ready.

Even if the technology is available, there must still be a perceived collective desire. The invention of the rocket occurred years after the materials were on hand. And despite the wheel's availability for five thousand years, the bicycle was not invented until the eighteenth century. The safety pin was invented in 2000 B.C., during the Bronze Age. But its major improvement, the ability to be held together firmly by a spring, was made by paper-clip wizard Walter Hunt in the early part of this century.

The automatic dishwasher didn't come onto the market until a hundred years after its invention was patented. First, there was too little hot water and too little electricity. Timing devices weren't ready. Efficient detergents weren't available. All these had to be developed to make the dishwasher a reality. But more important, no one really wanted a dishwasher at that time.

So ultimately, good ideas are less related to technology and more related to group desire. For an idea to be finally and fully accepted, a group consensus is necessary. Right timing just means that other people are thinking or are about to think your thought.

In discussing objective-versus-subjective knowledge, Sir Alan Cottrell writes that there is a collective subjectivity that is "intersubjective and refers to common or *public* experiences, as distinct from the private and idiosyncratic experiences of the individual. Scientific knowledge thus comes from intersubjective experience."[13] In this way a scientific idea, as well as all other ideas, must enter society's thinking to be made genuine. From the discovery of the individual scientist, it flows into societal awareness. In the early part of this century Einstein's theory of relativity was understood only by a handful of scientists; it was considered the height of erudition to comprehend it. Now, high-school students learn it (relatively) easily--the group "brain" has risen to the occasion and absorbed Einstein's thought.

Without group support, one could have a truly brilliant idea in a minute, build a model to demonstrate it in a week, and spend a lifetime trying to convince others of its value. Pasteur, after he discovered his vaccine, spent twenty years fighting the medical profession and the church before it was accepted. Many scientists have been deeply disappointed when they presented their discoveries to the world, only to find that no one was really interested and few could see the relevance.

The steam engine was invented in ancient Rome, but not developed until hundreds of years later. When Bell first offered his telephone for sale, it was turned down because there was "no need" for it. When Edison undertook the development of the electric light, a group of experts agreed that his efforts were "unworthy of the attention of practical or scientific men." In our own era, the Xerox copying process was available for four years before a backer could be found. So, even if we agree with Norman Douglas's observation that "no great person is ever born too soon or too late," we recognize that great ideas, like great people, need group support.

Synchronous Behavior

The extent to which we can get along with another person or group depends fundamentally on whether we can synchronize with them or not.

EDWARD HALL

We've shown how a large number of similar inventions, discoveries, or ideas occurring at once may be indicative of a highly coherent group consciousness in a given era. But it's also important to realize that such a phenomenon is really based on the very ordinary synchronicity that occurs in our daily lives. Synchronicity is a kind of social behavior as well as a mental function. Following Jung's description, anthropologist Edward Hall identified synchronicity in all human transactions. Hall suggests that if we don't synchronize with each other, we feel "out of step," as if we are stepping on each other's toes. Similarly, we may feel under foot and awkward. Infants learn to synchronize movement with adult voices, and eventually we all learn to synchronize the rhythms of speech and gesture. Each community has its own synchrony. Being in tune is a real phenomenon of social life. New Yorkers, for example, are several times quicker in pace and speech than other urbanites; forever after, in other places, unless they synchronize, they feel like 78-rpm records in a 33-rpm world.

Hall and his students conducted several intriguing experiments to observe the effects of synchrony in human behavior. In one experiment, the synchrony of children in a playground was found to have a distinctive coherent rhythm and beat, along with a "conductor":

> At first, they looked like so many kids each doing his own thing. After a while, we noticed that one little girl was moving more than the rest. Careful study revealed that she covered the entire playground. . . . Gradually, [we] perceived that the whole group was moving in synchrony to a definite rhythm. The most active child, the one who moved about most, was the director, the orchestrator of the playground rhythm! [14]

A related experiment of synchrony in behavior was devised by W. S. Condon:

> Two persons were hooked up to an electroencephalograph while engaged in conversation, with one camera filming the principals while another focused on the machine. During the entire period of conversation, the two EEG recording pens moved in such perfect unison as to appear "driven" by a single force; only when the talk was interrupted by a third person did the readings diverge. [15]

In light of such behavioral phenomena, we can surmise that groups of people whose brain waves are functioning in like manner may end up creating a more unified field of consciousness and a more coherent field of action than those whose brain waves are functioning randomly.

❖

Acting Together:
The Whole and Some of the Parts

As we observed earlier, nature has a tendency to enjoy things that are harmonized over things that are out of sync. If you put six grandfather clocks together against a wall, all with pendulums the same length, and set each pendulum swinging at a different time, in about two days all the pendulums will be swinging back and forth at the same time. It seems that the vibrations from the swinging pendulums penetrate the clocks, thus causing them to become synchronized. Similarly, a swarm of fireflies may start out flashing independently, but always end up flashing in unison. And schools of fish tend all to turn at the same time. Such collective phenomena are fascinating because they remind us how a biological system influences its parts, forming a behavior pattern that is universal but difficult to see when you're in it yourself! In fact, the similarity between human behavior and the collective and synchronous behavior of other life forms is so striking as to make us somewhat uncomfortable. Writes Lewis Thomas:

> . . . The bees and termites and social wasps seem to live two kinds of lives: They are individuals going about the day's business and . . . they are component parts . . . in the huge, writhing, ruminating organism of the Hill, the nest, the hive. . . . Four ants together, or ten, encircling a dead moth on a path, begin to look more like an idea. . . . It is because of this aspect, I think, that we most wish for them to be something foreign. We do not like the notion that there can be collective societies with the capacity to behave like organisms.[16]

This group integrity is perhaps best explained by a principle in physics known as the Meisner effect, whereby a small number of photons (the square root of 1 percent), lined up together, will cause the whole system to become synchronous. For example, in ordinary light, such as that emitted from a 60-watt bulb, the waves are random and unrelated. But in laser light, the waves move together syn-chronously, creating a steady beam of intense coherent light. Similarly, when all the components in any system act in phase with each other, and when circumstances cause a phase transition from scattered in-dividual concerns to a unified action, the collectivity pattern dra-matically emerges as a living, functioning unit, which then changes the behavior of the parts. Author Douglas Hofstadter explains:

> Phase transitions take place in physical systems--schools of fish, brains, countries--when there are sufficiently strong and numerous interactions between the components of the system, and when those interactions add up to large-scale correlations. When such effects occur, a new kind of entity springs up, on a higher level of organization than its constituents.[17]

One vivid illustration of this principle is the well-known story of "the hundredth monkey." In the 1950s scientists in Japan noticed a new behavior among wild monkeys: A few of the monkeys had un-dertaken to wash the dirt off sweet potatoes supplied them by the scientists. Over a period of six years, all the young monkeys learned this behavior; many of the adults did not. Then one day--the num-ber of monkeys washing potatoes at that point was uncertain--one more monkey began the behavior. Scientists dubbed her "the hun-dredth monkey" because a critical mass had just been reached; by that evening, *all* the monkeys were washing their potatoes before eating them. The fascinating part of the story is that colonies of monkeys in other places, on other Japanese islands and on the main-land, also began to wash their potatoes. The idea of washing pota-toes before eating them had been communicated somehow as a field phenomenon among the monkeys.[18]

Since all aspects of nature seem to enjoy and to benefit from pat-terns of harmonized behavior, from field effects, the question we must ask is, Don't we humans also benefit? And the answer is a definite "yes."

❖

We Are the World: Inner Networking

All power is one in source and end. . . . Years and distances, stars and candles . . . the craft in a man's hand and the wisdom in a tree's root: they all arise together. My name and yours, and the true name of the sun . . . all are syllables of the great word that is very slowly spoken by the stars. There is no other power. No other name.

URSULA K. LE GUIN, *Wizard of Earthsea*

You're not there as an individual. You're the representative of humanity at that point in history, having that experience for the rest of mankind.

ASTRONAUT RUSSELL SCHWEICKART, *on going to the moon*

Quantum physics gives us a basis by which to suggest that collective human functioning is a viable reality that offers some impressive opportunities. For example, great individuals could join together to form an infinitely powerful group mind or *collective consciousness* to achieve greatness. London University physicist David Bohm proposes that if even one hundred people could perceive this deeper stratum of reality and tap into their collective mind, "the ego would have vanished for these people, and they would form a single consciousness just as the parts of a highly integrated person are integrated as one." Since every particle of matter interconnects with everything else within what Bohm terms the "implicate order"--a level of absolute reality beyond space and time--it follows that our brains and, therefore, our conscious minds are all interconnected. In fact, he says, "We are more than interconnected. We are sort of interpenetrating."[19] Here is scientific confirmation of Emerson's understanding of a group mind.

Virginia Woolf recorded her awareness of this phenomenon as she experienced it at the death of a contemporary:

A curious feeling, when a writer like S.B. [Stella Benson] dies, that one's response is diminished . . . my effusion--what I send out--less porous and radiant--as if the thinking stuff were a web that were fertilized only by other people's (her, that is) thinking it too: now lacks life.[20]

In *Megatrends* John Naisbitt reports that by networking we can reach anyone in the world with only six person-by-person interactions. Amazing as that is, it's even more exciting to contemplate what "inner networking" in the quantum world would be like; not

only could we access Emily Smith in Toronto and Richard Jones in Las Vegas, but Socrates in Athens, Lawrence in Arabia, Helen in Troy, and Voltak on Planet 108.

Moreover, in this quantum universe of implicate-order awareness, people are automatically tuned into each other and can develop common notions at the same time. This explains how simultaneous thoughts can occur. This also explains why great societies produce more individual greats--the individual enjoys the quiet support of the developed group consciousness. But Bohm says these mental interconnections would occur only between people who had some coherent physical functioning:

> The ordinary relations between people are at such a high temperature--at such a degree of random, chaotic conflict--that their brains do pretty nearly work in isolation from each other. As long as there is conflict, we must expect that implicate-order awareness is unlikely.[21]

But when conflict is minimized and coherence maximized, the reality of "group greatness" emerges. In an ongoing "world peace" experiment being conducted by Maharishi Mahesh Yogi and scientists from a number of leading universities, seven thousand TM practitioners-- the square root of one percent of the population of the world, the number needed, according to the Meisner effect, to transform a population into a synchronously functioning system--are meditating together to achieve a predicted rise in coherence in world consciousness. Results are being observed on measures of the increased quality of life, on crime and warfare reduction, and on other indicators of rising consciousness.

On a smaller scale, there is evidence that group coherence is having beneficial effects on the success of certain excellent companies where, according to Peters and Waterman, "the whole company resonates to the tune of quality and reliability . . ." This is why a system of management that is more quantum than linear is so powerful. It features "lifetime employment, group decision making, collective responsibility, nonspecific career paths and wholistic concerns." By contrast, linear, segmented, specialized companies--modeled, it seems, after classical Newtonian physics--are becoming outdated and are having to shift gears.

"A Little Change in the Individual Makes a Big Change in the Society"

In practice, a few steps almost always represents a great leap for a big business.

PETERS AND WATERMAN

What is great can only begin great. Its beginning is in fact the greatest thing of all. . . . The great begins great, maintains itself only through the free recurrence of greatness within it and if it is great ends also in greatness.

MARTIN HEIDEGGER

We could say that quantum mechanics explains why a little change in the individual makes a big change in the society. The quantum theory of greatness as applied to the group is dramatically democratic. In this view, if a single quantum can make a huge difference in a given system, so can a single individual express the best of everyone. And because we each invent a particular world through a particular appreciation of it--how we see it and thereby enliven it is how we create it; the happiest of us genially make silk purses out of sow's ears.

The quantum approach structures the basis for profound agreement and provides an ideal setting for the best kind of winning--winning because someone else is winning, too. In this way the great companies, conclude Peters and Waterman, "create a broad uplifting shared culture, a coherent framework within which charged-up people search for appropriate adaptations." And even traditionally competitive enterprises can be successful yet oriented to a win-win situation. For example, the Dreyfus Third Century Fund, Inc., is one of several mutual funds that invest solely in ethically "clean" stocks rated on four counts: equal opportunity employment, product purity (firms that have never had product recalls rate highest), environmental protection, and occupational safety, and it chooses investments from the top scorers in each industry. According to a recent financial report, the fund has "more than tripled the value of its shares since it began

Melanie Brown

in 1972. That's twice as much growth as other stock market gauges--
such as the Dow Jones Industrial Average and Standard & Poor's
500--have shown."

Some economic areas are also shifting in response to this new supportive attitude: Economist Robert Axelrod and others have developed social strategies that break from the traditional zero-sum "I win,
you lose" routines and teach cooperative strategy. Writes William
Allman: "In a nonzero-sum game, the players are still trying to get
the most points, but often they can do better if others do better as
well." (To illustrate, he recalls the story of the Englishman watching
his first Frisbee game and wondering who was winning.) [22]

Group greatness begins with loving others and wanting the best
for them. If you give love, you get love, we are told, and it's true.
You start by being vigilant, alert to your own loving behavior. Your
thoughts become significant when you realize that you are living within
a larger territory than your own individuality. And thus you have
tremendous influence, because even a thought can heal or hurt. Once
you understand this, you begin to operate as if your thoughts were
transparent. Your images become the images you want for the whole
society. A great person considers the entire world to be full of great
people. So believes the economist-entrepreneur Paul Hawken, who
credits his outstanding successes to one simple understanding: "Human beings are brilliant and they all generally perform the way they're
expected to in a situation."

And when you behave with the greatness of others in mind, as a
consequence of your goodwill, no matter what else you do, you'll be
on the path to becoming great yourself. "It is one of the most beautiful compensations of this life," wrote Emerson, "that no man can
sincerely try to help another without helping himself."

In addition, when human cooperation is most effective and smooth,
nature seems most willing to cooperate with us. This is when we feel
the wonderful support of the environment, when meaningful coincidence or synchronicity becomes a way of life, both for the individual and for the group. The "frictionless flow" between individuals--
the Q phenomenon on a sociological scale--is perhaps a useful
description of the success of group enterprise and, ultimately, individual enterprise. It says that how I think and behave is very much

connected to how you think and behave. And if you are great, I have a much better chance to be great also.

Economist Peter Drucker explains that the emergence of our entrepreneurial society "may be a turning point in history." Perhaps this is because we are realizing the significance of self-creation within the framework of the quantum universe. As Hawken advises, "Don't study the market, *become* the market." We are an entire society, a global society really, moving away from the classical "me first" outlook to a quantum "all for one and one for all" view, from separateness to wholeness, from greatness for the few to greatness for the many.

With this understanding, *greatness represents a level of societal development--a sociocultural phenomenon as well as a psychology of individual creativity.* Like quantum systems, which are characterized by coherence within constituents that cause their individual function to coalesce into a collective state, collective greatness may result from the influence that is caused by the orderliness in the wave functions of great individuals.

This sociological coherence is a powerful collective benefit of what has been called the "group dynamics of consciousness." If we use it as a model for a sociology of greatness, it becomes a premier evolutionary system in which everyone can become great--we could say-- all at once. It starts with nature's evolutionary desire to make the most of each individual. It flows to the group, to the world, out into the universe, and back again to our most intimate selves, a self-referral support system dedicated to the development of personal greatness, to the best of everyone. And in the end, the operant principle of group greatness is the integrity of the individual, the perfection with which he or she represents us all.

> Realized in one man, greatness has its rise;
> Realized in a family, greatness multiplies;
> Realized in a village, greatness gathers weight;
> Realized in a country, greatness becomes great;
> Realized in the world, greatness fills the skies.
> And thus the greatness of one man
> You find in the family he began,
> You find in the village that accrued,

You find in the country that ensued,
You find in the world's whole multitude.
How do I know this integrity?
Because it could all begin in me.[23]

LAO-TZU

NOTES

CHAPTER ONE

1. Srully Blotnick, *Getting Rich Your Own Way* (New York: Jove Publishers, 1982), p. 73.
2. R. W. Emerson, "The Oversoul," *Selected Essays*, ed. Larzer Ziff (New York: Penguin Classics, 1985), p. 208.
3. Abraham Maslow, *Toward a Psychology of Being* (New York: Van Nostrand, 1962); *The Farther Reaches of Human Nature* (New York: Viking, 1971).
4. Interview in William Tucker, "Apocalypse Deferred," *Life*, January 1982, p. 125.
5. Ibid., p. 122.
6. Elizabeth K. Minnich, "On Excellence," *Ms.*, January 1985, p. 71.
7. Thomas J. Peters and Robert H. Waterman, Jr., *In Search of Excellence* (New York: Warner Books, 1982), pp. 95, 269.
8. Interview in *PSA*, May 1985, p. 84.
9. P. O'Toole, "Creative Thinking," *Vogue*, December 1983, p. 148. See also Teresa Amabile, "Effects of External Evaluation on Artistic Creativity," *Journal of Personality and Social Psychology*, 1979, 37, pp. 221–233.
10. S. Crichton, "Best Freshman Curricula for $167.25," in *Bostonia*, February 1982, p. 9.
11. In *Esquire*, September 1981, p. 46.
12. Elizabeth Haich, *Sexual Energy and Yoga* (New York: ASI Publishers, 1975), p. 87.
13. Virginia Woolf, *Women and Writing*, ed. Michele Barrett (New York: Harcourt Brace Jovanovich, 1979), p. 114.
14. Interview with Barry Farrell, *Playboy*, February 1972, p. 66.
15. Plato, *Symposium*, trans. M. Joyce, in E. Hamilton and C. Huntington, eds., *The Collected Dialogues of Plato* (Princeton, N.J.: Princeton University Press, 1973).
16. Harold Rugg, *Imagination* (New York: Harper & Row, 1963), p. 92.
17. Julian Jaynes, *The Origin of Consciousness in the Breakdown of the Bicameral Mind* (New York: Houghton Mifflin, 1982), p. 2.

18. Jeremy Bernstein, *Einstein* (New York: Viking, 1973), p. 11.
19. William Fifield, *In Search of Genius* (New York: William Morrow & Co., 1982), p. 116.
20. Stanley Rosner and Lawrence E. Abt, eds., *The Creative Experience* (New York: Grossman Publishers, 1970), p. 107.
21. Bill Moyers, "The Source of Creativity," *American Express Company Newsletter: "For Members Only,"* November 1982.
22. Gail Sheehy, *Pathfinders* (William Morrow & Co., 1981), p. 403.
23. Dag Hammarskjöld, *Markings* (New York: Ballantine Books, 1983), pp. 12, 41.
24. Fifield, *In Search of Genius*, p. 166.
25. Interview with Chaim Potok, Barbra Streisand and Chaim Potok," *Esquire*, October 1982, p. 124.
26. Norman Cousins, *Human Options* (New York: W. W. Norton & Co., 1981), p. 168.
27. *Playboy* interview, p. 61.
28. Sheehy, *Pathfinders*, pp. 359–360.
29. Rosner and Abt, *The Creative Experience*, p. 276.
30. William James, "Is Life Worth Living?," *The Will to Believe and Other Essays* (London: Longmans Green & Co., 1897).
31. Rosner and Abt, p. 130.
32. Horace Freeland Judson, "The Rage to Know," *The Atlantic Monthly*, April 1980, p. 113.
33. Interview with Paul Rosenfield, *San Francisco Chronicle*, October 7, 1979, p. 5.

CHAPTER TWO

1. Lewis Thomas, *The Lives of a Cell* (New York: Bantam Books, 1975), p. 27.
2. K. C. Cole, *Sympathetic Vibrations* (New York: William Morrow & Co., 1985), p. 230.
3. Anthony Campbell, *TM and the Nature of Enlightenment* (New York: Harper & Row, Perennial Library, 1976), p. 130.
4. *The Times* (London), October 12, 1981.
5. Peters and Waterman, *In Search of Excellence*, p. 98.
6. George Gilder, *Wealth and Poverty* (New York: Bantam Books, 1981), p. 290.
7. Albert Einstein and Leopold Infeld, *The Evolution of Physics* (New York: Simon & Schuster, 1938), p. 31.
8. Ronald Duncan and Miranda Weston-Smith, eds. *Lying Truths* (New York: London: Pergamon Press, 1979) p. 145.

9. Bertrand Russell, *Portraits from Memory* (London: Allen & Unwin, 1956), pp. 41–42.
10. Ken Wilber, ed., *The Holographic Paradigm and Other Paradoxes* (Berkeley, Calif.: Shambhala, 1982), pp. 62, 194.
11. Interview with K. C. Cole, *Discover*, June 1983, p. 49.
12. Duncan and Weston-Smith, *Lying Truths*, p. 166.
13. Campbell, *TM*, p. 176.
14. Ibid., p. 133.
15. Curtis Bill Pepper, "Saving the 'Last Supper,' " *The New York Times Magazine*, October 3, 1985, p. 44.
16. "Nature," *On Education*.
17. Peter Stoler, "A Conversation with Jonas Salk," *Psychology Today*, March 1983, p. 53.
18. Judson, *The Rage to Know*, p. 15.
19. Eudora Welty, *One Writer's Beginnings*, (Cambridge, Mass.: Harvard University Press, 1984), p. 100.
20. *Chronicle of Higher Education*, Vol. XXXII, No. 21, July 23, 1986.
21. Deepak Chopra, M.D., *Total Health: The Rediscovery of AyurVeda* (New York: Houghton Mifflin Co., forthcoming 1987).
22. Lawrence Domash, Introduction to *Scientific Research on T.M.*, *Collected Papers*, Vol. 1, D. Orme-Johnson and J. Farrow, eds. (Seelisberg, Switzerland: Maharishi European Research University Press, 1977).
23. E. Paul Torrance and Laura K. Hall, "Assessing the Further Reaches of Creative Potential," *Journal of Creative Behavior*, Vol. 14, No. 1, 1981, pp. 3–4.
24. Brewster Ghiselin, *The Creative Process* (New York: New American Library, Mentor Books, 1952), p. 45.
25. Jerry Cohen, "Superstars: How It Feels to Triumph," *The Los Angeles Times*, January 30, 1977, p. 3.
26. Ibid., p. 3.
27. Ibid., p. 20.
28. Virginia Woolf, *A Room of One's Own* (1929) (New York: Harcourt Brace Jovanovich, 1957), p. 101.
29. Cohen, *The Los Angeles Times*, p. 3.
30. Ibid., pp. 20, 22.
31. John J. O'Neill, *Prodigal Genius* (New York: Ives Washburn, Inc., 1944), p. 140.
32. H. Peterson, *Great Teachers* (New York: Vintage Books, 1946), Ch. 1.
33. Susanne Langer, *Philosophy in a New Key* (Cambridge, Mass.: Harvard University Press, 1957), p. 8.
34. K. C. Cole, *Sympathetic Vibrations*, p. 230.
35. Arthur M. Abell, *Talks with the Great Composers* (New York: Philosophical Library, 1979), pp. 20–23.

Notes

CHAPTER THREE

1. Woolf, *Women and Writing*, p. 131.
2. Woolf, *A Room of One's Own*, p. 71.
3. Quoted in Ashley Montagu, *Growing Young* (New York: McGraw-Hill, 1981).
4. C. N. Alexander, E. J. Langer, and R. Oetzel, eds., *Higher Stages of Human Development* (New York: Oxford University Press, forthcoming 1987).
5. C. N. Alexander, et al., "Transcendental Meditation and Mindfulness and Longevity: An Experiment with the Elderly," *Journal of Personality and Social Psychology* (in press).
6. Interview with Joan S. Wixen, *Modern Maturity*, January 1985, p. 96.
7. Woolf, *Women and Writing*, p. 45.
8. Woolf, *Room*, p. 101.
9. Kenneth Walker, *Women Saints: East and West* (Hollywood, Calif.: Vedanta Press, 1979), p. 227.
10. Woolf, *Women and Writing*, pp. 85, 10, 191.
11. Ibid., pp. 166–167.
12. Ibid., p. 47.
13. Ibid., p. 47.
14. Ibid., p. 75.
15. Betty Friedan, *The Second Stage* (New York: Simon & Schuster, Summit Books, 1982), p. 40.
16. Ibid., p. 144.
17. Montagu, *Growing Young*.
18. Friedan, *The Second Stage*.
19. Carol Gilligan, *In a Different Voice* (Cambridge, Mass.: Harvard University Press, 1982).
20. Walker, Introduction, *Women Saints*.
21. Phil Donahue, *Donahue* (New York: Fawcett Books, 1981).
22. *Newsweek*, May 28, 1984.
23. Rosner and Abt, *The Creative Experience*, p. 277.
24. Cohen, *Los Angeles Times*, p. 20.
25. Ibid., p. 20.
26. Hammarskjöld, *Markings*, p. 133.
27. Ibid., p. 9.

CHAPTER FOUR

1. K. C. Cole, *Sympathetic Vibrations*, pp. 101–102.
2. Rugg, *Imagination*, p. 121.
3. *Esquire*, December 1983, p. 574.
4. Peters and Waterman, *In Search of Excellence*, pp. 180–181.

5. Leonard Bernstein, *The Boston Globe*, November 21, 1982, p. 21.
6. Woolf, *Room*, p. 75.
7. Warren Bennis, *Working Smart Newsletter* (Stamford, Conn.: Xerox Learning Systems), Vol. 2, No. 37, July 1985, p. 1.
8. Plato, *The Symposium*, trans. Walter Hamilton (New York: Penguin Books, 1977), pp. 108–109.
9. Blotnick, *Getting Rich*, p. 24.
10. Albert Einstein, *The World As I See It* (Secaucus, N.J.: Citadel Press, 1979), p. 28.
11. *Selected Letters of George Edward Woodberry* (Associated Faculty Press, reprint of 1920 Edition).
12. *Esquire*, May 1985, p. 100.
13. Charles Lindbergh, *The Spirit of St. Louis* (New York: Scribner's, 1953).
14. Jerry Carroll, "Claire Bloom: A Reserved Look at Her Life Among Giants," *San Francisco Chronicle*, March 2, 1982, p. 16.
15. *The New York Times Magazine*, October 1, 1985.
16. Goethe, *Essay on Winckelmann*, from Introduction, Nietzsche, *Thus Spake Zarathustra* (New York: Penguin, 1977), p. 30.
17 Rosner and Abt, *The Creative Experience*, pp. 19–20.
18. Geoffrey Norman, "The Naked Sport," *Esquire*, May 1985, p. 185.
19. Daniel Seligman, "Luck and Careers," *Fortune*, November 16, 1981.
20. Gilder, *Wealth and Poverty*, pp. 298–299.
21. Rosner and Abt, pp. 200–201.
22. Dorothie Harrison, "Creative Intelligence and Music," *Creative Intelligence*, (London), No. 3, 1973.
23. Rosner and Abt, p. 325.
24. Ghiselin, *The Creative Process*, p. 37.
25. Calvin Tompkins, *The New Yorker*, May 1983, p. 118.
26. Judson, *The Rage to Know*, p. 116.
27. Cole, pp. 228–229.
28. *People*, August 18, 1980, p. 33.
29. Rex Reed, *Conversations in the Raw* (New York: New American Library, 1970), p. 51.
30. Ashley Montagu, *The Practice of Love* (Englewood Cliffs, N.J.: Prentice-Hall, 1975).
31. David McClelland, *Psychology Today*, May 1982, p. 56.
32. Helen Dukas and Banesh Hoffman, eds., *Einstein: The Human Side* (Princeton, N.J.: Princeton University Press, 1979), p. 18.
33. Interview in *Omni*, July 1982, p. 116.
34. Cousins, *Human Options*, p. 106.
35. Interview with Michael Bandler, *American Way*, September 1981, p. 12.
36. Personal interview.

37. Abraham Maslow, *The Farther Reaches of Human Nature* (New York: Viking, 1971), p. 279.
38. Ibid., p. 295.
39. Jeremy Bernstein, *Einstein,* pp. 206–207.

CHAPTER FIVE

1. Maslow, *Farther Reaches,* p. 295.
2. Lewis Terman, in P. E. Vernon, ed., *Creativity* (Middlesex, England: Penguin Education Books, 1970), Ch. 2.
3. Catherine Cox, ibid., pp. 28–30.
4. *Time,* March 23, 1981.
5. David Owen, "The Limits of Excellence," *Inside Sports,* November 1981, p. 64.
6. Ibid., p. 69; see also Natalie Angier, "How Fast, How High, How Far," *Discover,* November 1981, pp. 29–30.
7. Geoffrey Norman article, *Esquire,* p. 186.
8. Rosner and Abt, *The Creative Experience,* pp. 109, 216.
9. O'Neill, *Prodigal Genius,* p. 264.
10. *Discover,* May 1984, p. 40.
11. Lecture at the Science of Creative Intelligence Symposium, Queens College, Toronto, Canada, June 1971.
12. W. S. Ray, *The Experimental Psychology of Original Thinking* (New York: Macmillan, 1967), p. 46.
13. C. W. Taylor and F. X. Barron, *Scientific Creativity: Its Recognition and Development* (New York: John Wiley & Sons, 1963), p. 16.
14. D. E. Berlyne, *Aesthetics and Psychobiology* (East Norwalk, Conn.: Appleton-Century-Crofts, 1971), p. 70.
15. S. J. Parnes and H. F. Harding, *A Sourcebook for Creative Thinking* (New York: Scribner's, 1962), p. 124.
16. Ellen J. Langer, "Automated Lives," *Psychology Today,* April 1982, p. 64.
17. Paul MacCready, "The Floating Needle," *Science Digest,* March 1983, p. 52.
18. Taylor and Barron, *Scientific Creativity,* p. 17.
19. Peter Russell, *The Brain Book* (New York: E. P. Dutton, 1979), p. 7.
20. Ibid., p. 7.
21. *Omni,* July 1982, p. 63.
22. Connie Zweig, *Brain-Mind Bulletin,* March 4, 1985, p. 2.
23. See Daniel Goleman, "Science Times," *The New York Times,* July 30, 1985; September 24, 1985.
24. Goleman, *The New York Times,* July 30, 1985, p. C7.
25. Ibid.

26. Ibid.
27. See Campbell, *TM*, pp. 78–79, 94.
28. See Goleman, *The New York Times*, September 24, 1985; also PBS television series, *The Brain*.
29. PBS, *The Brain*.
30. Atuhiro Sibatani, "The Japanese Brain," *Science 80*, December 1980, pp. 24–26.
31. *Newsweek*, February 7, 1983, p. 43.
32. PBS, *The Brain*.
33. *Newsweek*, p. 48.
34. *The New Yorker*, January 10, 1983, p. 25.
35. *Newsweek*, p. 41.
36. Ibid., p. 41.
37. N. A. Lassen, "Brain Function and Blood Flow," *Scientific American*, October 1978, pp. 50–59.
38. Campbell, p. 93.
39. Thomas Verny, M.D., and John Kelly, *The Secret Life of the Unborn Child* (New York: Simon & Schuster, Summit Books, 1981), p. 39.
40. Lewis Thomas, "Autumn Leaves," *Science 80*, September 1980, pp. 18–20.
41. Ulric Neisser, *Psychology Today*, May 1982, p. 45.
42. J. Eccles, "Evolution and the Conscious Self," *The 1967 Nobel Conference: The Human Mind*, J. Rolansky, ed. (Amsterdam: North Holland Publishers, 1967).
43. Lecture at the Science of Creative Intelligence Symposium, Amherst, Mass., July 1971.
44. Vernon, *Creativity*, Ch. 3.
45. *Bostonia*, February 1982, p. 10.
46. *Esquire*, October 1982, p. 92.
47. A. R. Luria, *The Mind of a Mnemonist* (New York: Basic Books, 1968), pp. 23, 28.

CHAPTER SIX

1. H. F. Crovitz, *Galton's Walk: Methods for the Analysis of Thinking, Intelligence and Creativity* (New York: Harper & Row, 1970), Ch. 1.
2. H. J. Campbell, *The Pleasure Areas: A New Theory of Behavior* (New York: Delacorte Press, 1973), p. 208.
3. Marghanita Laski, *Ecstasy* (Bloomington: Indiana University Press, 1961), pp. 196–197.
4. Ralph Waldo Emerson, "The Poet," *Selected Essays* (New York: Penguin Classics, 1985), pp. 262–263.
5. Rosner and Abt, *The Creative Experience*, p. 235.

6. Ibid., p. 271.
7. John Naisbitt, *Megatrends* (New York: Warner Books, 1982), p. 101.
8. Rosner and Abt, p. 190.
9. Sheehy, *Pathfinders*, p. 98.
10. Vernon, *Creativity*.
11. Rugg, *Imagination*, p. 262.
12. Joseph Pearce, *The Crack in the Cosmic Egg* (New York: Pocket Books, 1973), pp. 36, 58.
13. Peters and Waterman, *In Search of Excellence*, p. 264.
14. James, *The Will to Believe*.
15. Blotnick, *Getting Rich*.
16. Haniel Long, trans., *The Marvelous Adventure of Cabeza de Vaca* (Dallas, Tex.: Southern Methodist University Press, 1972), pp. 10–11, 23–24.
17. Kissinger, *The Times* (London), October 12, 1981.
18. In Farrell article, *Playboy*, p. 198.
19. Center for the Study of Social Policy Report, *Changing Images of Man*, Stanford, Calif.: Stanford Research Institute, October 1973, p. iii.
20. Ibid., p. iii.
21. Stoler, "Conversation with Jonas Salk," p. 55.
22. E. Paul Torrance and R. E. Myers, *Creative Learning and Teaching* (New York: Harper & Row, 1970).
23. *The Newsweek Poll, 1983, Newsweek* magazine.
24. Alvin Toffler, *The Third Wave* (New York: Bantam Books, 1981), p. 381.

CHAPTER SEVEN

1. From Havelock Ellis, *Selected Essays* (London: J. M. Dent and Son, 1936).
2. Samuel G. Freedman, "How Inner Torment Feeds the Creative Spirit," *The New York Times*, November 17, 1985, Sect. 2.
3. Sheehy, *Pathfinders*, p. 305.
4. Rosner and Abt, *The Creative Experience*, p. 337.
5. Ibid., p. 274.
6. Ibid., p. 227.
7. Anthony Storr, *Dynamics of Creation* (New York: Atheneum, 1972), p. 94.
8. Parnes and Harding, *A Sourcebook for Creative Thinking*, p. 195.
9. Rosner and Abt, p. 91.
10. Alex Osborn, *Applied Imagination* (New York: Scribner's, 1953).
11. See Frank X. Barron, *Creative Person and Creative Process* (New York: Holt, Rinehart, & Winston, 1969).
12. Torrance and Hall, "Assessing the Further Reaches of Creative Potential," p. 10.

13. Parnes and Harding, pp. 65–66.
14. Eugenia Zuckerman review of *Mademoiselle* (New York: Carcanet, 1985) in *The New York Times Book Review*, October 6, 1985, p. 14.
15. Carl Sandburg, *Abraham Lincoln: The Prairie Years and The War Years* (New York: Harcourt Brace Jovanovich, 1974).
16. Fred M. Hechinger, "How Talent Can Be Nurtured," *The New York Times*, February 12, 1985.
17. Vernon, *Creativity*, p. 97.
18. O'Neill, *Prodigal Genius*, pp. 256–257.
19. T. S. Eliot, *The Four Quartets*.
20. Paul Bohannan, "The Eloquence of Silence," *Science 80*, January/February, 1980, pp. 17–18.
21. J. Allen Boone, *The Language of Silence*, Paul and Blanche Leonard, eds. (New York: Harper and Row, 1970), p. 58.
22. Hammarskjöld, *Markings*.
23. See *Scientific Research on T.M.: Collected Papers*, Vol. 1, eds. D. Orme-Johnson and J. Farrow (Seelisberg, Switzerland: Maharishi European Research University Press, 1977). Also R. Keith Wallace, *The Maharishi Technology of the Unified Field: The Neurophysiology of Enlightenment* (Fairfield, Iowa: Maharishi International University Neuroscience Press, 1986).
24. *Creating an Ideal Society* (Seelisberg, Switzerland: Maharishi European Research University Press, 1976).
25. For a further description of these principles, see Maharishi Mahesh Yogi, *Commentary on the Baghavad-Gita* (New York: Penguin Books, 1969). Also *The Science of Being* (International SRM Publishing, 1963).
26. *Omni*, July 1982, p. 88.
27. *Creating an Ideal Society*.
28. Interview in *Science Digest*, January 1985, pp. 64–65.
29. Rosner and Abt, pp. 143–144.
30. Personal interview.
31. Peters and Waterman, *In Search of Excellence*, p. 194.

CHAPTER EIGHT

1. Duncan and Weston-Smith, *Lying Truths*, p. 32.
2. Ralph Waldo Emerson, *Journals*.
3. Paul Bohannan, "The Gene Pool and the Meme Pool," *Science 80*, November 1980, pp. 25–28.
4. Haich, *Sexual Energy and Yoga*, p. 87.
5. Duncan and Weston-Smith, pp. 238–240.
6. Henry Steele Commager, "Brilliant Originals," *Washington Post Magazine*, October 10, 1982, p. 33.
7. Rosner and Abt, *The Creative Experience*, p. 277.

8. Thomas, *Lives of a Cell*, p. 53.
9. Rudy Rucker, "The Powers of Coincidence," *Science 85*, February 1985, p. 54.
10. Ibid., p. 57.
11. A. Campbell, *TM and the Nature of Enlightenment*, p. 194.
12. Joseph Rossman, *Psychology of the Inventor* (Washington, D.C.: Inventor's Press, n.d.).
13. Duncan and Weston-Smith, p. 167.
14. Montagu and Matson, *The Human Connection*, p. 152.
15. Ibid., p. 153.
16. Thomas, p. 12.
17. Douglas Hofstadter, "To Be of One Mind," *Science 85*, May 1985, p. 56.
18. Ken Keyes, Jr., *The Hundredth Monkey* (Vision Books, 1985).
19. John Gliedman, "Mind and Matter," *Science Digest*, March 1983, p. 70.
20. Woolf, *Women and Writing*, p. 27.
21. Gliedman, "Mind and Matter," p. 72.
22. William Allman, "Tit for Tat," *Science 84*, October 1984, p. 27.
23. Adapted from translation by Witter Bynner, *The Way of Life According to Lao Tzu* (Capricorn Books, 1944), p. 59.

BIBLIOGRAPHY

Abell, Arthur M. *Talks with the Great Composers*. New York: Philosophical Library, 1979.

Alexander, C. N., E. J. Langer, and R. Oetzel. *Higher Stages of Human Development*. New York: Oxford University Press, 1987.

Barron, Frank X. *Creative Person and Creative Process*. New York: Holt, Rinehart, & Winston, 1969.

Bernstein, Jeremy. *Einstein*. New York: Viking, 1973.

Blotnick, Srully. *Getting Rich Your Own Way*. New York: Jove Publishers, 1982.

Boone, J. Allen, *The Language of Silence*, Paul and Blanche Leonard, eds. New York: Harper and Row, 1970.

Bruner, Jerome S. *On Knowing: Essays for the Left Hand*. Cambridge Mass.: Belknap Press, 1962.

------. *The Process of Education*. Cambridge, Mass.: Harvard University Press, 1961.

Burns, James MacGregor. *Leadership*. New York: Harper & Row, 1978.

Campbell, Anthony. *TM and the Nature of Enlightenment*. New York: Harper & Row Perennial Library, 1976.

Campbell, H. J. *The Pleasure Areas: A New Theory of Behavior*. New York: Delacorte Press, 1973.

Campbell, Joseph. *The Hero with a Thousand Faces*. Princeton, N.J.: Princeton University Press, 1968.

Campbell, Joseph, ed. *The Portable Jung*. New York: Viking, 1971.

Capra, Fritzhof. *The Tao of Physics*. Berkeley, Calif.: Shambhala, 1975.

Chopra, Deepak. *Total Health: The Resdiscovery of AyurVeda*. New York: Houghton Mifflin, 1987.

Cole, K. C. *Sympathetic Vibrations: Reflections on Physics as a Way of Life*. New York: William Morrow & Co., 1985.

Cousins, Norman. *Human Options*. New York: W. W. Norton & Co., 1981.

Crovitz, H. F. *Galton's Walk: Methods for the Analysis of Thinking, Intelligence and Creativity*. New York: Harper & Row, 1970.

Dawkins, Richard. *The Selfish Gene*. New York: Oxford University Press, 1976.

Donahue, Phil. *Donahue*. New York: Fawcett Books, 1981.

Dukas, Helen, and Banesh Hoffman, eds. *Einstein: The Human Side*. Princeton, N.J.: Princeton University Press, 1979.

Duncan, Ronald, and Miranda Weston-Smith. *Lying Truths*. New York and London: Pergamon Press, 1979.

Edwards, Betty. *Drawing on the Right Side of the Brain*. Los Angeles: Tarcher, 1979.

Einstein, Albert. *The World As I See It*. Secaucus, N.J.: Citadel Press, 1979.

Ferguson, Marilyn. *The Aquarian Conspiracy: Personal and Social Transformation in the 1980s*. Los Angeles: Tarcher, 1980.

Fifield, William. *In Search of Genius*. New York: William Morrow & Co., 1982.

Friedan, Betty. *The Second Stage*. New York: Simon & Schuster, Summit Books, 1982.

Ghiselin, Brewster, ed. *The Creative Process: A Symposium*. New York: New American Library, Mentor Books, 1952.

Gilder, George. *Wealth and Poverty*. New York: Bantam Books, 1981.

Gilligan, Carol. *In a Different Voice*. Cambridge, Mass.: Harvard University Press, 1982.

Goldberg, Philip. *The Intuitive Edge: Understanding and Developing Intuition*. Los Angeles: Tarcher, 1983.

Gordon, William J. J. *Synectics*. New York: Harper & Row, 1961.

Haich, Elizabeth. *Sexual Energy and Yoga*. New York: ASI Publishers, 1975.

Hall, Edward. *The Silent Language*. Garden City, N.Y.: Doubleday, 1959.

Hammarskjöld, Dag. *Markings*. New York: Ballantine Books, 1983.

Huxley, Aldous. *The Perennial Philosophy*. New York: Harper & Row, 1945.

James, William. *The Varieties of Religious Experience [1902]*. New York: Mentor Books, 1985.

------. *The Will to Believe and Other Essays*. London: Longmans Green, 1897.

Jaynes, Julian. *The Origin of Consciousness in the Breakdown of the Bicameral Mind*. New York: Houghton Mifflin, 1982.

Jencks, Christopher. *Who Gets Ahead? The Determinants of Economic Success in America*. New York: Basic Books, 1979.

Keyes, Ken, Jr. *The Hundredth Monkey*. Vision Books, 1985.

Koestler, Arthur. *The Act of Creation*. New York: Macmillan, 1964.

Kubie, Lawrence S. *Neurotic Distortion of the Creative Process*. New York: Noonday Press, 1965.

Kuhn, Thomas. *The Structure of Scientific Revolutions*. Chicago: University of Chicago Press, 1962.

Langer, Susanne. *Philosophy in a New Key*. Cambridge, Mass.: Harvard University Press, 1951.

Laski, Marghanita. *Ecstasy: A Study of Some Secular and Religious Experiences*. Bloomington: Indiana University Press, 1961.

Lewis, C. S. *The Four Loves*. London: Collins, 1960.

Lifton, Robert Jay. *The Broken Connection: On Death and The Continuity of Life*. New York: Simon & Schuster, 1979.

Lindbergh, Charles. *The Spirit of St. Louis*. New York: Scribner's, 1953.

Long, Haniel. *The Marvelous Adventure of Cabeza de Vaca*. Dallas, Tex.: Southern Methodist University Press, 1972.

Luria, A. R. *The Mind of a Mnemonist*. New York: Basic Books, 1968.

Maharishi Mahesh Yogi. *On the Bhagavad-Gita: A New Translation and Commentary*. New York: Penguin Books, 1967.

------. *The Science of Being*. Los Angeles: International SRM Publishing, 1963.

Maslow, Abraham. *The Farther Reaches of Human Nature*. New York: Viking, 1971.

------. *Toward a Psychology of Being*. Princeton, N.J.: Van Nostrand, 1962.

May, Rollo. *The Courage to Create*. New York: W. W. Norton & Co., 1975.

Montagu, Ashley. *Growing Young*. New York: McGraw-Hill, 1981.

------, and Floyd Matson. *The Human Connection*. New York: McGraw-Hill, 1979.

------, ed. *The Practice of Love*. Englewood Cliffs, N.J.: Prentice-Hall, 1975.

Naisbitt, John. *Megatrends: Ten New Directions Transforming Our Lives*. New York: Warner Books, 1982.

O'Neill, John J. *Prodigal Genius: The Life of Nikola Tesla*. New York: Ives Washburn, Inc., 1944.

Orme-Johnson, D., and J. Farrow, eds. *Scientific Research on T.M.: Collected Papers*, Vol. 1. Seelisberg, Switzerland: Maharishi European Research University Press, 1977.

Ornstein, Robert. *The Psychology of Consciousness*. New York: Viking, 1972.

Osborn, Alex. *Applied Imagination*. New York: Scribner's, 1953.

Parnes, S. J., and H. F. Harding. *A Sourcebook for Creative Thinking*. New York: Scribner's, 1962.

Pearce, Joseph C. *The Crack in the Cosmic Egg*. New York: Pocket Books, 1973.

Peters, Thomas J., and Robert H. Waterman, Jr. *In Search of Excellence: Lessons from America's Best-Run Companies*. New York: Warner Books, 1982.

Peterson, H. *Great Teachers*. New York: Vintage Books, 1946.

Piaget, Jean. *The Moral Development of a Child*. New York: Kegan Paul, Trench, Trubner, 1932.

Polyani, Michael. *Personal Knowledge*. Chicago: University of Chicago Press, 1958.

Ray, W. S. *The Experimental Psychology of Original Thinking*. New York: Macmillan, 1967.

Rosner, Stanley, and Lawrence E. Abt, eds. *The Creative Experience*. New York: Grossman Publishers, 1970.

Rugg, Harold. *Imagination*. New York: Harper & Row, 1963.

Russell, Peter. *The Brain Book*. New York: E. P. Dutton, 1979.

Sheehy, Gail. *Pathfinders*. New York: William Morrow & Co., 1981.

Sheldrake, Rupert. *A New Science of Life*. Los Angeles: Tarcher, 1981.

Taylor, C. W., and Frank X. Barron. *Scientific Creativity: Its Recognition and Development*. New York: John Wiley & Sons, 1963.

Thomas, Lewis. *The Lives of a Cell*. New York: Bantam Books, 1975.

Toffler, Alvin. *The Third Wave*. New York: Bantam Books, 1981.

Torrance, E. Paul, and R. E. Myers. *Creative Learning and Teaching*. New York: Harper & Row, 1970.

Toynbee, Arnold J. *A Study of History*. New York: Oxford University Press, 1946.

Vernon, P. E., ed. *Creativity: Selected Readings*. Middlesex, England: Penguin Education Books, 1970.

Verny, Thomas, M.D., and John Kelly. *The Secret Life of the Unborn Child*. New York: Simon & Schuster, Summit Books, 1981.

Walker, Kenneth. *Women Saints: East and West*. Hollywood, Calif.: Vedanta Press, 1979.

Wallace, R. Keith. *The Maharishi Technology of the Unified Field: The Neurophysiology of Enlightenment*. Fairfield, Iowa: Maharishi International University Neuroscience Press, 1986.

Wallas, Graham. *The Art of Thought*. New York: Harcourt Brace Jovanovich, 1926.

Welty, Eudora. *One Writer's Beginnings*. Cambridge, Mass.: Harvard University Press, 1984.

Wilber, Ken, ed. *The Holographic Paradigm and Other Paradoxes*. Berkeley, Calif.: Shambhala Press, 1982.

Wilson, Edward O. *On Human Nature*. Cambridge, Mass.: Harvard University Press, 1978.

Woolf, Virginia. *A Room of One's Own* (1929). New York: Harcourt Brace Jovanovich, Harvest, 1957.

------. *Women and Writing*. Michele Barrett, ed. New York: Harcourt Brace Jovanovich, Harvest, 1979.

Zukav, Gary. *The Dancing of Wu Li Masters*. New York: Bantam New Age Books, 1980.

ACKNOWLEDGMENTS

In acknowledging the great people who helped to bring this book to fruition, it is with deep gratitude that I first thank the major contributor, His Holiness Maharishi Mahesh Yogi, that best of teachers, who has been a continual source of pure knowledge and loving inspiration. Through his unified field-based technology, Transcendental Meditation (T.M.) and the T.M.-Sidhi program, he has provided a profound means to uncovering greatness, as well as the unforgettable guidance to seek the highest in ourselves and others: His teachings, like all real truths, are "living ideas"--ideas to be lived and used, not simply to be thought.

I next wish to thank deeply my friend and colleague Bryan Aubrey, whose crystal-clear intelligence and unfailing attention to the ever-changing versions of this manuscript enabled me to organize and complete it. Heartfelt thanks also go to my editor, Lisa Drew, whose editorial acumen, loving encouragement, and willingness to take on this particular project were a real blessing. I also thank her assistant, David Means, and my delightful agent, Jonathan Dolger.

I am very grateful to Larry Domash for the remarkable depth of his initial advice; to Peggy Tsukahira Norris for her helpful comments; to Maureen Kelleher for her generous organizing power; to Enloe Willingham for two of his thoughts, and to those great individuals whose experiences and ideas have inspired so much of this book; In particular, I acknowledge the profound contributions of Virginia Woolf and Ralph Waldo Emerson; and also the important contributions of Skip Alexander, Alaric Arenander, Anthony Campbell, K. C. Cole, Norman Cousins, Marilyn Ferguson, Rashi Glazer, John Hagelin, Edward Hall, Marghanita Laski, Ashley Montagu, Bevan Morris, David Orme-Johnson, Rhoda Orme-Johnson, Tom Peters and

Acknowledgments

Robert Waterman, Debra Poneman, Peter Russell, Jonas Salk, Robin Ticciati, R. Keith Wallace, Eudora Welty, and my students.

I also wish to thank the following dear friends whose quiet and noisy encouragement and support for this book has meant so much to me: Marcia Abrahams, Skip and Vicky Alexander, Rogers and Candace Badgett, Jim Belilove, Cheryl Bianchi, Steve Blake, Gerry Bodeker, Shirley Bonchef, Terry Braunstein, Nancy Breidenthal, Allan Y. Cohen, Tom Cole, Tina Conway, Michael and Susie Dillbeck, Henry Eckstein, Richard Eidson, Bill Fitelson, Paula and Ralph Gilbert, Nancy Gross, Monty Guild, Sonia Gunderson, Julie Guttman, Madeline de Joly, Paul Kapiloff, Kurleigh King, Judy Lamar, Ellen Langer, Mosie Lasagna, Emily Levin, Michael and Jan McCutcheon, Heidi Mage, Emilie Marks, Janet Nichols, Elaine Noble, John and Lisa Olmstead, Debra and Fred Poneman, Ron Posner, Victor and Judy Raymond, Eric Rosenfeld, Joncie Rowland, Jonathan Sabin, Ronnie Sanders, Richard Schneider, Sally Schwartz, Tony Smith, Tina Sterling, Steve and Sheila Terry, Pamela Thomas, Michael Tompkins, Ben and Bev Voogt, Nini White, Maureen Wynne, Robin Zabel, Moki and Stuart Zimmerman, Connie Zweig, my mother, Annabelle Brown, and my other precious friends for all the large and small reasons.